Between Earth And Heaven

雲蒸霞蔚

陈督兮
CHEN DUXI

Contents

目录

Essay

水纟文

陈督兮的绢本绘画有着一种独特的客体导向性，他描绘物，尤其是构成纹理的物的细节，在这些纹理细节上，绘画通过线条与物统一了起来。但他的再现方式既不是宋代写生那般去描绘一种恒定的客体，也不似西方文艺复兴传统那样去描绘一时一处的主体所见，陈督兮描绘的是一种客体化的主体认知：视角是主观的，但描绘却是客体导向的，仿佛摄影，并不去格物，而只图致知。

这种知是向内的，类似于沉思，甚至沉迷，在很长一段时间内，陈督兮一直喜欢描绘水流、石纹、叶脉等流体的事物，有趣的是，在这些案例中，他着重的是这些表面（字面意义上）的性状，这是一种轻逸的认知，它“滑”过客体。这里的“滑”隐喻的是一种线性的，亦是一种线描的观看方式。线在这些作品中占据着绝对主导的地位，这些线在描绘客体，也在追寻空间，更在呈示自身，以及其所意味的运笔时段的专注——观者的目光也因此被牵引。

这一批作品都是在描绘流体，大致有水流、水波、水蚀、水成岩，形态各异的流动、卷积与沉淀。它们放在一起有着类型学的意味，也构成了视觉谱系。在这个意义上，它们既是水文主题，又是水纹题材，带来某种理性主义的审美。

题材往往是语言所选择的，在陈督兮这里，自然物成为他的主题或许是线描性语言的选择。“线”是一种及物的视觉语言，在沃尔夫林的分析中，“线”包含着触觉，因此用“线”去描绘便如用目光去触摸对象。换句话说，再现性绘画中的“线”具有一种客体认知性，线描风格更适合于科学图像，反之，提香或者印象派那样的涂绘风格更便于表现某种主观所见。但陈督兮的线描并不是白描，他的线条在重复中不断变换延展，线条本身构成了一种抽象的繁复，似乎是对世界万千客体的礼赞，物理与心性合二为一。

鲍栋

Shui Wen ("Water Patterns"/"Hydrology")

Chen Duxi's silk paintings are uniquely object-oriented. He depicts objects, especially the details that make up the objects' textures. On these texture details, paintings unify with the objects through lines. However, his representation method is different from the Song Dynasty sketches that depict a permanent object or the Western Renaissance tradition that depicts what the subject sees at a specific time and place. What Chen Duxi depicts is an objectified subjective perception, meaning the perspective is subjective, while the description is object-oriented, almost like photography, which does not investigate things but only seeks to extend knowledge.

This kind of knowledge goes inward, similar to contemplation or even addiction. For a long time, Chen Duxi has been fond of depicting fluid objects like water flow, stone veining, and leaf veins. Interestingly, in these cases, he focuses on the superficial (literally "on the surface") qualities, which form a free and lofty perception that "skids" over the object. The word "skid" here metaphorically refers to a linear and line-drawing way of viewing. Lines absolutely dominate these works. These lines depict objects, pursue spaces, and present themselves and the implied concentration of the brushstrokes, guiding the viewer's attention.

This batch of works depicts fluids, including water flow, water waves, water erosion, and sedimentary rocks. Gathering these forms of flow, suspension, and precipitation gives a typological meaning and also constitutes a visual lineage. In this sense, the works represent themes of both hydrology and water patterns, forming a type of rationalist aesthetics.

The chosen language often decides the subject matter. In Chen Duxi's case, natural objects constitute his subject, perhaps because of his choice of line-drawing language. The line is a transitive visual language. In Heinrich Wölfflin's analysis, lines suggest the sense of touch, and using lines to depict is like using eyes to touch objects. In other words, the lines in representational paintings embody object perception, and line drawing works with scientific images. On the contrary, the free coloring used by Titian or impressionists works better for expressing subjective views. Nevertheless, Chen Duxi's lines are not minimalist outlines. His lines are constantly changing and extending through repetition. The lines themselves form an abstract complexity, almost a tribute to the multitude and vicissitude of the world's objects, integrating the physical with the mental.

Bao Dong

遥远的共鸣

在上有淡墨的绢本背景上有一双手，苍白的皮肤上，一些淡红色的线条若隐若现，这是艺术家陈督兮 2020 年的作品《手》。如果凑近看的话，可以看到这些细密的线条描绘的是手上的纹路。对我来说，这些线条看上去既合情合理又令人困惑：它们让几乎毫无血色的皮肤具有体积感，但它们的颜色与日常所见的掌纹和指纹并不一致。事实上，这些红色的线条更像血管和肌肉，而血管和肌肉是在皮肤下面的，而不是皮肤表面。这让我产生一种特殊的、接近于诡秘（uncanny）的感觉，这种强烈的感觉让我得以从新的角度理解陈督兮的创作。本文将从《手》这件作品出发，尝试对艺术家创作中的几条脉络做一个梳理。

这种诡秘的感觉并不是立刻产生的，而是在画面细节逐渐进入视野的过程中浮现出来的。我渐渐发现：我并不是在看一双手外在的样子，我的视线似乎可以穿过皮肤的表层，直抵下面的血管和肌肉。换句话说，陈督兮似乎是从身体里面在画这双手，让身体内部的细节出现在皮肤表层之上。此外，手指的一些细节也令人费解，两手的小拇指和左手的中指都弯曲得有些过度，再有，左手与右手的位置被调换了。如果这是一双平放在水平面上的手，唯一的解释是双手是交叉放置的。当然，也存在另一种可能性，即观者在面对一双伸向空中的手。事实上，观者很难明确自己是从哪个角度在观看。除了手之外，大部分的画面是空白的。方形的构图因为长宽等长，本来就容易让人失去明确的方向感，视觉语言的高度精简和画面中的空白更强调了这种失重感。

陈督兮近年来的创作在不断变化，而《手》代表了一个特定的方向。这个方向可以通过将《手》和他的另一件作品《以息相吹》（2019）相比较来说明。《以息相吹》呈现的是一双站在水里的脚。两张作品创作时间接近，也有诸多共同之处。与《手》中似乎被拉长的手指类似，一些脚趾也被略微拉长；同时，脚和腿部的皮肤也是苍白无血色的。不过那种覆盖整个画面的奇特的诡异感显然并不属于《以息想吹》带给人们的观感。《以息想吹》的标题来自于《庄子》的“生物之以息相吹”，意思是生物之间以气息相联系。与这个标题相对应，画面呈现了人体和水两种物质形态，由此可以引发观者对于一系列关系的联想。这包括人体与水之间的关系，也包括观者的视觉（看到两种物质形态）和触觉（对于站在水中的感觉的联想）之间的关系。与此不同，《手》并不直接涉及事物间的关系这个主题。如果一定要找到某些共同点的话，《手》呈现的是不同观看角度之间的关系，其线条和空间的模糊性让观者在几种观看模式之间徘徊不定、反复摇摆。

《手》与《以息相吹》的创作时间相差约一年。它们之间的区别暗示着艺术家在这一年之间的创作上的一些变化。在视觉层面上，这主要表现为一种新的处理线条的方式：线条从水的运动延展为身体上或身体内的纹路。换另一个角度看，这也可以看作一种观看模式的转变，即从外在的观察变为内向的探索。

为了理解这个转变，下文将转向陈督兮更早一些的作品，以此来理解艺术家在 2019 年前后对水和人体的描绘发生的变化。从 2013 年到 2018 年，"水"是陈督兮作品中最为常见的主题，其出现的形式多为流水，也有山间的雾气，以及游鱼所暗示的无形的水。陈督兮将他对"水"的持续描绘追溯至 2013 年的一次都江堰写生。据艺术家描述，因为当地没有办法买到油彩和白纸，他在写生中用了中国画的勾线笔和宣纸。在此之前，传统绘画的题材和材料已经在陈督兮的作品中多次出现，而这次写生加速了他向传统的转向。

从陈督兮基于这次都江堰写生的作品中可以看出他在 2013 年视觉语言上的转变。这些绢本水墨作品中，艺术家以细密蜿蜒线条描绘了流水复杂的动态。陈督兮让构图集中在流水上，画面中很少出现明确的前景和背景之间的区分，也没有诸如用云雾、山石的细节点明周围环境或地理的特点。水流的运动相对平缓，画面中看不到浪花、泡沫这样的细节。画中的线条似乎可以随时蜕变为另外一种形态，比如声音的视觉化形式、木纹或抽象图案。

在 2013 年之前，由线条组成的抽象构图已经在陈督兮的作品中多次出现。在 2011 年和 2012 年之间，受到建筑设计软件的启发，陈督兮创作过一个基于几何式抽象图形的《穹顶》系列。他在画布上钉上钉子，然后将鱼线固定在钉子上，形成复杂交错的线条。他所使用的尼龙鱼线可以反光，有光照的时候，鱼线也会在画布上投下影子，这让画面上线条和空间的关系更趋繁复。艺术家在回顾这个时期时提到，这个系列让他形成了一种特定的观察和处理线条的方式，对他后来的创作也产生了一定影响。

不过，陈督兮有关都江堰的作品与《穹顶》系列也存在不同。《穹顶》中的空间是属于想象层面的，而在描绘都江堰的作品中，水流的动态与艺术家在实地的观察息息相关。每个线条都在向不同的角度延伸，而构图中，每一部分的水流动态与其他部分都不尽相同。

艺术家既描绘了水向前运动的状态，也呈现了一种微妙的静态。无论观者靠近还是远离画面，都很难同时看清楚画面的各个部分。在我的观看经验中，当我将视线放在整体构图上，一些局部的运动就很难看清楚；而当我将视线移到一个局部，其他部分的水流就退入视野角落，并开始变得模糊，甚至开始缓缓地旋转或运动起来。其他部分的水流就退入视野角落，并开始变得模糊，甚至开始缓缓地旋转或运动起来。

这种对于复杂运动的描绘是基于陈督兮对水的观看。更进一步说，它们更像是来自于对水的长期的、专注的凝视，而非对水在某一时刻形态的捕捉。在陈督兮的一篇文章中，他描绘过他画水时的观察方法:“应和水的运动表达，或者说是对所有流动体的表达，必须提取最大的运动趋势与运动规律的总和。”这段话将“观看”描述为一种分析、提炼、思考的过程。与此相关的一个细节是，陈督兮后来将有关都江堰的作品归入《持颐》系列，“持颐”的意思是托腮沉思，这也同样指向一种陷入思考的凝视。在中国画论中，这种审视性的观看不只与视觉有关，也与理念有关。《易经》中将世界看作永恒变动的过程，且这个过程与水类似，是连续的、持续变化的、绵绵不断的。在面对陈督兮有关水的作品时，道家有关变化的理念是很难被忽视的理解框架。

在 2013 年之前，来自于道家和传统中国绘画的题材已经在陈督兮的作品中出现了。如果将 2013 年作为一个转折的话，这个转折主要表现为艺术家作品与传统绘画之间更加紧密的、确定的联系。这表现在主题和绘画材料的选择上，也表现在构图上。出现在陈督兮早期绘画中的视觉并置在他 2013 年之后的作品中已经很少见到，他的构图更趋简洁，水、动物、古代人物直接出现在单色背景或接近于平面的空间中。这种转变中可以看到艺术家更为笃定的个人视野，以及随之而来的对画面空间更为深入的掌控能力。从另一个角度看，并置视觉元素，创造出具有冲突感的或梦境般的空间是国际当代艺术中更为常见的语汇。陈督兮的这个转变这也可以看作一种在“当代”和“传统”这两个艺术领域中重新定位自己创作的过程。

回到《手》这幅画，画中的手纹可以看到陈督兮水图的影子。与水的运动类似，这些线条是静止的，但又呈现动态的趋势，它们是静止的人体的一部分，又似乎如水一般流转。在这个意义上，这件作品让我联想到有关身体的运动的微妙之处，即内部永不止息的流动、生长以及衰败和外表的平静。

有关身体的线条在陈督兮 2019 年的作品中多次出现。在《持颐 7》（2019）中，大部分的构图是淡红色或肉色的线条。与艺术家对都江堰的描绘类似，画面中并没有线索点明流体的物质属性及运动方向，这些曲线看上去既像流水，也像人体的内部。画中所呈现的空间的基本形态也是模糊的，比如，观者很难确定画面的右下方是凸出来还是凹进去的。同年，陈督兮开始创作两个新的系列的作品。其中一个是肖像画《基因表达的肖像》系列 ，与陈督兮其他的人像不同，这些作品描绘的不是历史或神话人物，而是全部以艺术家的朋友为主题。另一个 2019 年开始创作的系列名为《尔躬》。这个系列的作品描绘了包括人物、植物、动物和水在内的主题，将该系列中不同作品勾连在一起的是画面中的一种不稳定的能量，或一种不安的情绪。比如《尔躬》系列中，水的纹路不再是平滑的、蜿蜒的，而是紧张的、刻意的、神经质的。在最下面一层浅色的细密线条之上，覆盖着一些起伏更大的线条，其中有些线条甚至接近于锯齿状。如果说上文所述的有关都江堰的作品呈现的是一种平静的、深入的审视，《尔躬》则让人们透过一双悸动不安双眼去观看，画面中颤抖的线条仿佛这个人波澜起伏的内心投射。

在上一段中，我试图将陈督兮在 2019 年的变化总结为生物性的、来自日常经验的比重的增加以及更为个人化的视觉语言。同时，我也意识到这些变化发生距离本文写作不过一年的时间，而艺术家还在持续创作上述几个系列的作品，在现在这个时间点还很难完整把握其意义。因此，我仅就我自己的观看体验中最为明确的几个部分展开下面的论述。首先，我在观看时体验到了一种被悬置的感觉，因为我很难将我看到的视觉语言与我对几种绘画类别的粗略印象对应起来，这些类别包括中国绘画、欧洲绘画、传统和全球现当代绘画等等。因此，在这个短暂的悬置感之后，我的观看并没有受到太多既定观念和框架的影响。我意识到，要继续看下去，我只有依赖视觉本身。

在观看陈督兮 2019 年的作品过程中，我发现作品与我之间的距离不再确定，它看上去既远又近。他们遥远，是因为它们很难被归类，我一时无法找到合适的分析框架。它们的切近感则来自于视觉层面和除视觉之外的感知层面。不同于陈督兮画水时经常使用的空中视角，这些作品将观者拉近到可以看清楚植物和生物的细节的位置。在一些作品中，我似乎在透过放大镜观看事物，这会模糊我对整体的观感，而放大一些细节带给我的影响。如作品《尔躬》呈现的是一朵玫瑰的茎，刺正在从茎的表层密集地生长出来，以极具侵略性的方式进入我的视野。我认为它们具有侵略性，是因为它们外形尖锐、数量众多，也因为它们的表层类似于肌肉的颜色和肌理，仿佛某种有关人体的噩梦般的景象。经由视觉语言的刺激，《尔躬》在某个时刻让我产生近乎反射性的恐惧。我认为艺术家有关生物性的一段论述在这里值得回顾：“……我们的身体有基因的记忆是不需要通过理性认知来形成判断的……这种语言的魅力，让我十分着迷，我认为这才是一种根源性语言。”事实上，陈督兮淡化特定文化框架的尝试和强调生物性的视觉语言是互为表里的。不管是将观者推远还是拉近，都可以看作在艺术家所说的“寻找根源性语言”这个方向上所做的努力。

《手》创作于 2020 年的夏天，这个特殊的时间点让作品的阴暗气质与当下产生了直接的联系。病毒让人们进一步认识到了身体的脆弱性，这种认知虽然是跨文化的，也与各个地方的具体文化形态息息相关。在过去十几个月的公共记忆中，文化和生物已经如此紧密相连，以至于人们也许永远无法再以同样的方式来观看身体以及有关身体的视觉描绘。我在观看《手》的时候所感到的不安也许不仅仅来自于本能，也来自于被过去一年所改变的认知。不过，身处于 2020 年底，我们还不到回顾历史的时候。人们可能需要很长时间才能经由各种途径了解到这个改变的深度和广度。我现在所能做的，只能是指出《手》和现实的这种联系，或者说将《手》看作当下正在变动的有关身体认知的一个视觉表征。

回到上述那种既近又远的感觉，这种感觉在观看《手》的时候也出现了。我无法将《手》归入我所熟悉的绘画类别之中。同时，《手》既吸引我，又让我觉得很难靠近。这种摇摆不定的感觉可能与皮肤和水纹的重叠有很大关系，因为看流水的方式显然和看掌纹的方式是不同的。另外，这些红色的线条类似于血液、肌肉，让人联想到人体内部的景象。我到底是在手外面观看还是在里面观看？我是在读取掌纹中的信息，进入他人的梦境，还是在从医学的角度观看一张手的透视图？对这两个问题的不同回答可能带来完全不同的观看方式，将画中的线条置于完全不同的结构之中。在实际观看过程中，上述不同的模式交替或一同出现，这让我感到画面难以琢磨，由此可能产生了本文最开始提到的诡秘（uncanny）的感觉。

在本雅明的文章《摄影小史》和后来的数篇作品中，他用“光晕（aura）”来描述一种观看自然或艺术品原作时既近又远的视觉体验。本雅明将光晕视作一个有空间也有时间维度的概念。“它可以离得很近，却是一定距离之外的无与伦比的意境，”他这样写道，“某个夏日正午，站在远处一座山峦或一片树枝折射成的阴影里，休憩着端详着那山或那树，直到与之融为一体的片刻或时辰降临。”观看《手》的体验与本雅明所描述的光晕类似，因为离画面越近，越容易产生一种距离感；而即便远观画面，那种心理层面上的强度依然挥之不去。

就我所知，光晕和陈督兮的实践诞生于完全不同的语境之中。然而在我的感觉中，它们的确是有联系的。为了进一步明确这种联系的意义，我想短暂地引入另一个概念，即超现实主义。在他的有关超现实主义的重要著作 Compulsive Beauty 中，艺术史学者哈尔．福斯特认为，光晕与超现实主义作品中的诡秘感有着内在联系。借助于对本雅明《论波德莱尔的几个母题》的解读，福斯特认为光晕所代表的的视觉经验的核心在于：将人与人之间的感情转移到人对物体的感受中。这点让光晕这个概念和超现实主义非常相似。通过佛洛依德有关诡秘（uncanny）的理论，福斯特总结了超现实主义理论、文学和艺术创作中，与诡秘有关的体验的三个面向，即现实和非现实、动态和静态、内部和外部世界之间差别的消失。《手》并不是一张超现实主义作品，但福斯特所总结的这三个面向在我观看《手》的经验中全部存在。光晕、诡秘、超现实主义这三个内在相关的概念似乎组成了一个概念的星丛，而与《手》相关的视觉体验在这个星丛中得到了一种遥远的共鸣。

说这是“遥远”的共鸣，是因为超现实主义并不是陈督兮所参考的视觉语言或理念框架，光晕在他的创作和写作中也没有被提起过。我认为陈督兮是通过完全不同的途径，唤起了这些二十世纪早期曾经引起欧洲学者和艺术家关注的美学经验。此处我想对超现实主义和陈督兮作品之间的关系做进一步的辨析，因为我想这个参照点或许可以照亮陈督兮实践中容易被忽视的一部分。如上所述，陈督兮的视觉语言很难被既定的风格类别所涵盖，这与超现实主义对不受文化约束的表达方式的追求有类似之处。另外，陈督兮对来自不同文化的早期绘画有广泛的兴趣，而超现实主义和民族志在二十世纪初期的发展也有诸多交集。在二者之中，我看到一种相似的人类学式的热情，即对图像的兴趣不止于视觉层面，也涉及到对图像所处的精神、心理、文化和社会环境的理解，这一点和上述超越特定文化框架的倾向是相辅相成的。对于他文化的理解有助于对自己所处的文化产生新的、更具包容性的视角，进而脱离特定文化的桎梏。虽然视觉语言和理念有诸多不同，超现实主义者和陈督兮在这一点上的思考方向是一致的。

使用超现实主义这个参照点也许会造成“陈督兮从传统绘画转向现代绘画”这个错误的且高度简化的结论。事实上，陈督兮在近期的写作中依然会直接引用古籍，他在继续创作看上去更为接近传统绘画的作品，《宋画全集》也是他经常翻阅的一本画册。可以说，陈督兮在 2019 年的创作更像是他 2013 年到 2018 年之间创作的一种特定方向上的延伸。这个延伸让他之前的一些思路以更为直接地方式呈现了出来。在描述他画水的思路时，他写道："这是需要一种训练，手在纸上的运行如同流速。而且还需要取消主体与对象的对立，让主体身处在对象体内。"这段话不仅强调了艺术家的身体与视觉之间的关系（手的运动和对流速的观察），也隐含了观察者和所观察对象之间、内部与外部之间界限的模糊。这两个问题都与上述艺术家在 2019 年的转变紧密相关。这段写作完成于 2020 年，也许在这个时间点艺术家在思考画水的方法的时候更为明晰地意识到了这两个问题；也许这是艺术家创作中一以贯之的思路，在 2019 年前后，这条思路在新的能量的刺激下生成了新的视觉语言。无论是哪种具体情况，对于陈督兮来说，2019 年前后他创作中的变化是具有内在连续性的，是以前思考的推进。

延续这个思路，我想将《手》这件作品与艺术家本人的关系推进一步。如上所述，在观看 2019 年的作品时，我可以明确感到我在透过他人的眼睛观看。我说"明确"，是因为这个感受中的"他人"更接近于普通人日常的状态，而不是一个沉思中的、进入内在精神世界中的人。这个人处于生活之流中，对他的朋友有细致的观察（如在人像系列中所呈现的），也会受到情感、冲动和本能的影响（如《尔躬》系列所呈现的）。我想艺术家也许是清楚这一点的。《尔躬》这个标题来自于《论语 · 尧曰》中的"天之历数在尔躬"，意思是"你自己"。这可以看做陈督兮对于观看者的一个提示，也可以看做艺术家对于绘画与自身关系的思考。

《手》的主题本身也具有自画像的性质。手在早期基督教绘画中经常作为指涉上帝的符号出现，因而具有了创造者的意涵。除了这层含义之外，手也是画家和作品中间最为重要的介质，因而在文艺复兴时期的绘画中，对于手的刻画也经常成为代表画家自身的符号。抛去西方绘画这段历史，仅仅去想象艺术家用自己的手去描绘画中的手这个场景，也很难不将两者联系起来。我倾向于认为，《手》带有这种自我反身性，与陈督兮对于自己的创作的理解有关。在我的想象中，这双手曾经在艺术家的视野中反复变化，它是熟悉的，也是陌生的；是流水，也是皮肤；是审视的对象，也是艺术家自己。基于对陈督兮过去创作的了解，我想在那一刻，这些可能性会在艺术家那里共存，他并不急于选择。

郭欣然

Distant Resonance

Hands (2020) portrays just what the title suggests—a pair of hands against a monochromatic background. Shades of red appear here and there on the pale white skin. Upon closer inspection, these are fine red lines representing palm prints. These meticulously rendered lines look both revealing and perplexing. They are revealing, for they endow the pale skin with a sense of texture; they seem perplexing, for hand lines are rarely red. Against the almost colorless skin, this web of lines is suggestive of blood veins or some kind of muscle tissues. While palm prints are part of one's skin surface, blood vessels are embedded in flesh beneath the skin. As I was looking at the piece, the visual conflation between the two aroused an uncanny feeling of both familiarity and strangeness. This peculiar yet mesmerizing quality of the work drove the writing of this essay, in which I will attempt to provide a preliminary framework for understanding this painting by tracing past developments of the artist's practice.

To be sure, the uncanny feeling did not come instantly. It gradually emerged as various details of the painting came into my sight. I realized that I was not only looking at the hands, but also *through* the skin at the veins and flesh. It seems that the artist did not portray hands as they appear in plain sight; instead, he seems to have painted the hand from inside out, layering the veins and muscles on top of the skin. Moreover, several fingers, the pinkies of the two hands and the middle finger of the left hand in particular, seem to be curved in an arbitrary manner. This uncanny feeling also had something to do with the way that the hands are placed. Chen has left more than half of the composition empty. This void around the hands seems to draw as much attention as the painting subject itself. The square format further underlines a sense of groundlessness, of the lack of a clear sense of direction. It is unclear, in plain sight, if the hands are reaching upward or placed horizontally on a table.

The intriguing quality of *Hands* is obvious when compared with one of Chen's earlier pieces Breathing amongst Beings (2019), in which the artist depicted a pair of feet in water. Similar to the portrayal of hands, certain physical features of the feet, especially the thumbs, seem slightly elongated; the skin is also painted pale white, with detailed depiction of the hair on the legs. Yet that haunting vision of things not being quite right, like a veil cast over the picture plane, is not there. The title, *Breathing between Beings*, is drawn from the Taoist classic *Zhuangzi*, in which invisible connections between things are described poetically as "living creatures are blown about amongst each other". In line with the title, the physical contact between body and water prompts thoughts about the relationship between various living entities, as well as that between the vision of water and the feeling of water.

Hands, in comparison, is devoted to a singular subject matter. The abovementioned connection between skin and flesh in Hands is more implicit. It only becomes clear to someone in the process of viewing, as this connection is essentially about how one's state of looking alternates, rather than about something portrayed directly in the work.

Judging from these two paintings done one year apart, Chen may have went through a transition around 2019. At the most basic level, this transition entails a different way of dealing with lines. While he used undulating lines to represent water in *Breathing amongst Beings*, these wavering lines are painted into the skin in Hands. From another point of view, this transition involves a different way of looking, replacing thoughtful reflection with visceral feelings that gradually unfold in time.

To understand this transition, I will take a retrospective look at Chen's earlier works, especially how he approached the depiction of water and human body before and after 2019. Between 2013 and 2018, the theme of water is constantly present in Chen's oeuvre. It sometimes takes the form of rippling water, running stream, or amorphous mist; it is sometimes indicated by swimming fishing. Chen turned to the theme of water after a sketch trip to Dujiangyan in Sichuan in 2013. Having no access to oil paint and paper in local stores, he used rice paper and Chinese brush. According to Chen, this change in painting materials facilitated his move towards a more traditional way of rendering lines and space.

Chen's paintings based on this sketch trip bespeak the new direction he was moving to. These works feature running water with meticulously rendered sinuous lines that coils and uncoils, bends and unbends, convenes and disperses. Chen sometimes left the space above water blank, sometimes filled the whole composition with water patterns. In either case, there are few details that orient the viewer spatially. A clear differentiation between the foreground and background is also unnoticeable. The artist focused solely on depicting water, without adding elements such as cloud, mist, or rocks indicative of atmospheric effects or landscape features. The movement Chen captures is rarely drastic or tumultuous, leaving few traces of big waves, foam, or splashes. The abstract compositions certainly remind viewers of the sight of running water, though this vision is abstract to a degree that it can easily morph into something else, be it sound visualization, wood texture, or imaginary landscape. It seems as if that the paintings are less about the sight of running water than about the complex physics behind the movement of liquids.

Chen had gained much experience working with lines and abstract shapes by the time he started working on water paintings. Between 2011 and 2012, Chen had taken a detour in geometric abstraction. Prompted by his foray into architectural design software, Chen formed a unique way of arranging lines to form imaginary spatial constructs. He realized his vision by attaching reflexive fishing nylons to nails drilled into the painting canvas. The light reflections on the nylons and the shadows these lines cast on the canvas create a complex interplay between abstract forms and material traces. When asked about if these earlier experiments with lines had an impact on his later water paintings, Chen said that he had formed a certain way of observation and of working with lines in this period, which paved the way for his later works.

Meanwhile, Chen's paintings of Dujiangyan depart from these earlier works in the visual language of abstraction. While the earlier pieces resemble constructs of imaginary space, these later paintings feature the palpable motion of interacting water currents. Each line follows a slightly different direction, and each part of the composition maps a fraction of the overall labyrinthine movement. In fact, a sense of movement and a subtle suspension of movement are both present in these works. Gaining a commanding view of the movement is not an easy task. Whenever I focused on one area of the painting, the other parts of the composition started to rotate, turn, and flow at the periphery of my vision.

It would be difficult, if not impossible, for the artist to arrive at such complex dynamics via theorization or speculation alone. Despite their abstract features, Chen's Dujiangyan paintings signal a mode of viewing dependent upon, albeit not confined by, sensory perception. They look more like the result of a long and focused gaze, rather than the sight of water at a specific moment. In his own writing, Chen described his perception of water with attentive observation. After describing various states of water, he wrote about the way to distill visual expressions that capture all kinds of liquid movement, "One has to seize the momentum of movement at its peak and the sum of the rules of movement." In line with this, he titled the series of water paintings, including the Dujiangyan pieces, *Chi Yi* (持 颐), which, drawn from the Taoist classic *Zhuangzi*, means the act of contemplation by putting hand on one's chin.

In Chinese painting theory, such investigative gaze reaches beyond the visual into the realm of the ontological. According to the Taoist classics *Yijing*, water patterns can be seen as visual manifestations of a cosmic flow that involves all the parts of the universe in a never-ending, self-generating momentum. This Taoist notion of change has a rather pervasive impact on how Chinese approach the notion of change. The commonly used Chinese expression *liubian* (flowing change), for example, captures the Taoist conception of fluid, continuous change. This notion of change frames how some viewers, especially those familiar with Chinese culture, approach Chen's portrayal of water. Whether such reading is sufficient to understand Chen's practice is another story. I will come back to this issue later in the article.

Threads drawn from Taoism and pre-modern Chinese painting had appeared in Chen's works before 2013. From 2009 to 2011, Chen had painted a number of works on subjects with Taoist underpinnings; he had also started using Chinese contour brush and silk as painting support. After 2013, the affinity between Chen's oeuvre and Taoism became more definite and evident. Apart from the change in themes and painting materials, Chen's compositions became simpler, more straightforward, and more poised. The artist had given up works that feature contrasting visual juxtapositions or constructions of imaginary space. Water, animals, and ancient figures appear against monochromatic backgrounds or within space with limited spatial recession. This simplicity is indicative of a stronger artistic vision and a more systematic conceptualization of pictorial space. In a way, this can be described as a move away from tropes of international contemporary art and a move towards the language of pre-modern Chinese painting.

In *Hands*, the thin red lines are reminiscent of the toiling water in Chen's Dujiangyan works. Similar to the patterns of water, these lines appear both animate and inanimate. The suggestion of water curling and twisting is obvious; yet this reference is conditioned by the fact that these lines essentially belong to the human body. Taking this into consideration, Hands reminded me of the dialectics between the perpetual movement of fluids and microorganisms inside human body and the seeming stillness on the outside.

Organic lines resembling human body emerged in Chen's works in 2019. In one work Contemplate 7 (2019), Chen applied various shades of pink and red to most part of the composition, while mixing in several streaks of darker color. Few details of the work suggest the physical quality of the painting subject, the direction of its movement, or if the lower right corner is protruding or receding from the surface. The result is a highly ambiguous composition that may remind one of water, wood, and human body at the same time. Also in 2019, Chen started two series of figurative works. One portrays his friends and acquaintances against monochromatic, circular backgrounds. Unlike Chen's earlier portrayals of religious deities or philosophers, these portraits of ordinary people are devoid of symbolic meanings. The other series, titled *Ergong*, focuses on a range of living forms including plants, animals, and human beings. Different from the smooth serpentine movement of water featured in the *Chi Yi* series, works of the *Ergong* series are more unsettled, more complicated, seemingly agitated by an immanent force. The Order Of Body – Refrain of this series, for example, portrays water with jagged lines that rise and fall in a rather arbitrary manner. Right in the middle of the painting, where the color of the water turns lighter and the seascape gives way to the sky, Chen added a serrated line that stands starkly against the background. Below this detail, more jagged lines appear on top of a web of light blue lines. If Chen's Dujiangyan works evolve around a calm and thoughtful gaze at water, The Order Of Body - Refrain portrays water through the eyes of an anxious observer, whose nervous impulses reverberated with the trembling lines Chen painted.

I have the feeling that this shift towards the organic and the bodily in 2019 is a significant one, yet I don't think now is the right time to elaborate on this significance. This change started less than one year ago. Writing about a change while it is still unfolding risks overlooking threads and propensities that would surface years or decades later. Therefore, I am going to focus on parts of my reactions that appear most acute at this moment. First and foremost, I was drawn by the temporary moment of suspension in my viewing process, when I failed to anchor the works by categories such as Chinese, European, traditional, or contemporary. Despite Chen's use of traditional painting materials, his visual language, quite obviously, does not fit neatly into any of these categories. My viewing had to proceed without the conditioning or hints of a certain interpretive framework. I had to focus on the act of looking itself.

One effect brought by this heightened emphasis on looking is that these latest works seems close and afar at the same time. The distance comes from the fact that the viewer is not able to pin down the theme or style to an artistic lineage. The feeling of closeness takes place both in a literal and metaphorical manner. For one, they move the viewer much closer to the painting subject. Viewers no longer look down from a position in mid-air, as in his Dujiangyan paintings; the view, whether of plants or human beings, becomes more direct and close-up. In some cases, I felt as if I was looking through a magnifying glass, which partially obscures the physical quality of the painting subject. When examining the blown up details of *Contemplate 45*, for instance, the swerving lines morph from a plant to rock formations to wrinkles on human skin. In some other cases, the biomorphic visual language provokes a visceral feeling from me. This is most obvious in Rose, as spikes on the stem of the rose seem to protrude into our vision in a rather menacing manner. This is not only underlined by the spikes' pointed outlines, but also by their surface texture reminiscent of human flesh. This anthropomorphous detail obscures the biological feature of the flower. Even with the knowledge of this being a representation, I had a fleeting feeling of apprehension. In fact, Chen's withdrawal from existing cultural frameworks and his heightened emphasis on biomorphic features as two sides of the same coin. Visceral reactions of fear and disgust to certain visual forms are written deep into our biological instincts. The provocation of instinctual reactions, in most cases, liberates one from the confines of human culture.

In the case of *Hands*, however, it would be a stretch to say that the morbidity of the work, painted in the summer of 2020, evades cultural confines. The fear of the pandemic and the heightened awareness of human fragility have become something shared across cultures. The biological and the cultural have become so deeply entangled in the past twelve months that it may have permanently altered our general perception of human body. The dreadfulness that flickers on and off in my viewing of Hands cannot be separated from this fear and this altered perception. It may take longer for people to fully grasp and extrapolate the implication of this pandemic on our collective consciousness. For now, I think it is suffice to say that the connection between the painting and the grave reality exists. In its own way, Hands indexes the visuality being shaped by this reality.

Meanwhile, I encountered a similar feeling of aporia in *Hands* as in his 2019 works. The lack of an obvious interpretive framework is certainly present in Hands; and the visceral reaction it evokes is no less poignant than in Transmit. This aporia also has something to do with the overlay of water patterns on human skin. While patterns of water movement implies the examination of an external observer, the suggestion of hand lines, blood veins, and muscle tissues trigger different modes of viewing, such as palm reading, surgical examination, and a dreamlike vision. Each mode of viewing entails subordinating the lines to a completely different way of approaching human skin and flesh. The incongruities between these ways of looking may partly explain the uncanny response *Hands* stirred within me.

This feeling of both near and far finds a distance echo in Walter Benjamin's concept of aura. In his seminal essay "A Short History of Photography" and a number of later articles, Benjamin used aura to describe the visuality of both near and far. When explaining the unique experience of encountering an original work of art, he defined aura as a temporal experience that creates "the unique appearance of a distance, however close at hand." The viewing of Hands is auratic precisely because the closer one moves to the canvas, the more distant he or she feels. At the same time, even one moves away, the psychic intensity of the work still haunts one's vision.

To talk about aura here is not out of context, for this concept intersects with the uncanny feeling I had. Art historian Hal Foster, in his book *Convulsive Beauty*, draws a connection between aura and surrealism. Citing Benjamin's "On Some Motifs in Baudelaire", Foster points out that inherent in the auratic experience is the transfer of encounters between humans to that between human and objects, which strikes a chord with the uncanny experience that lies at the center of the conglomeration of theory, experiments, literature, and art associated with the term surrealism. Through a reading of Freud, Foster extrapolates three aspects of the uncanny that are congenial to Surrealist objects and methods. The uncanny is the blurring between the real and the unreal, the mobile and the immobile, as well as a conflation between the external and internal worlds. All of these sets of opposite qualities, quite surprisingly, are present in my encounter with *Hands*. In other words, my perception of this painting strikes a chord with the visuality associated with aura and surrealism.

Admittedly, Chen's latest works stem from concerns completely different from the early twentieth-century exploration of the unconscious and the liberation of human psyche. Yet it would be productive to take a look at this connection. After all, surrealists rarely affiliated their practice to psychoanalytic theories of the uncanny, while, as Foster compellingly demonstrates in his book, the uncanny provides a crucial lens to understand the experience associated with surrealism. Surrealism, as a reference point, may illuminate aspects of Chen's visual logic that would otherwise be overlooked. As explained above, Chen is moving towards a way of looking unfettered by existing cultural values, which share some similarities with the surrealist exploration of the unconsciousness. Along the same line, one may also draw parallel relationships between Chen's wide-ranging interest in ancient images of various cultures and the intersection between surrealism and ethnology as exemplified in works of Georges Bataille and Michel Leiris. For surrealists and Chen alike, the anthropological interest in how images are conceived and made in vastly different situations contribute to their search for a way of unconstrained expression.

Chen's pursuit of an unfettered visual language is by no means a negation of his previous practice. Rather, he seems to sift through various cultural resources, including pre-modern Chinese painting, to re-conceptualize looking and painting. In 2020, Chen described this shift as the transition from the postionality of an outside observer to an exploration oriented towards the internal. "I then realized that the subject of observation is the essence. And the subject is a human being with a body. The body is essentially a physical being," he wrote. These words cannot be detached from the Taoist notion of change, which sees the world as an all-embodying cosmic flow. In this flow, the divide between the observing subject and the observed object, as well as that between the internal and external worlds, disappears. Notably, Chen did not draw on Taoist concepts in his writing, despite the fact that he has kept a steady interest in Taoism for years. It is possible that he had internalized Taoist ideals to such a degree that he, consciously or unconsciously, found no need to underline them in his writing. It Is also possible that the artist prefers to frame his artworks in a more inclusive way. In either case, an interpretive framework solely based on Chinese philosophy would be a necessary yet not sufficient condition to read his work.

Chen's oeuvre exemplifies a constant move to and from motifs and styles commonly deemed traditional. Most obviously, Chen painted a number of works that do not look much different from ancient Chinese paintings after 2013. Some of them may remind one of Song-dynasty paintings of water; some are portraits of religious figures or auspicious animals reminiscent of Yuan-dynasty ink line (*baimiao*) works. Yet the visual similarities do not necessarily place the works within the lineage of traditional painting. The fact that they were created conterminously with works such as *Hands* bespeak the necessity of a more complex understanding of "tradition". I use quotation marks to refer to how the word often functions as an umbrella term for a wide range of aesthetic concepts and visual language derived from the pre-modern period. From my understanding, Chen is interested in steeping himself in "tradition" while simultaneously moving away from it, with the aim of letting his own vision and structure take shape in his painting practice.

Artists invariably inherit things from the past; the problem is to comprehend this inheritance with the awareness that inheritance always stems from present-day concerns. It is totally sensible to interpret some of Chen's works by referencing Taoism and ancient water paintings. Such introduction is even more necessary for viewers unfamiliar with ancient Chinese aesthetics. Yet such interpretive framework might cloud the artist's multifarious engagement with visual and intellectual resources that lie outside the realm of "tradition". As mentioned above, Chen has a broad interest pre-modern paintings around the world. The list is long, including Maya mural, Lascaux cave painting, ancient Indian painting, Assyrian mural, ancient Egyptian art, Greek pottery, among others. What did an image mean for its creator and viewers? What kind of social, cultural, and psychological conditions made a certain mode of painting possible? These are some of the questions Chen raised in our conversation and in his online posts. These are inquiries geared at understanding the past, though the way these questions were posed essentially belongs to the present.

Finally, I want to think about Hands in relation to Chen himself. When viewing his works created in 2019, viewers may become aware at some point that they are looking through the eyes of another individual. Through the portrait series, viewers gain access to an individual's perception of his friends. Via works of the *Ergong* series, viewers obtain an intimate understanding of an anxious and unsettled observer. This observer, following the visual cues, is not much different from ordinary people. He has a keen observation of people; he can be swayed by emotions, impulses, and instincts. The fact that some of these works arouse visceral reactions reveals that the observer shares the instinctual defense mechanism that others have. The presence of this observer and that of the artist tend to overlap as one looks on. And I don't think the artist is unaware of this. The title *Ergong*, drawn from the ancient Confucian classics *The Analects*, literally translates to "yourself". This can be read as a reminder for viewers to be aware of their own physical body; it can also be an allusion to the presence of the artist himself.

This acknowledge of the painter looms large in the viewing of *Hands*. A pair of hands is a symbol laden with religious and cultural meanings. It has functioned as a reference to the God in early Christian art and a gesture towards the artist in art of the renaissance and later times. Aside from its religious connotations, hand is seen as an intermediary between the artistic creator and his work. Regardless whether Chen had tapped into this trope of Euro-American painting, the fact that he centered the whole composition on a pair of hands is telling. Imagine that physical proximity between the hands being painted and the hands executing the act of painting. It is likely that the artist was aware of the self-referential quality of the symbol. Here it is worth mentioning that, while a friend of Chen's posed her hands for the painting, the lines on the palms are based on those of the artist. I speculate that there might have been a moment when the lines in Chen's eyes shifted back and forth between familiar and unfamiliar, between water and skin, between an object of observation and a part of himself. Judging from his artistic developments over the years, I suppose that, at that particular moment, the artist knew better than to pin these lines down to one single state.

Guo Xinran

且战且学仙

——陈督兮《云蒸霞蔚》的艺术意志

“一画之法，乃自我立”，“有我之境”的创生，源出于心与世界的最初战斗。

石涛用“一画”形容天地初开的原初立法行动，而立法需要力量。落笔于纸的“一画”，彰显着心物对待的力学现象学。通过观物，世界以气势撼人之态向“我”施加作用力，“我”则用心的构型力量在同一时间反作用之，将自然把握为真理并表出为笔法。笔法的运作让山川成为有序表象，所谓“惟听人之握取之耳”——“握取”是执笔有力的直观形态。换句话说，绘制万物，是为了呈现心与物相待的力学体验过程。画家应当且必须在这个过程中逐渐经历并超越与自然各层级事物的“有待”关系，以求企及终极的“无待”境界，返回最初的“太朴”，亦即热力平衡的状态。

这种绘画现象学，是陈督兮这样的画家必然曾经体验过的：在各种媒介的平面上“用力”运笔，看似飘逸、绵长的笔触，实则需要首先克服笔墨和纸面之间无情的摩擦阻力。逆锋、出锋是力的凸显，藏锋、裹锋是力的包容，力量在操练中让身体与自然贯通。与古人一样，《云蒸霞蔚》直面山水草木竹石进行造型艺术创作，让蓬勃生生的“物势”与森郁雄强的“笔势”在力学逻辑上获得了类比性的关联。在艺术作品当中，曲折顿挫的力学效果结构为线条的绵延，由此仿佛直接呈现万物之不断生长的有机体貌（竹节、年轮、石纹、虫壳、矿石晶体……）。万物生生不息，而生命之力首先体现为对现有世界、同时也对自我的一种冲破和进攻。用一种黑格尔主义的腔调来说，生长等同于自我超克，而新生的部分总是对过去部分的否定。步步高升的竹节否定了尚未露头的笋尖，层峦叠嶂的奇峰否定了一览无余的平原，眼前的浪花总会被另一波浪花替代，18 岁的生日意味着 17 岁的死亡……万物冥冥之象当中无处不见这种否定 - 肯定的有机图式。当陈督兮沉迷于观察并用笔墨模仿这些生命有机体的自然图式时，万物森然之力也就似乎涌入了他的笔端，让他能够用纸笔交战的现象学，模仿天人交战的现象学。

你我的实然生存，总是基于“与物相刃相靡”的辩证过程。没有摩擦就不会生热；没有受动就没有能动；没有抵牾就不会有顺应。作为无限流体的生命在否定世界和否定自我的过程中体现着更为强力的肯定，也让更强的势能得以作为法则显现出来。尼采讲狄俄尼索斯精神，旨在重新召唤无限否定着的肯定意志。在此基础上，里格尔的“艺术意志”

学说才超出具体艺术史问题而具有哲学高度：每个具体历史地理处境当中的“相刃相靡”，总会让某一个有限但完善的“自身”获得肯定。造型从石头中浮现，光感从颜料中绽放，作品逐步克服最初无形无色的状态而“立志”，成长为自由个体。立志是获得方向，是获得道路。绘画的体感中伴随着技术的成熟，画家打磨自身，砥砺自身，作品因此成了“自由探究”和“自然生成”两种志向的共同见证。

《云蒸霞蔚》当中满是无机物的晶状层累、有机物的蠕动变态，千变万化，不仅模拟着物象的伸展，还揭示着陈督兮本人作为格物者的格斗式成长。对大物的端详，属于“从善如流”，所谓“参差荇菜，左右流之”；对细物的刻画，则属于“参差荇菜，左右芼之”，大把采撷自然素材以营构气韵，这种积极的格物活动，让画家、画作与氤氲本体似乎连贯为一体，也为新形式和法度的来临提供基础。由此才能理解笔触连绵的自然画家陈督兮何以还是力感丰沛的礼乐鼓手陈督兮，才能理解采野菜和“钟鼓乐之”在文明史层面的联系。

这样看，《云蒸霞蔚》里试图模仿的自然气息，实则能够揭示出世间你我成长为文明化个体的生命韵律。宗白华把“气韵生动”讲成有节奏的你我生命，并不会减弱“气”作为宇宙本体的意义，也不是为了向西方美学低头，而是为了在一个战乱频繁、世道艰难的环境下，让你我众人能够普遍获取力量的立志途径通过艺术经验得到直观显现。在 20 世纪 40 年代强调“充实之为美”，强调宇宙的“豪情”，显然是为了迎接即将到来的天地玄黄时刻。在宗白华那里，美的可静观特性并不与生生不息的存在节奏相违背，二者似乎是花朵和根系的关系。

在《云蒸霞蔚》里，美的图式与郁郁蒸腾的创作豪情也并行不悖——我们不能像极端的观念论者那样认为言象世界只是形骸，只是对神髓天光的暗喻。每一次带有生机的言象操演当中，总会存在着一些尝试精确把握否定 - 肯定之力学原理的图示，总会存在着以爱欲和意志追溯真我的踪迹。正如诗歌追踪时间，图式追踪空间，出身蜀地的督兮从四川高山上的道观找到“云蒸霞蔚”四个字，为自身营造图式的艺术意志立象，是因为“笼罩感极强”。这也意味着，唯有立志营造神秘的广大空间（无论是自然洞天还是政治苍天），创世的力量才会流溢到恭敬朝天的画家的身心之际。这并非对萨满巫术的一种猎奇式返回，而是旨在让凿路开山的壮士心志以雄浑瑰奇的方式登场。“地崩山摧壮士死”，这种斗争中的死亡带来的是更为宏大且完整的自然 - 政治大空间秩序。

要开辟新的道路，通向新的秩序，就得预演各式各样的战斗。就此而言，陈督兮面朝神性山水的画作，不免让我们回想起种种积极格斗且其乐无穷的政治传统。这或是因为神性山水本在作为政治中心的“汾水之阳”:“轩辕、尧、孔、广成、大隗、许由、孤竹之流，必有崆峒、具茨、藐姑、箕首、大蒙之游焉。”（《画山水序》）山水中的超越维度和在世的纵横维度之间总有着经纬关系。《史记·封禅书》记载了齐人关于轩辕黄帝“且战且学仙”的传说。造指南车乃至于预测风雨洪旱的技艺看似仙术，也可能是通过格物而获得的自然技术，其动机和心志都在于不断地投身战斗并获得胜利。这一可能源出于战国的传说实则说明，文明的旋涡模式伴随着和平与战争的辩证，亦即礼物与格物的辩证。“礼”在乎敬，“格”在乎免于耻，即免于战败。为了免于战败，技术文明和制度文明都需要发展，你我的艺术意志也就在嵌入自然的过程中通达自然。西方的文艺复兴有马基雅维利也有达芬奇，战争的艺术和艺术的战争并行不悖。同属于战乱时期的晋唐之际，也曾涌现“艺术 - 技术 - 思想”的突破。到了 20 世纪初，梁启超要求业已嵌入世界历史的中国来一场轰轰烈烈的“文艺复兴”，引发百家争鸣，“且战且学仙”在这个时期也就意味着让技术获得实质性进步、进而让国家获得自由的艺术意志。

“云蒸霞蔚”莫不是一种仙境氛围？可仙境氛围何以显现于人间？众所周知，任何战争中的第一体验，都是生存空间的稀缺。“人生在天下，困难确实大。”在阻力极大的乱世，水平的政治维度当中满是他者业已设立的成法。求仙访道者或可援引格物经验破除成法，但这要求极大的力学成本。若是愿意思索“且战且学仙”之人何以在面向山水造化之际转向“心源”，就不难发觉，他们或许是为了在纵横天下的同时，于垂直维度发生超越，让格致的技艺能够跃迁为心意的技艺，继而让你我的生存之道获得更高的整全性视野。

探究“心源”的过程，是《庄子》中借助“卮言日出”不断环绕终极道体的过程。藐姑射之山和四子是寓言，也是尧的心象。督兮在绘画中以繁复如云的物象和人像叩问自然，莫非他的心中也有着“且战且学仙”的志愿？那么，他的作品也就成了“和以天倪”的卮言，成了“若垂天之云”的鲲鹏之躯。

在战国的诗赋文章中，“云”的意象层出不穷。由幽冥虚静之处升腾而起的“鹏”好似居间于天地的“云”，为万物垂范，演示着内圣外王的奥义。外王的覆盖面越大，体量越大，所待之物也就越大，力量的对峙和迸发强度也就越大，运动的幅度和频率也就越宏观:“抟扶摇而上者九万里，去以六月息者也。”“云蒸霞蔚”，是极大尺度，也是极大力度，但却汇聚在极小方寸之间。这是中国艺术精神的魅力，也是“云”的魅力。荀子《赋篇》有云:

> 有物于此，居则周静致下，动则綦高以钜。圆者中规，方者中矩。大参天地，德厚尧禹。精微乎毫毛，而大盈乎大寓。忽兮其极之远也，攭兮其相逐而反也，卬卬兮天下之咸蹇也。德厚而不捐，五采备而成文。往来惛惫，通于大神，出入甚极，莫知其门。天下失之则灭，得之则存。

这是在歌颂战国时期儒道互补的云游壮士们，也是在为后世君子锤炼诗性的模仿典范。与此相似，《楚辞》中的“云中君”（对应作为本体的“云蒸”）-“东君”（对应作为万象的“霞蔚”）形象，就彰显着居间天地的垂天之姿，或是“览冀州兮有余，横四海兮焉穷”，或是“青云衣兮白霓裳，举长矢兮射天狼”。在此我们发现了战国经验抑或中国艺术精神的秘密：成为云就是成为自然，亦即：

（一）朝向无定和流动，因为政治事态永远不定。

（二）朝向美丽与雄浑，因为超越境界永未来临。

陈督兮的《云蒸霞蔚》投射给我们的正是一部流动且雄浑的力学之法。“法”代表着原初暴力，也代表着滋养万物、赋予天地纹理的好生之力。当生杀大权集于一体之际，“云中君”-“东君”的显白意象也就转义为“少司命 - 大司命”的秘密意象，居间于自然与人，也就转义为了居间于生存与死亡。至此，我们必须感谢督兮笔下的万象，它们让“且战且学仙”的居间体验如上古神灵一般活现于当今，这是一种对古典心灵的现代临摹。若屈原再生，得见其作，或许会问：无乃吾当年所呵之壁乎？

冯庆

Fight and Attain Immortality

——The Artistic Will of Chen Duxi's *Between Earth And Heaven*

"The law of the first stroke of painting is self-establishment." (Shi Tao, a Chinese painter) The creation of "the realm of self" originates from the initial battle between the mind and the world.

Shi Tao used "the first stroke" to describe the inceptive law-setting when the world was first formed, and law-setting requires strength. The "first stroke" on the paper demonstrates the dynamic phenomenology of the artist's mind and body. Through observing objects, the world exerts overwhelming force on "me" while "I" reacts to it at the same time with the structural power of the mind, grasping nature as the truth and expressing it as brushwork. The operation of brushwork gives the mountains and rivers an orderly appearance. As Shi Tao said, "They are available for the artist to grasp," and "grasping" is the intuitive form of strongly holding the brush. In other words, painting all things presents the dynamic experience of the relationship between the mind and things. In this process, the artist should and must gradually experience and transcend the "relying on something" relationship with things at all levels of nature to reach the ultimate state of "relying on nothing"and return to the original "grand simplicity," the state of thermal and dynamic balance.

This kind of phenomenology of painting is an experience that artists like Chen Duxi must have had. Applying "force" on the surface of various media with seemingly elegant and long strokes actually requires first overcoming the ruthless frictional resistance between pen, ink, and the surface. Reversing and displaying the stroke demonstrate strength. Hiding and wrapping the stroke show the tolerance of strength. In constant practice, strength allows the body to connect with nature. Like the traditional Chinese artists, *Between Earth And Heave*n directly depicts the mountains, rivers, trees, bamboo, and rocks to create art forms so that the vigorous physical postures and the lush and powerful brushstrokes gain an analogical connection in the logic of dynamics. In the works of art, the twists and turns of the dynamic effect are structured as continuous lines, seemingly directly representing the constantly growing organic patterns of all objects (bamboo joints, growth rings, stone patterns, insect shells, ore crystals...). All things grow and multiply with no end, and the power of life is firstly reflected as a breakthrough and attack on the existing world and, at the same time, on the self. In a Hegelian tone, growth is equivalent to self-transcendence, and the newly grown part always negates the past. The rising bamboo joints negate the shoot tips that have not yet grown, the mountains and peaks negate the unobstructed plain, the waves we see always get replaced by another round of waves, and the 18th birthday means the death of the

17th. All things, unpredictably and mysteriously, show this organic visual schema of negation and affirmation. When Chen Duxi was obsessed with observing and using pen and ink to imitate the natural schemata of these living organisms, the power of all orderly things seemed to flow into his brush, allowing him to use the war-like phenomenology between paper and pen to imitate the phenomenology of the war between nature and humans.

Your and my positive existence are always based on the dialectical process of "in conflict with things or in harmony with them." Without friction, there would be no heat; without being acted upon, there would be no action; without conflict, there would be no harmony. Life, as an infinite fluid, experiences negating the world and self, embodies a more powerful affirmation, and allows the stronger potential energies to appear as the laws. Nietzsche talks about the passion of Dionysus, aiming to reawaken the infinitely negated affirmative will. On this basis, Riegl's theory of "artistic will" transcends specific art history issues and reaches philosophy: the "conflict and harmony" in each specific historical and geographical context will always affirm a certain limited but perfect "self." The shape emerges from the stones, and the sense of light blooms from the paint. The work gradually overcomes the initial formless and colorless state and "determines" to grow into a free individual. Setting an aspiration aims to gain direction and path. The physical experience of painting goes along with the maturity of the technique. The artist polishes and fortifies himself. Therefore, the work witnesses the two ambitions of "free inquiry" and "natural generation."

Between Earth And Heaven is full of crystalline layers of inorganic matter and the wriggling and metamorphosis of organic matter. These ever-changing images not only simulate the expansion of objects but also reveal Chen Duxi's own fighter-style growth as an investigator of objects. When he studies large objects, he "following the good like a flowing river," like "Water flows left and right, Of cresses here and there"; in the depiction of small objects, he Is more like "Feast friends at left and right, On cresses cooked tender!" (from *Shijing*, *The Book of Poetry*), picking a great many natural materials to create a sense of charm. His proactive investigation makes the artist, painting, and rising clouds coherent and integrated, providing a foundation for new forms and laws. Only from this investigation can we understand why Chen Duxi, a natural artist with continuous brushstrokes, is also a powerful promoter of ritual music and understand the connection between picking wild vegetables (cresses) and "O bells and drums, delight!" as part of the history of Chinese civilization.

Looking at it this way, the natural breath *Between Earth And Heave*n attempts to imitate reveals the rhythm of life in which the world's people grow into civilized individuals. Zong Baihua sees the "vivid *Qi* and charm" as the rhythmic life of you and me. This interpretation does not weaken the significance of "*Qi*" as the entity of the universe, nor does it surrender to Western aesthetics. In an environment with frequent wars and hardship, Zong tried to show a path of determination that allows people like you and me to universally gain strength and directly reveal that path through artistic experience. In the 1940s, the emphasis on "fullness is beauty" and the universe's "grand passion" was obviously to welcome the coming moment of significant changes and revolutions. In Zong's view, the contemplative nature of beauty does not conflict with the endless rhythm of growth and multiplying. The two attributes are akin to flowers and roots.

In *Between Earth And Heaven*, the beautiful visual schema and the blooming creative passion go hand in hand. Unlike extreme conceptualists, we do not see that the world of images is just a skeletal body, a metaphor for the divine essence and heavenly light. In every energetic verbal and visual performance, we always see attempts to accurately grasp the dynamic principles of negation and affirmation, and there are always hints of tracing the true self through love and will. Just as poetry tracks time, a visual schema tracks space. Duxi, who was born in Sichuan, found four characters, "Yun Zheng Xia Wei" (meaning "rise and gathering of glowing clouds") from a Taoist temple in a Sichuan mountain, and created a visual schema of his own artistic will because the four characters show a "strong sense of envelopment." This also means that only by having the will to create a mysteriously vast space (whether a natural cave-like space or a political sky-like order) can the power of creation eventually flow into the body and mind of the artist who respects the sky. This is not a curious return to shamanic witchcraft but an attempt to make a majestic ushering in the heroic mind and will of the brave warriors who build a road on a dangerous mountain. "Under the crumbled peak the brave warriors died." Death in struggles creates a grander and more complete natural-political large-space order.

To open up new roads and lead to a new order, one has to rehearse all kinds of battles. In this regard, Chen Duxi's paintings that face the divine landscape ("mountains and rivers") cannot help but remind us of various traditions of enjoying proactive political struggles. This may be because the divine landscape is originally located in the "Yang of Fen River," the ancient political center: "People like Huangdi, Yao, Kongzi, Guangcheng, Dawei, Xuyou, and Guzhu must have traveled to the mountains of Kongtong, Juci, Miaogu, Jishou, and Dameng." (*Preface to Painting Mountains and Rivers*) The transcendent dimensions of landscapes and the vertical and horizontal political dimensions form a geographic relation. The "Book of Fengshan" of *Shiji* (*Records of the Grand Historian*) records the Qi people telling Huangdi's legend of "fight and attain immortality." Huangdi's skills of making a compass cart and even predicting wind, rain, floods, and droughts may seem like magic, but they might also be skills obtained through investigating natural objects, with the motivation and will were to constantly fight and win. This legend, which might originate from the Warring States Period, actually illustrates that the whirlpool development pattern of civilization is accompanied by the dialectics of peace and war, that is, the dialectics of rituals and investigation. Rituals are about respect, and investigation is about avoiding shame, that is, avoiding defeat. To avoid defeat, both technological civilization and institutional civilization need to develop, and your and my artistic will gains access to nature as it becomes embedded in nature. The Western Renaissance presented Machiavelli and Leonardo da Vinci. The art of war and the war of arts went as parallels. China saw art, technology, and thought breakthroughs during the Jin and Tang Dynasties, both war-torn periods. At the beginning of the 20th century, Liang Qichao, the activist, demanded that China, which had already been embedded in world history, start a vigorous "Renaissance," triggering much debate on the issue. "Fight and attain immortality" in this period would mean making substantial technological progress, allowing China to gain free artistic will.

Is "Yun Zheng Xia Wei" a kind of immortal atmosphere? But how can the atmosphere of immortals appear in the human world? As we all know, the first experience in any war is the scarcity of living space. "A human life in the world is full of hardship." In troubled times with great resistance, politics in the horizontal dimension sees a world full of established laws. Those seeking Taoist immortality may use their experience in investigating objects to break the established order, but this requires a huge cost in applying dynamics. Suppose one is willing to think about why people who "fight and attain immortality" turn to the "mind source" when facing the great changes in the mountains and rivers, it is not difficult to find that they may be trying to transcend the vertical dimension while traversing the political world, so that their skills in investigating objects can be transformed into skills about the mind, and then they will allow you and me to gain a higher and holistic vision in our way of survival.

Exploring the "source of the mind" is continuously going around the ultimate Tao entity with the help of the "daily mindless water like language" as described by *Zhuangzi*. The story of the Four People in the Mountain of Miaogushe is a fable and also the mental image of Emperor Yao. In his paintings, Duxi uses complex cloud-like objects and figures to question nature. Could it be that he also has the desire to "fight and attain immortality" in his mind? Then, his works have become the water-like words "tempered and harmonized by the Heavenly element in our nature" and the bodies of great fish and bird (*Kun* and *Peng*) "like clouds all around the sky."

In the poems and articles of the Warring States Period, the image of "cloud" emerges endlessly. The great *Peng* bird rising from the vacant and stillness is like the "cloud" between heaven and earth, acting as the model of all things and demonstrating the secret of "inwardly forming the sage and externally the king." The greater the coverage and size of the "external king," the greater the things they are relying on, the greater the intensity of the power of confrontation and explosion, and the more macroscopic the amplitude and frequency of movements: "Then it ascends on a whirlwind 90,000 li, and it rests only at the end of six months." "Yun Zheng Xia Wei" is grand in scale and strength, but the force stays in a tiny area. This is the charm of the Chinese artistic spirit and the charm of clouds. Xunzi's "Fu Pian" says:

> There is an object, when it stops, it stays quietly at the lowest, when it moves, it is high and boundlessly expansive. It can be either round or square, as if it is drawn perfectly by a compass or a ruler. It is as great as heaven and earth, as virtuous as Yao and Yu. It can be as tiny as a hair or as large as a huge space. Quickly, they become extremely far away; divided, they chase each other and return; when risen, people live a life of hardship. It is virtuous, leaves no one behind, and has patterns formed by five colors. Its comings and goings are through darkness and unpredictable like the great gods. They enter and exit so quickly that no one knows the door. If the world loses it, the world perishes. If the world has it, the world lives.

This poem is a tribute to the cloud-like wandering elites who practiced both Confucianism and Taoism during the Warring States Period, and it also sets for later generations of gentlemen to refine their poetic nature. Similarly, the characters of Yunzhongjun (corresponding to "Yun Zheng," as the entity) and Dongjun (corresponding to "Xia Wei," as the multitude of images) in *Chu Ci* (*Verses of Chu*) show the appearance of someone living a life of greatness between heaven and earth, either "I see beyond the known world, and I have traveled to many places in the four seas," or "I wear blue clouds and white neon as clothes, I am holding up a long arrow to shoot at the evil wolf star." Here we discover the secret of the Warring States experience, or the spirit of Chinese art: to become a cloud is to become nature, meaning:

1. Toward uncertainty and fluidity because political events are always uncertain.
2. Toward beauty and majesty, for transcendence never arrives.

What Chen Duxi's *Between Earth And Heaven* projects to us is a fluid and powerful law of dynamics. Law represents the original violence and the power of nurture that nourishes all things and gives texture to heaven and earth. When the power of life and death is integrated into one body, the explicit images of Yunzhongjun and Dongjun are transformed into the secret images of Shao Siming and Da Siming, mediating between nature and people, which also translates into mediating between survival and death. At this point, we must thank Duxi for all the phenomena in his works, which make the intermediate experience of "fight and attain immortality" come alive today like ancient gods. This is a modern copy of the classical mind. If Qu Yuan was to be reborn and could see his work, he might ask: is this the same wall I wrote my emotional words on?

Feng Qing

模进与迭奏

乍看之下，陈督兮不同系列作品所呈现出的视觉主题可谓各异其趣，彼此之间似乎并无必然的逻辑关联。但若抛开这种表象，转而进入其创作观念内部，便会探知到若干如草蛇灰线般潜伏、贯穿于各类画面中的持续、深入的探索，这关乎对生命的观照、对本质规律的探寻，以及对认知结构的连接。显然，艺术家并未遵循一种形式语言层面上所谓的创作“进化论”原则，而是有意将自己反复抛入到一种智识与经验的陌生之境中，从而不断激发自身对其所关切问题的多维度体察。

如果依照视觉语言上的粗浅划分，陈督兮的作品包含了抽象性与具象性两种特质。以其创作的《虚静》、《尔躬》系列为例，前者以延绵不断、变幻万千的抽象线条为基本形式语言，后者则以偏于“写实”的手法对生物体的多元形态加以个性化的呈现，分别体现出对这两种不同风格形式的侧重。事实上，抽象性与具象性在其诸多画面中往往以一种彼此交融的方式相互渗透，这典型体现在以《持颐》系列作品为代表的画面中。该系列由线条所勾勒的形态时而偏于抽象、时而偏于具体，隐约指向江河、山丘、星空、云霞，在似与不似之间突显出一种生生不息的流动感。

在其早期创作的一系列以缠绕交织的丝线构成的具有抽象形态的作品中，陈督兮似乎已经完成了其对某种本质规律的观念传达，然而艺术家并未在这一形式框架中继续以固有模式进行“衍生”，而是转入到绘画——这一更具主体性与行动力的表现方式中，并不断在所谓的“具象”与“抽象”之间反复横跳。这种实践方式颇像是一种对终极理念的倒推与反证。换言之，艺术家摒弃了“进化论”式的创作模式，转而试图将一种对本质规律的认知转化于形态迥异的视像之中，以一种“不着相”的方式测试某种放之四海而皆准的法则。

不难发现，陈督兮一直以来对各类生物所展现出的浓厚兴趣在其绘画作品中得到了充分的体现。在《尔躬》系列的创作中，艺术家有意抽离了其所表现生物的具体情境，并选择以或整体、或局部，甚或是微观局部的视角，通过一系列主观的语言转化，有效强化了存在于具体生物中的、易于被忽视的个性化特质与细部的万千变化。但与其说陈督兮画面中形态各异的生物，折射出的是一种对生命体复杂建构与美学显现的惊叹，不如说是一种对生物实在性及其所蕴含的生命可靠性的认知与思考，一种对生物个体本自具足的天然之态的凝视与呈现。

与此同时，艺术家对蕴含于万物之中的生命力的体察与表现，亦未单纯停留在一种可视的表象上，而是进一步深入到对物质之间能量集结、交换、共生的抽象理念上，这或可理解为一种类似对“气韵”的表现。《虚静》与《持颐》系列中，充满动势的线条在蜿蜒回转间犹如旋律般起伏跌宕、不绝如缕。其间，艺术家试图捕捉的并非是一个个现实中不可片刻留驻的瞬间景象，而是那种存在于可见形态背后的、推动物质世界运行的流动不居的能量。

在这类以线条为主体语言的作品创作中，陈督兮采用了一种非预设性的绘画方式，在对整体画面意境具备一个基本想象的前提下，以笔随心走的方式完成对形态的具体构建。每一根线条的走向都是笔墨与心境的当下交融，不可预知、亦不可重复。创作的过程颇似一次即兴的音乐演奏，在心手往来之间编织出节奏的疏密与旋律的起伏。需要指出的是，这种“即兴”式的创作并非如脱缰之马，而是被恰当地控制在一个稳定的框架之中，正如音乐内在的理性基调，即一种建立在乐理结构上的有约制的发挥。这恰如观看其作品时所感受到的某种内敛的气质，某种寓“意”于“工”的细密心思。

应当说，几乎任何一种创作都包含着主体因素，在陈督兮的作品中也同样体现了这种来自创作者的主体在场。无论是《虚静》、《持颐》系列中那些由蔓延回旋的线条以及单色调构成的极具想象力的自然景象，抑或是《尔躬》系列中以微妙的形变以及表现性色彩所呈现的生物体，皆证实了这种主体性的在场。值得注意的是，在追寻某种可靠性依据的过程中，艺术家在有意无意中尽可能地抽离了自我的情绪与意识。故而，其作品中的主体性指向的并非情感层面的抒发，而更多的是有关观看视角的选择与绘画性的考量，而其对后者的巧妙运筹又对前者生成了加持，从而使其获得了更为有效的强化与显现。

当然，这种主体性所可能连带的范围，可以进一步辐射至艺术创作者自身的文化背景、趣味趋向、成长环境等一系列相互作用的远端溯源当中。尽管陈督兮从未刻意强调某种文化身份，但其对工笔这一绘画形式的选择，及其作品中所透露出的东方美学倾向，均提示了这种内在的文化基因对其艺术创作所产生的潜移默化的影响力及推动力。但同时需要强调的是，艺术家并未将自身囿于这种环境与基因，所赋予的文化敏感性当中，而是以一种颇具好奇心的方式，将其所关注的问题及与之相关的思考，置于更为宽泛的文化、风格以及学科类型当中。

正如陈督兮作品中所显现出的尚古之趣，不仅体现在对古典绘画风格元素的运用上，对古朴幽远意境的向往上，也同样体现在对部分古生物题材的选取上。换言之，这种对远古的幽思同时指向了人文及自然两个层面。而单就文化及其所派生的绘画风格而言，陈督兮亦采取了多元借鉴的手法。如果说《动物》系列以富于想象力的表现方式，更为明显地呈现出对中国古典绘画语言及其意境的挪用，那么《肖像》系列则以一种全然不同的题材，显示出对宋元人物绘画及波斯人物细密画表现元素的糅合。

若从这种对语言风格的借鉴角度，更为细致入微地检视陈督兮的画面，观者甚至可以捕捉到部分《尔躬》系列作品中，那些以较粗线条勾勒形态，并采用更多纯色绘制的主体形象所附带的现代主义元素，或是《肖像》系列作品在人物塑造中所提取的些许尼德兰肖像绘画表现手法，抑或是其整体创作中所隐隐透露出的某种超现实感。

所有这些来自不同维度的元素在陈督兮的画面中以一种和谐自洽的方式彼此交织、自然融合，并生成属于画面自身的逻辑。或许，任何所谓风格、形式，乃至学科、文化、思想，在某种意义上不过都是一种对真实的片面性解读，它们所能代表的正是个体或群体对本质规律展开的种种无限接近真相的主观认知。艺术家正是通过将自身的视角与观念不断置于其所关注的一系列领域的认知边界，试图搭建彼此间可能存在的连接与共识，寻找一种内在的通感，并借此传达一种对生命最初生成的无尽神往与想象。

王薇

Sequence and Refrain

At first glance, the visual themes presented in Chen Duxi's different series of works are diverse, without any inevitable logical connection between them. But if one goes beyond the surface and enters his creative concepts, one will discover traces of continuous and in-depth explorations that lurk and run through various images. Such inquiries concern the observation of life, the seeking of essential laws, and the connection with cognitive structures. Obviously, the artist does not follow a creative "evolutionary" principle at the formal language level but intentionally throws himself repeatedly into an unfamiliar realm of knowledge and experience, thus constantly stimulating his multi-dimensional concerns about issues.

A rough classification of visual languages would see Chen Duxi's works as both abstract and concrete. For example, in his *Vacuous Silence* and *The Order Of Body* series, the former uses continuous and ever-changing abstract lines as its primary formal language, and the latter uses a more "realistic" approach to depict the diverse forms of living beings. The two series reflect the different emphasis using these two different styles. In fact, abstraction and concreteness often interpenetrate in many of his paintings, and the typical examples are manifest in the *Contemplate* series. The forms sketched by lines in this series are sometimes abstract and sometimes concrete, suggestive of rivers, hills, starry skies, and clouds but not exact copies of these natural objects, highlighting a sense of endless liquid flow.

In his early series of abstract works, composed of entangled threads and lines, Chen Duxi might have conveyed his concept of a certain essential law. However, the artist did not continue to use this formal framework. Instead of "deriving" from the existing patterns, he moved on to painting, a more subjective and proactive way of expression, and constantly hopped between the "concrete" and the "abstract." This practice method is like backward reasoning and proving by disproving the contrary. In other words, the artist abandoned the "evolutionary" creative model and instead tried to transform an understanding of the essential laws into diverse visual images, testing a universal law in a way that does not stick too closely to a particular method.

Apparently, Chen Duxi fully displays his strong interest in all living beings in his paintings. In creating the *The Order Of Body* series, the artist intentionally abstracts away the specific context of the presented living beings and chooses to take a whole, partial, or even microscopic perspective. Through a series of subjective language transformations, he effectively strengthened the easily overlooked individual traits and the multitude of detail variations in specific living beings. But rather than saying that creatures of varied shapes and sizes in Chen Duxi's paintings reflect amazement at the complex construction and aesthetic manifestation of organisms, it is better to say that the objects are a recognition and reflection of the reality of living beings and the reliability of their lives, a gazing and presentation of the natural state of individual living beings.

At the same time, the artist's observation and expression of the vitality contained in all things does not simply stop at the visible appearance but goes further into the abstract concepts of energy collection, exchange, and symbiosis between matters. One may see this as an expression of "*Qi* and charm." The twists and turns of the dynamic lines in the *Vacuous Silence* and *Contemplate* series are like timeless melodies with ups and downs. In them, the artist is trying to capture not the momentary scenes in reality that never stay for a moment but the flowing energy that exists behind the visible forms and drives the movement of the material world.

In the creation of this kind of work using lines as the primary language, Chen Duxi takes on a non-preset painting. After having a bare imagination of the overall creative concept, he completes the concrete form of the painting in a free-flowing way. The direction of each line is the current blend of brush and ink and state of mind, unpredictable and unrepeatable. The creative process is quite like an impromptu musical performance, weaving the density of rhythm and the ups and downs of melody between the mind and the hand. To highlight, this kind of "improvised" creation is not wild, like a runaway horse, but adequately controlled within a stable framework. His work, like music, is inherently rational, a restrained expression based on the structure of music theory. When one views his works, one feels a restrained temperament, a certain meticulous planning that uses artisan "work" as metaphors for his "ideas."

The key is that almost any creation contains subjective factors, and Chen Duxi's works also reflect the artist's subjective presence. The highly imaginative natural scenes formed by crawling, convoluted lines, and monochromatic colors in the *Vacuous Silence* and *Contemplate* series, or the organisms presented using subtle deformations and expressive colors in the *The Order Of Body* series, confirm the subjective presence. Importantly, in pursuing a reliable basis, the artist intentionally or unintentionally detaches his emotions and consciousness as much as possible. Therefore, the subjectivity in his works is not directed at the expression of emotions but more about the choice of viewer's perspective and the consideration of painting, and his ingenious management of the latter has added weight to the former, thus gaining more effective reinforcement and manifestation of the choice.

Of course, we can trace the possible scope of this subjectivity to the artist's cultural background, interests and preferences, and childhood environment, which form a remote series of mutually interactive sources. Although Chen Duxi has never deliberately emphasized a cultural identity, he has chosen the *Gongbi* technique, and his works are geared toward Eastern aesthetics, suggesting the influence and driving force of this inherent cultural genes on his artistic creation. But at the same time, it needs to be emphasized that the artist does not confine himself to the cultural sensitivity endowed by the environment and genes but uses a curious way to express his concerns and related pondering within the broader cultures, styles, and disciplines.

As shown in Chen Duxi's works, his interest in the ancients is reflected in the use of classical Chinese painting elements, his longing for the ancient minimalist styles, and the choices of paleontological themes. In other words, this contemplation of ancient times points to both the humanistic and natural levels. In terms of cultures and their derived painting styles, Chen Duxi also draws lessons from multiple sources. The *Animals* series clearly shows the appropriation of Chinese classical painting language and artistic conception in an imaginative expression. On the contrary, the *Portrait* series, with a completely different subject matter, shows a mixture of the Song and Yuan portraits and Persian miniatures.

Suppose one examines Chen Duxi's paintings more from the perspective of his borrowing of language styles, the viewer can even catch the modernist elements in the *The Order Of Body* series, thicker lines to outline the subject forms and solid colors to paint them, the Netherlandish portrait painting techniques used for the characters in the *Portrait* series, and the sense of surrealism implicitly revealed in all his works.

In Chen Duxi's paintings, all these elements from different dimensions are intertwined and naturally Integrated in harmony and consistency, thereby generating the inherent logic of each painting. Perhaps any so-called style, form, discipline, culture, and thought, in a sense, is an incomplete interpretation of reality. These may represent the individual or group's subjective perception of the essential laws, with the perception being infinitely close to the truth. By constantly placing his perspective and concepts at the cognitive boundaries of a series of fields that he is concerned about, an artist attempts to build possible connections and consensus between each other, find inner resonance, and thereby convey a sense of endless fascination and imagination for the original birth of life.

Wang Wei

Artist's Statement

关于生物

最近几年，因为常常到户外活动的缘故，又重新激发了我对自然科学相关方面的兴趣。我并不是有意要从生物的角度去解释艺术，而是在一种非常放松的状态下偶然关注到有关生物演化的历史，于是开始搜集一些古生物和海洋生物的资料以及纪录片。此刻我发现我的好古之趣在这方面获得了极大的满足，好古似乎成为了一种探索的动力。

自然界并不会因为文明而改变它运行的法则。从冥古宙之始，到太古宙、元古宙、显生宙，然后是古生代、中生代、新生代，再然后是下面若干的纪，纪下分世，世下分期，期下分时。在这样一个近 40 亿年的反反复复的演化过程之中，我们不难发现，人类其实是一种非常年轻的生物，但是他与各种各样的生物之间都存在联系。我逐渐在绘画中倾注对于对象生物性的观察，突出它们的生物特征以及这些特征的原始表达。

“生物性”最终回归的是身体这个认知中枢。对外部观察地再为透彻，最终还是要回到主体身上。身体的历史与奥秘是打开所有问题的钥匙。这是一个巨大的探索空间，对我而言也是一个新的视角。当我看到那些 3 ～ 5 亿年前的三叶虫时，它们的身体里存在着与我们相同的某些东西，至少在繁衍这件事情上我们没有区别。

我并不想用一种猎奇的心态去描绘它们的身体，它们的价值远比我们想象的要大得多。在我们熟悉或者不熟悉的动植物或是人之中，我采用一种与生物性相关的视角再去观察对象，会发现有些许不同。

试想，当我们与这些古生物相遇时，它们会散发什么样的气息？它们的活动只是为了将外界的物质转化为自身的物质，同时分解自身的物质提供生命所需的能量？它们与单细胞生物并没有多大的区别。进化虽然越来越复杂，功能越来越强大，体积从小到大，又从大到小，一切都是为了适应生存。这些问题，在我看来是关乎生命根本的问题，虽然目前我也没有找到答案。

人类所有的意识活动都来自于必然的、为适应生存的生物性。人的精神性追求与生物性的关系是什么？难道这些追求有跳脱出生物性的范畴吗？我们常常被精神的力量撼动，认为人活一代又一代，只有精神是具有超越性的，不受时空的阻隔可以长久的传递，视其为某种神圣。但这一切都需要以具备生物的基本属性为前提。因此，我对生物性的客观视角仿佛有了一种更为可靠的信任。它不同于物理和数学。并非所有的因果逻辑在生物界中都有所依据，无序和错误的基因传递导致的生物多样性的演变才是真相，所以人们主观的渴望秩序带来的安全感与可靠性。世界必须是可认知的愿望，在那股支配万物的力量面前显得无力，就像我们永远无法完全认知我们的身体里所有的潜能。在无知中学会充分的运用有限的已知，可能才是生命生存迫切需要面对的具体问题 。和光同尘并不是境界，它只是回到起点。生物性也包含着心性，也许认知的终极是一种面对世界的态度，而不是认知的多与少。

古生物学家与基因学家们的探索，对整个生物变化莫测序列的传递而言，犹如宇宙中的微尘，即使我们有了很多线索，也无法描绘出整幅图景。所以，艺术的视角也仅仅只是尘埃的另一面，但这并不会影响探索带来的惊喜。

在童年对于世界的认知还有许多空白，但在玩耍的时候突然看见一只彩色的蜘蛛、或是通体斑斓的昆虫时，我当然会本能地警惕，这说明我们的身体有基因的记忆是不需要通过理性认知来形成判断的。当你看到这些毒虫的长相，它们的身体正在传达它们行为习惯的信息。这种语言的魅力让我十分着迷，我认为这才是一种根源性语言，没有任何沟通的障碍，不受时间的限制。这也正是我在绘画中试图探讨的语言。因为有时候，我在想生命根本的问题是不是也就是绘画根本的问题。

植物有植物的世界，昆虫有昆虫的世界，海洋有海洋的世界，微生物、鸟类、都有自己的世界。如果你进入，都会沉迷，但最后还是要回到人的世界，即使有时候我并不想回来。

我认知的重点一直在变迁和纷繁中寻找一种相对稳定和可靠的东西。 我开始关注传统，关注水的流变，关注运动，以为这些就是本质。后来意识到所有这些关注的主体才是本质，主体就是肉身就是身体，身体就是生物性的。

生物演化与流变的目的是适应性的。为什么去适应？因为外部也在变化，外部的运动我们更加无法理解，于是有了宗教的解释。宗教把这些运动的轨迹和交织解释为信仰统一性的集合，然后这个集合有了不同的名字。 这一系列内外的变化我们无法呈现出整全的解释。但这个世界却是整全得不需要解释。天地无言是矣。艺术正是在这种无言之中进行交流，用运动观察运动，用无言诉说无言，在本位中动察本体。

陈督兮

On Biology

Due to my recent interest in outdoor activities, I have become familiar with several topics of natural science. I do not mean to explain art from a biological perspective. I came across the history of biological evolution quite accidentally. This led me to the research and documentary films of prehistoric animals and sea creatures, which helped me to fulfill my interest in antiquity. I find that this interest has become a momentum for my exploration.

The rules of nature are not altered by human civilization. Geologic time begins with the Pyeozoic, the Archean, the Proterozoic, and Phanerozoic. Then it comes to the Paleozoic, the Mesozoic, and the Cenozoic. Each eon can be subdivided into eras; each era can be sub-divided into periods. These are followed by epochs, ages, and chrons in terms of the length of time. Human being, a relatively young species within the natural evolution that lasted for over four billion years, is interconnected with various biological organisms. I started to pay more attention to the biological aspects of my painting subjects and emphasize them, as well as their pristine expressions, in my work.

Our perception of biological features relies on the cognitive organs in our body. No matter how acute our observations are, the center of our attention has to return to the observing subject. The history and mystery of human body is the key to understanding everything. When I look at trilobites from three to five million years ago, I think about the biological features that they and human beings. At least, in terms of reproduction, trilobites and humans are not much different.

I don't want to depict human body to seek novelty, as the value of human body is much more meaningful than we can imagine. If I look through the lens of biological features, living organisms and human beings will appear to us in a slightly different way.

Imagine encountering one of such ancient creatures, what kind of breath would they have? Do their activities simply stem from the need to digest things and turn them into energy to continue their life? These ancient creatures are not essentially different from single cell organisms. Evolution has rendered creatures more complicated and tougher. The size of living organisms changes from small to big, or from big to small, with the sole aim of survival. For me, these are fundamental issues of life, though I have not reached a final conclusion yet.

All cognitive activities of human being are derived from our biological features that help us adapt to the environment. What is the relationship between humans' spiritual pursuit and biological features? Do spiritual pursuits exceed our biological confines? We are oftentimes moved by spiritual forces. We tend to think that, throughout generations, only spiritual pursuits can transcend temporal and spatial limits; therefore, their power can be transmitted through ages and can be seen as divine. Yet all of this is predicated on our basic biological features. For this reason, I become more convinced about the biological perspective. Unlike physics or mathematics, in the biological world, not all causes and logics are based on evidence. The truth is: disorder and incorrect gene delivery lead to the evolution of biodiversity. For this reason, humans, out of their innate need, yearn for the security and reliability brought by order. Just as we can never fully recognize the potential of our body, our desire to turn the world into a cognizable object would appear feeble in the face of the power that governs everything. Learning to make full use of the limited known part of the world while recognizing our ignorance may be the most urgent task in our life and survival. Being in harmony with light and dust is not an otherworldly realm; it merely returns us to where we first began. Biological features entail characteristics of our mind. Perhaps, ultimately, cognition more about a way of dealing with the world than about how much we cognize.

Compared with the highly capricious biological sequences, the work of paleontologists and geneticists is like dust in the whole universe. Even if we have found multiple clues, we can hardly paint the whole picture. The perspective that art offers is not much different from such dust. Meanwhile, this does not affect the wonder our exploration brings.

When I was a child and did not know much of the world, I would be instinctively alerted when, while playing, I saw a colorful spider or a bright-colored insect. This shows that our genetic memory does not make judgements by relying on rational cognition. When a human being encounters these venomous insects, he or she learn about the information about these insects' behavior and habits directly through their appearance. The charm of this visual language deeply fascinates me. I see it as a rudimentary language unobstructed by communication barriers or temporal limits. This is the language I am exploring in my paintings. Sometimes I wonder if the fundamental issue of life and the fundamental issue of painting are the same.

Plants have a world of their own; insects have a world of their own; and oceans have a world of their own. Microbes and birds all have their own worlds. If one enters any of these worlds, one will be deeply enchanted. Yet eventually we have to return to the world of human beings, despite the fact that sometimes we don't want to come back.

My work has been centered on the searching for things that, amidst various changes, are relatively stable and reliable. I initially payed attention to tradition, the flow of water, and movement, as I thought that these represented the essence of things. Then I realized that the subject paying attention is the essence. The subject is a body and is constituted of flesh. It is biological.

The aim of biological evolution is adaptation. Why adaptation? Because the outside world is perpetually changing. And it is difficult for us to understand these changes external to us. Therefore, we created religious explanations. We unite interpretations of multiple movements into singular belief systems and give each system a different name. We can hardly interpret all internal and external changes thoroughly. And, after all, this self-governing world does not require our explanations. As the old Chinese saying goes, heaven and earth are silent. Art communicates in this silence. In art, we observe movement through movement; we express silence through silence; we observe the subject in a subjective manner.

Chen Duxi

Works

Vacuous Silence

最重要的还是对于绘画目的性的消解，和对自我主体性的弱化。让自然物本身来给你一种启示，这是整个作品最重要的一部分，也是我对“虚静”思想的践行。身在其中的时候，要致虚，守静，才能归根，复命。“虚是一个开始，虚心就是虚掉它的目的性，我也不知道我为什么要做，怎么做。对象会给我的启发，带我进入”。

The most important things are dissolving the purpose of painting and weakening of self-subjectivity. Let the natural objects themselves give you an inspiration, which is the utmost crucial part of the whole work and also my practice based on the idea of “vacancy and stillness.” When I am in it, I must become vacant and remain still, so that I can return to my root and fulfill the appointed end. “Being vacant is a beginning. Having a vacant mind means losing its purpose. I do not need to know why or how I am doing this. The objects will inspire me and lead me inside.”

Vacuous Silence #5

170×130cm
Oil Painting
2013

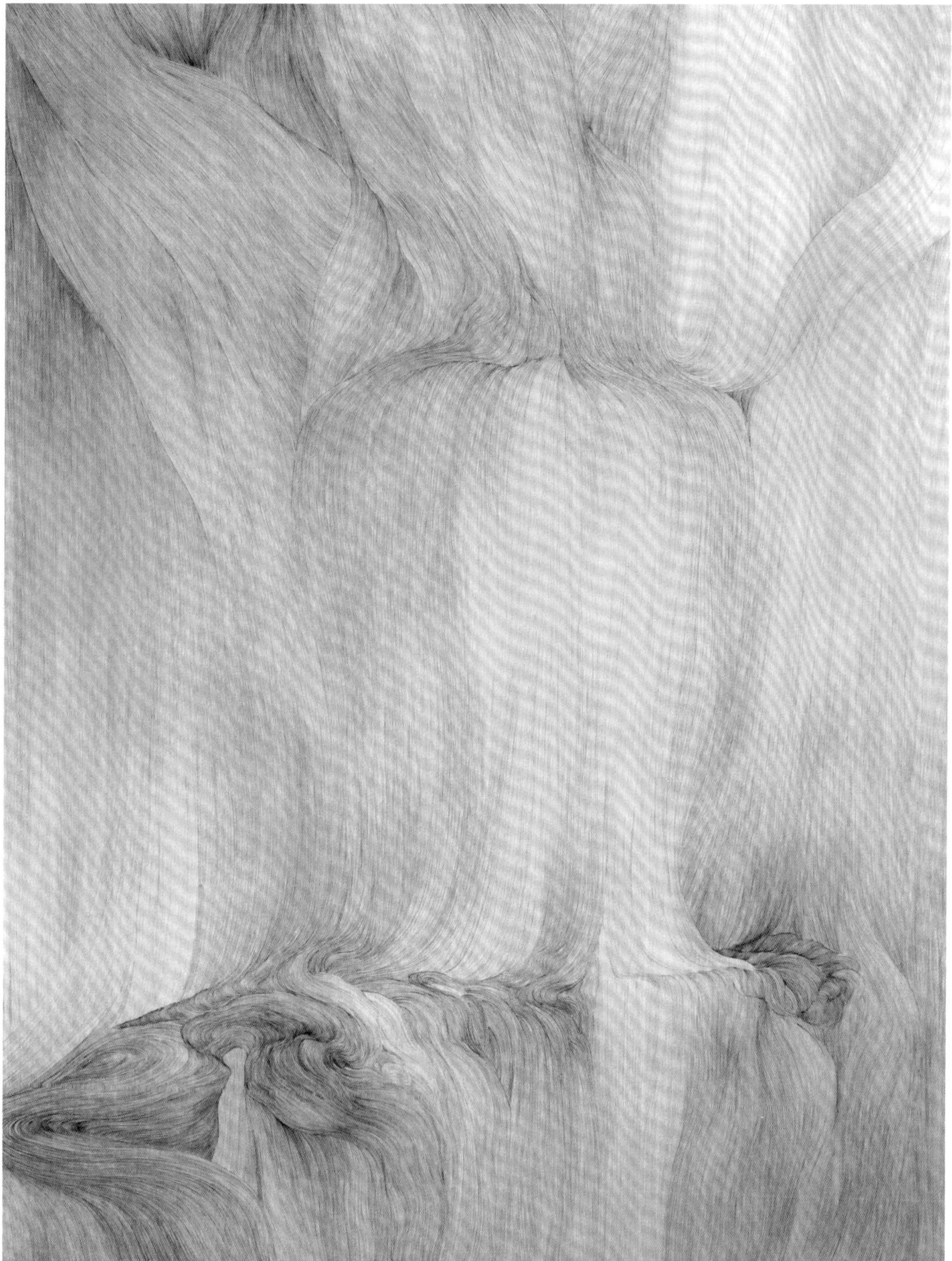

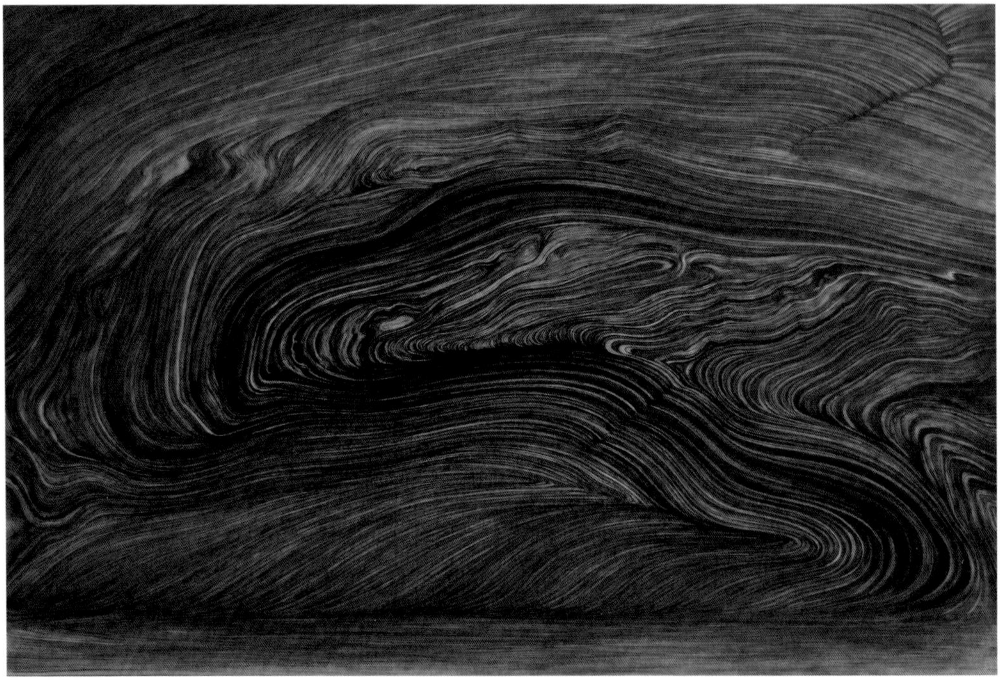

Vacuous Silence #1

120×80cm
Oil Painting
2013

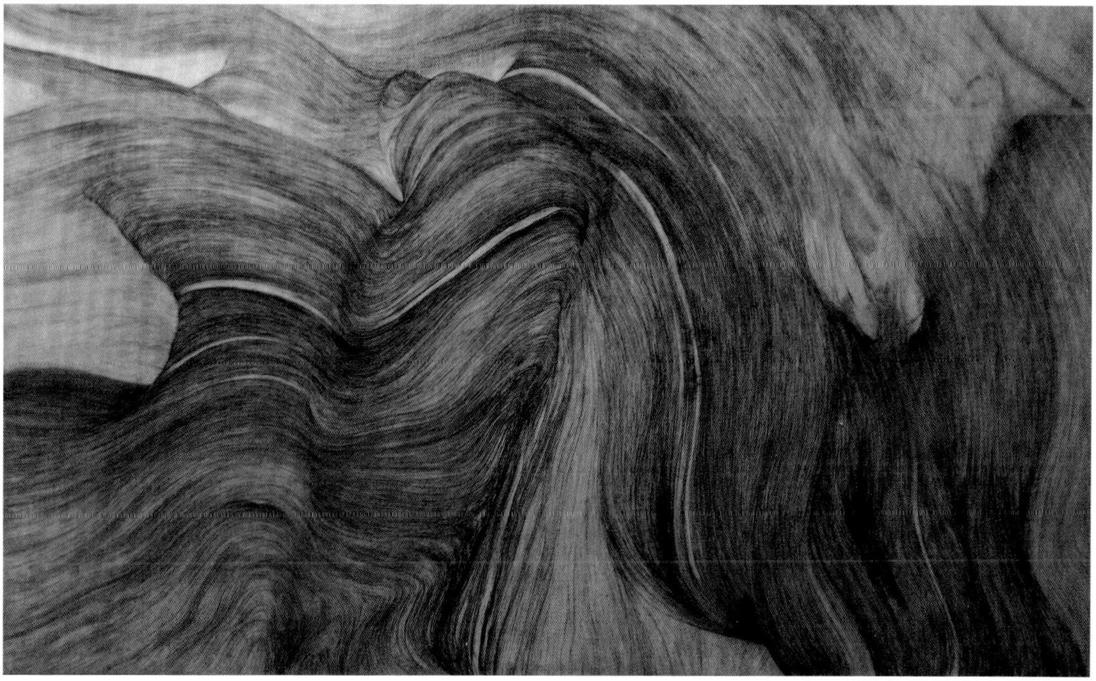

Vacuous Silence #2

100×60cm
Oil Painting
2013

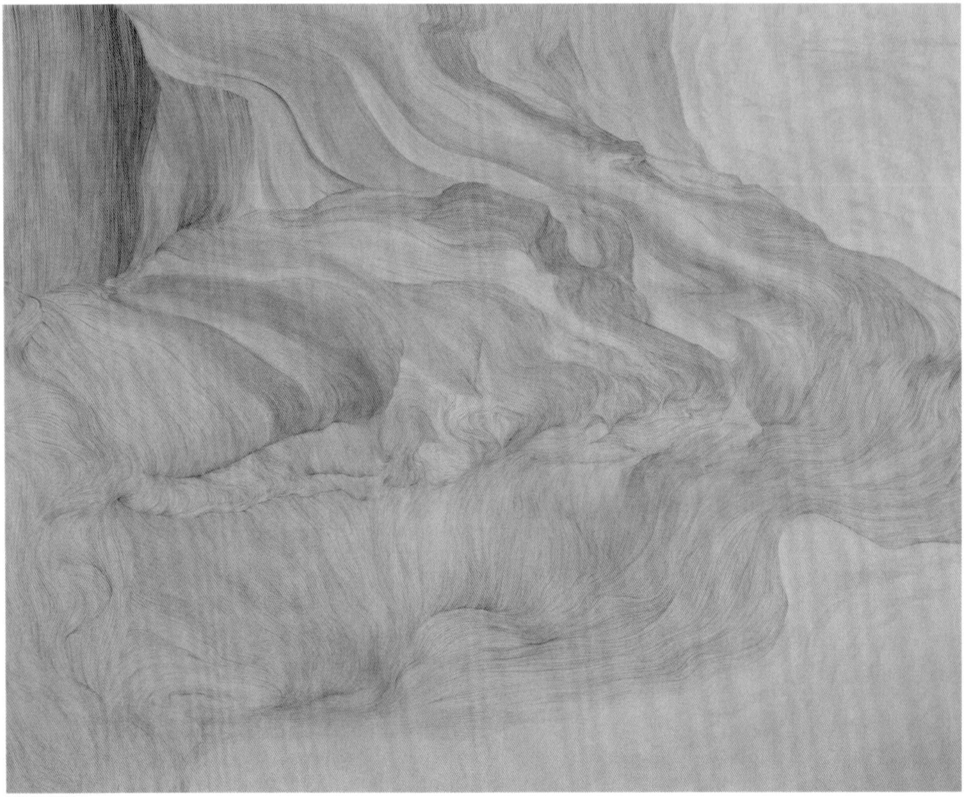

Vacuous Silence #4

160×100cm
Oil Painting
2013

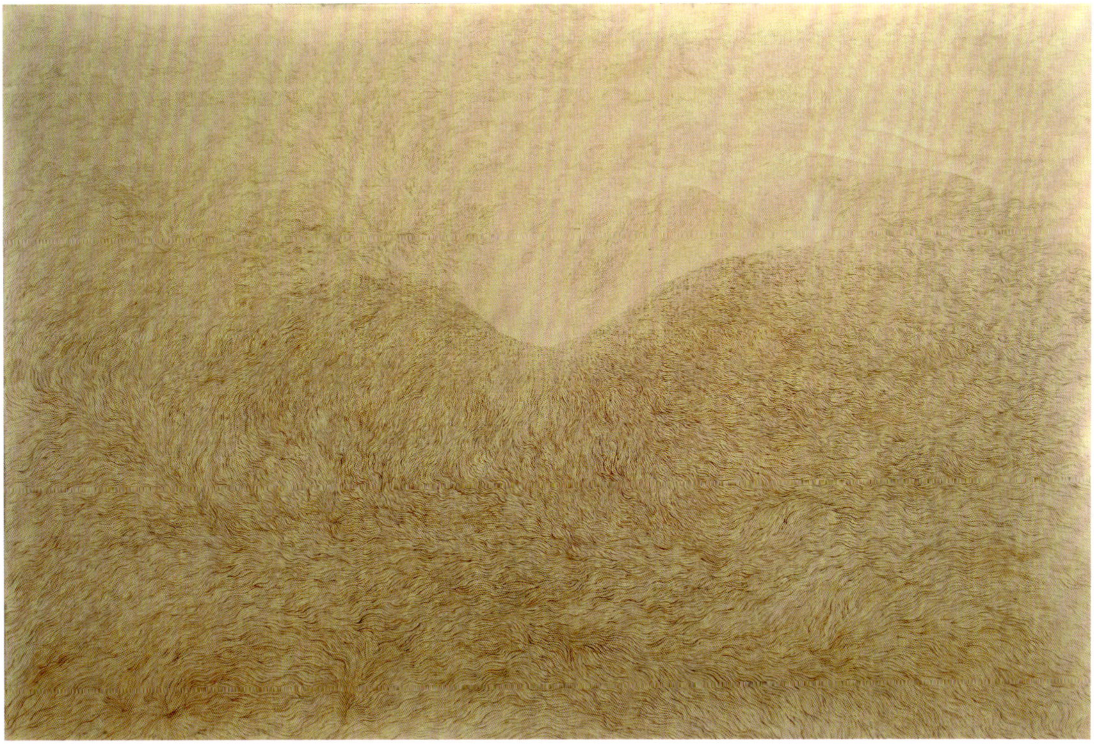

Vacuous Silence #3

120×80cm
Oil Painting
2013

Vacuous Silence #7

200×100cm
Oil Painting
2013

Vacuous Silence #6

100×200cm
Oil Painting
2013

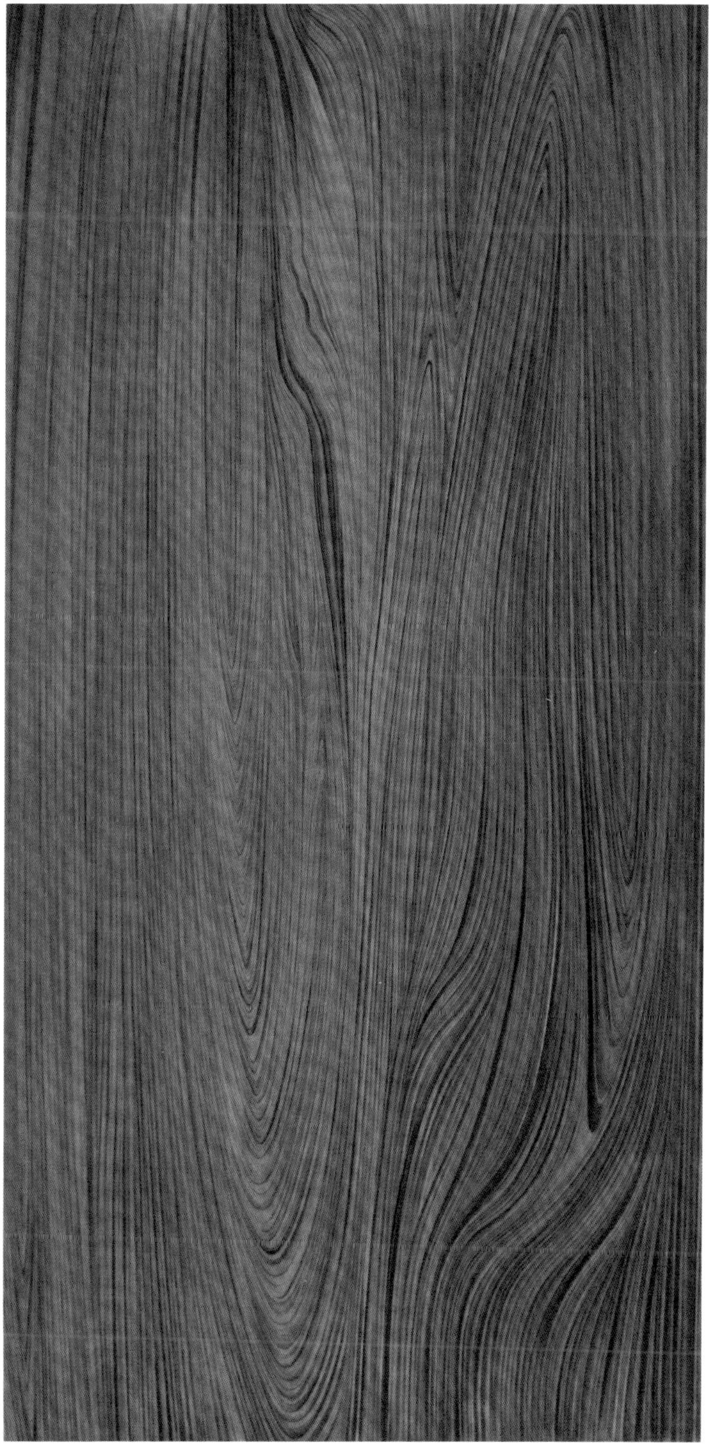

Contemplate

我认为肌理就是一种对时间的压缩，这种压缩形成的痕迹，就好像我们的记忆一样。它不光是我们这一生的记忆，还有无数代的记忆的累积和叠加，如同是时间的标本。

在人类出现以前，地质的历史挤压和沉淀，形成肌理的一种图像，我觉得它蕴藏了大量丰富的信息。

比如说我们看到的一些化石、树木的树皮、河流的水波纹，它有非常清晰的、重复的纹理。你会随着这些肌理纹路延展的方向，去试图找到一个跟时间相关的入口，然后打开一个新的空间。

I think all textures form a compression of time, and the traces formed by this compression are like our memories. It is not only the memory of our lifetime but also the accumulation and superposition of countless memories created by generations before us. It is like a specimen of time.

Before humans appeared, the geological history was squeezed and precipitated, forming an image full of textures. I feel those textures contain a lot of information.

For example, we see fossils, bark of trees, and ripples of rivers, all of which have clear and repetitive textures. You will follow the extension of the lines on these textures, trying to find a time-related entrance, and then open a new space.

Contemplate #25screen

200×180 cm
Silk Mineral Pigment
2018

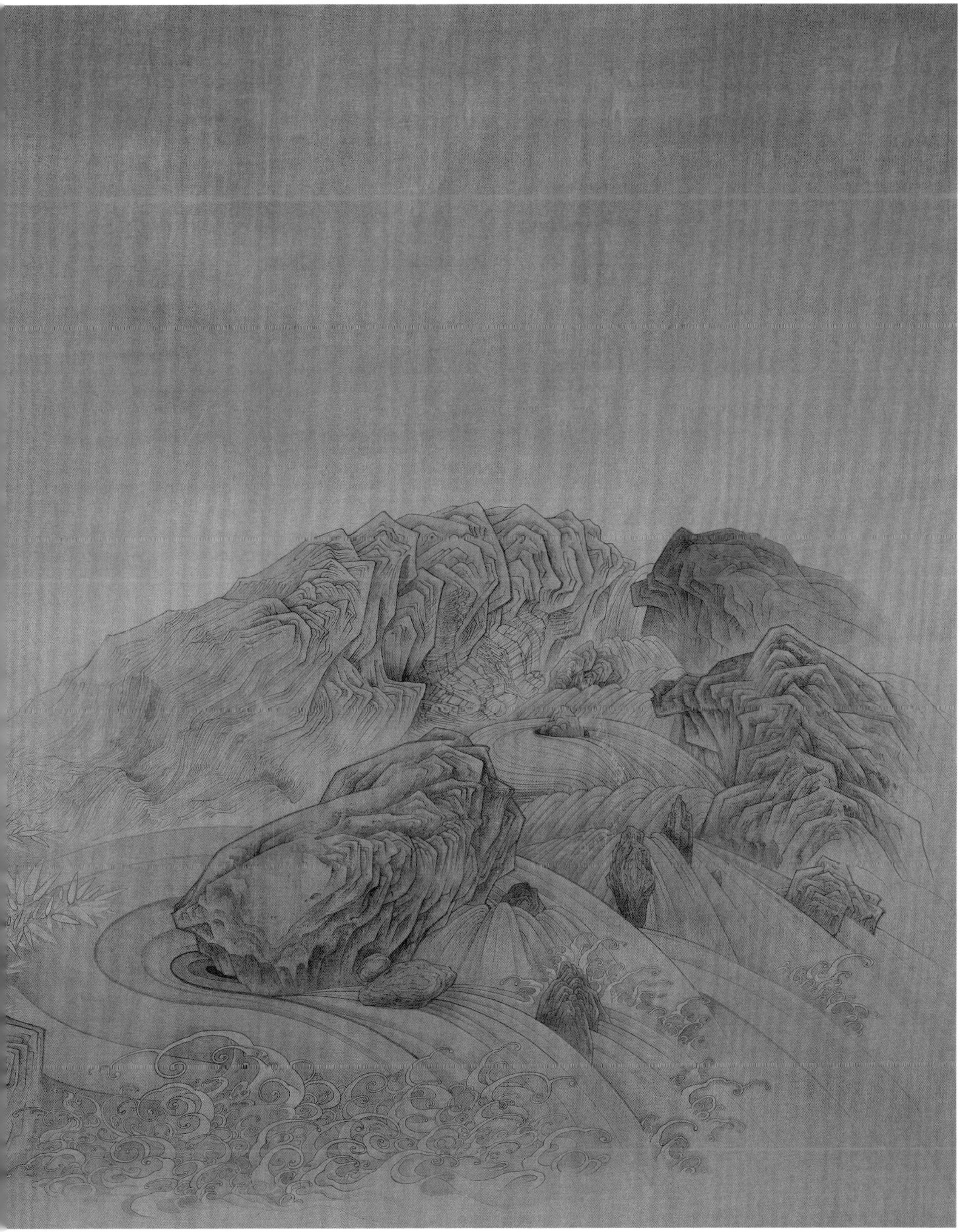

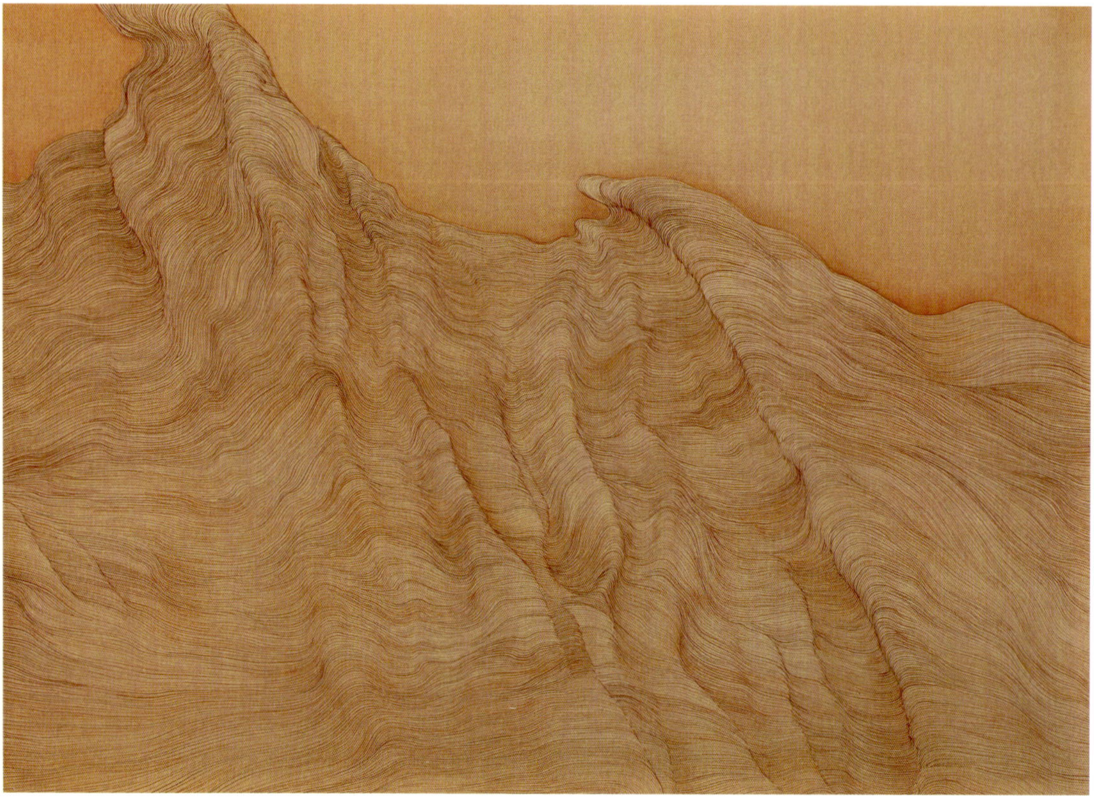

Contemplate #27

70×50 cm
Silk Mineral Pigment
2018

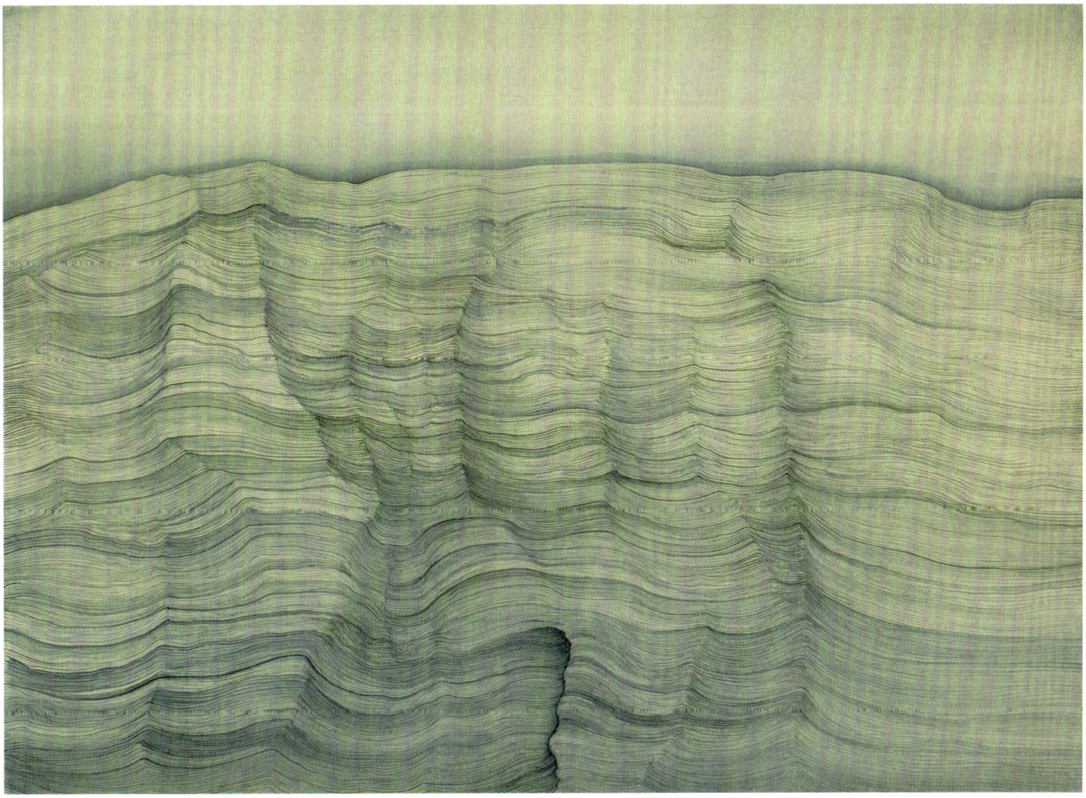

Contemplate #24

70×50 cm
Silk Mineral Pigment
2017

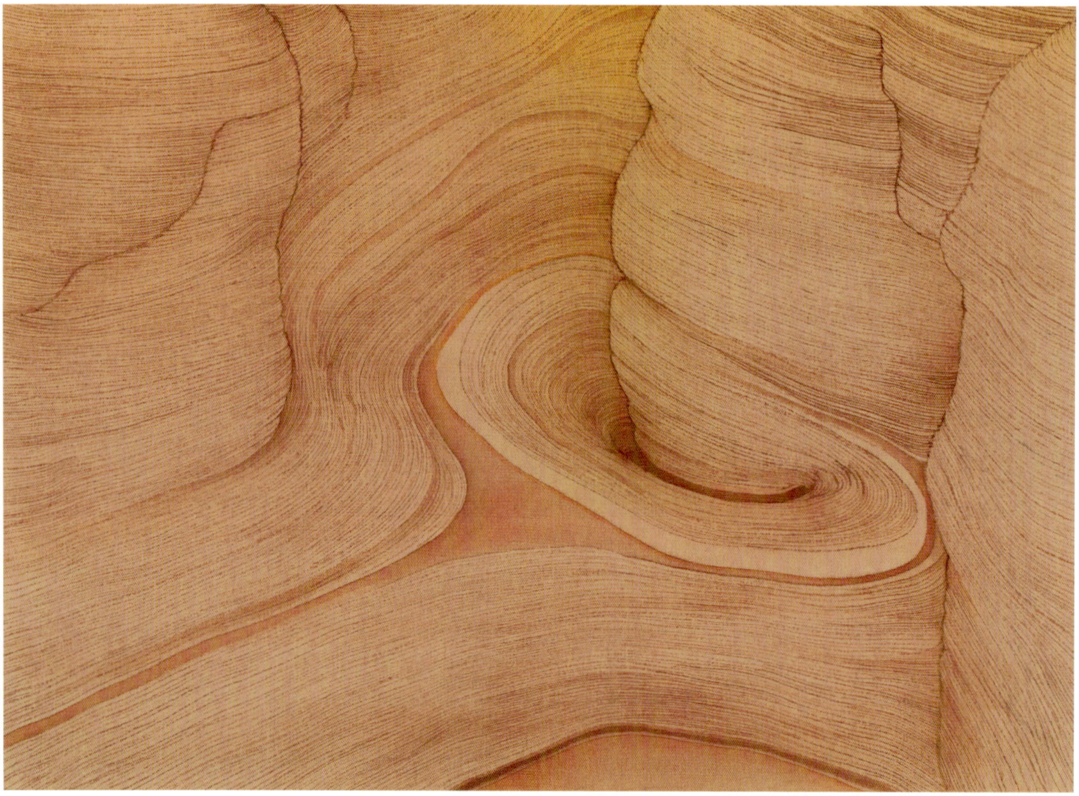

Contemplate #77

47×33 cm
Silk Mineral Pigment
2021

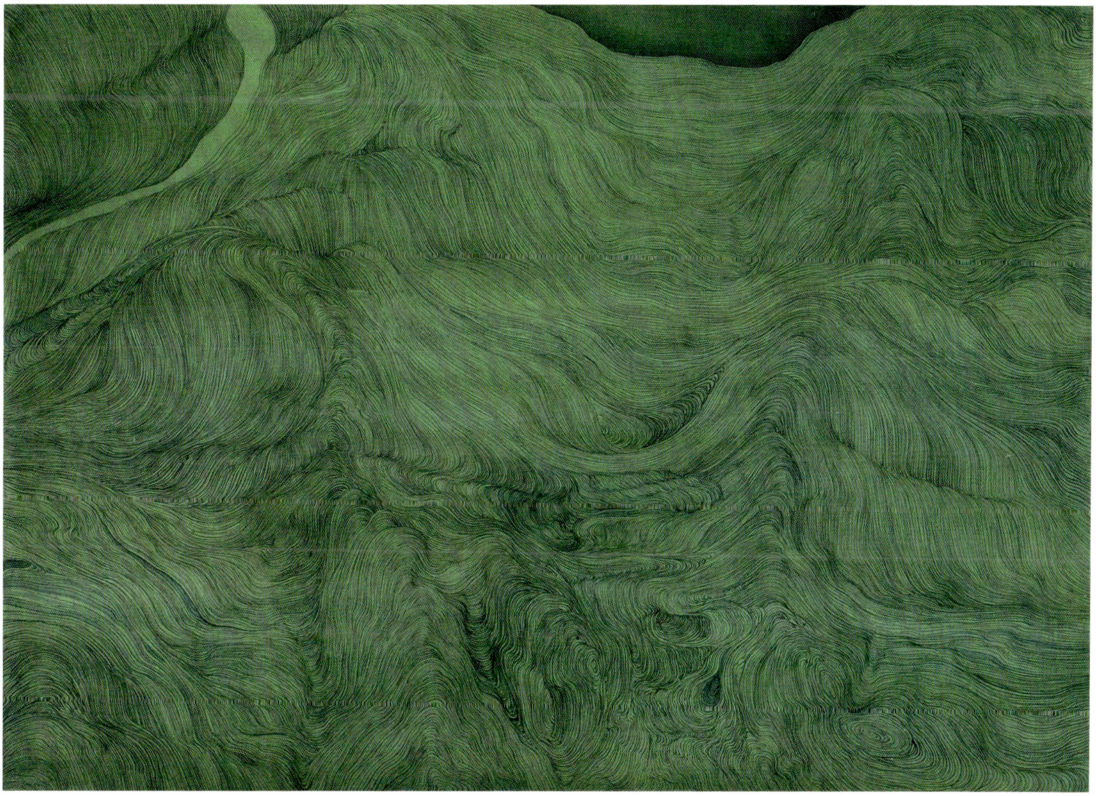

Contemplate #53

70×50 cm
Silk Mineral Pigment
2017

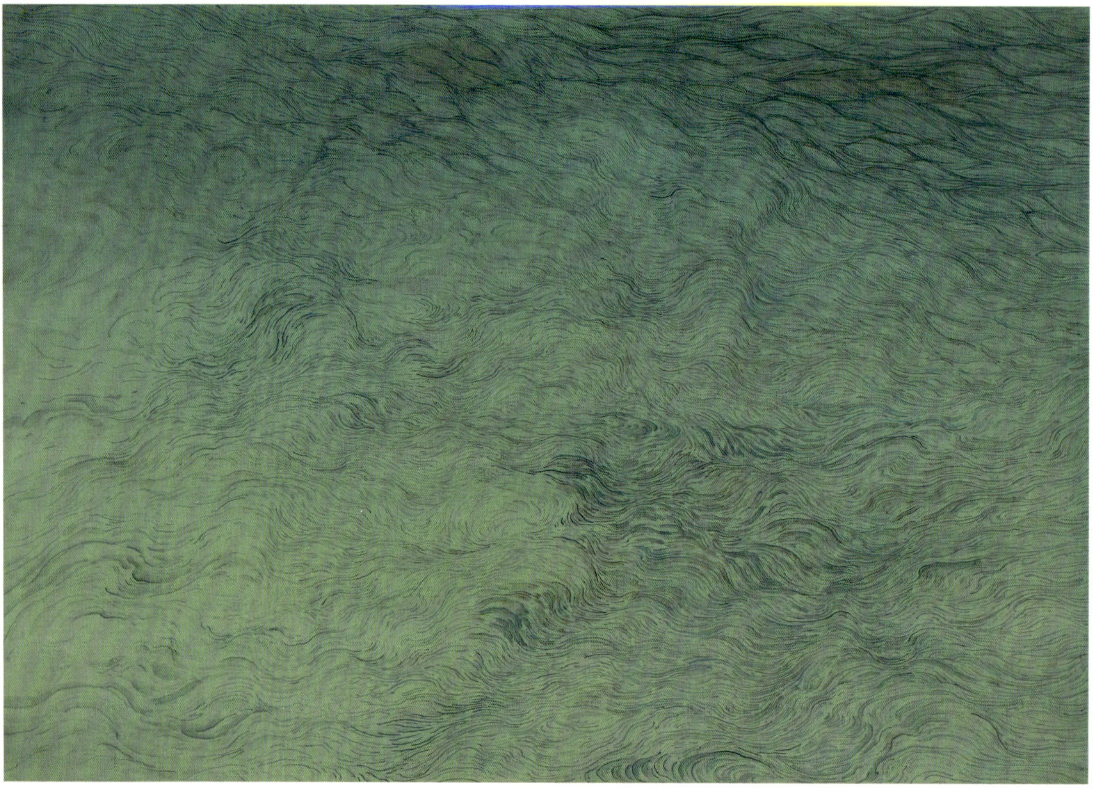

Contemplate #51

70×50 cm
Silk Mineral Pigment
2017

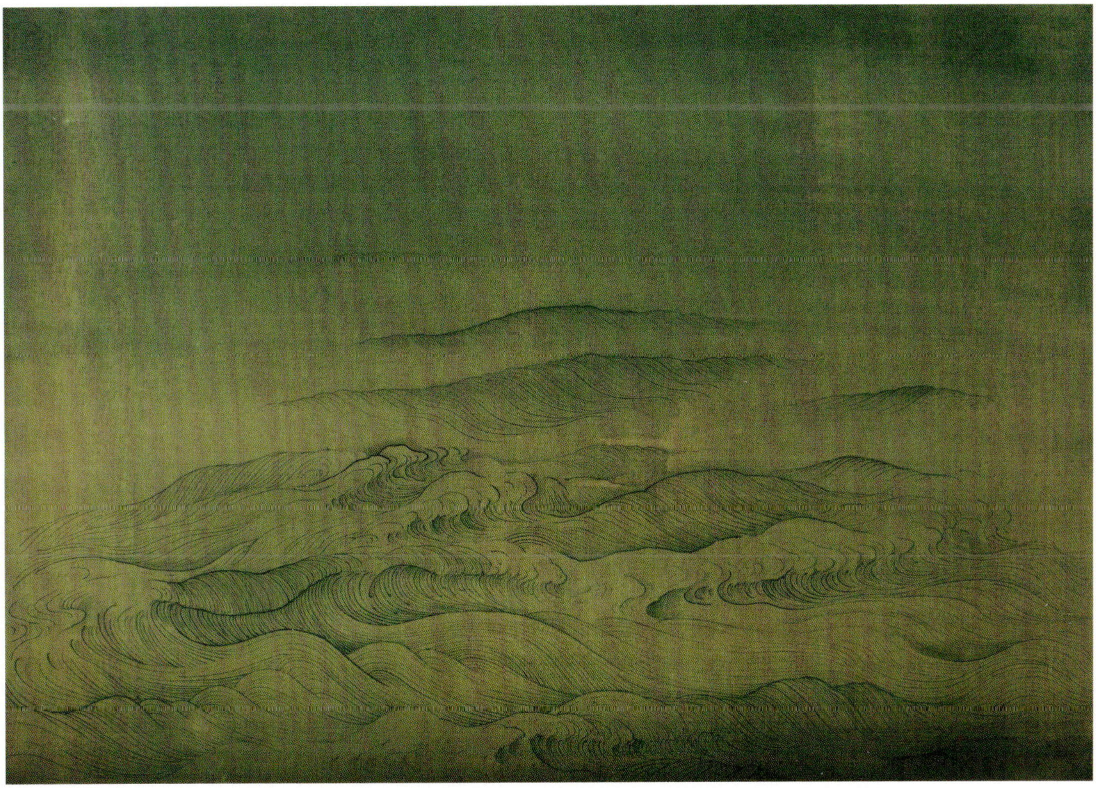

Contemplate #52

70×50 cm
Silk Mineral Pigment
2017

Contemplate #31

70×50 cm
Silk Mineral Pigment
2018

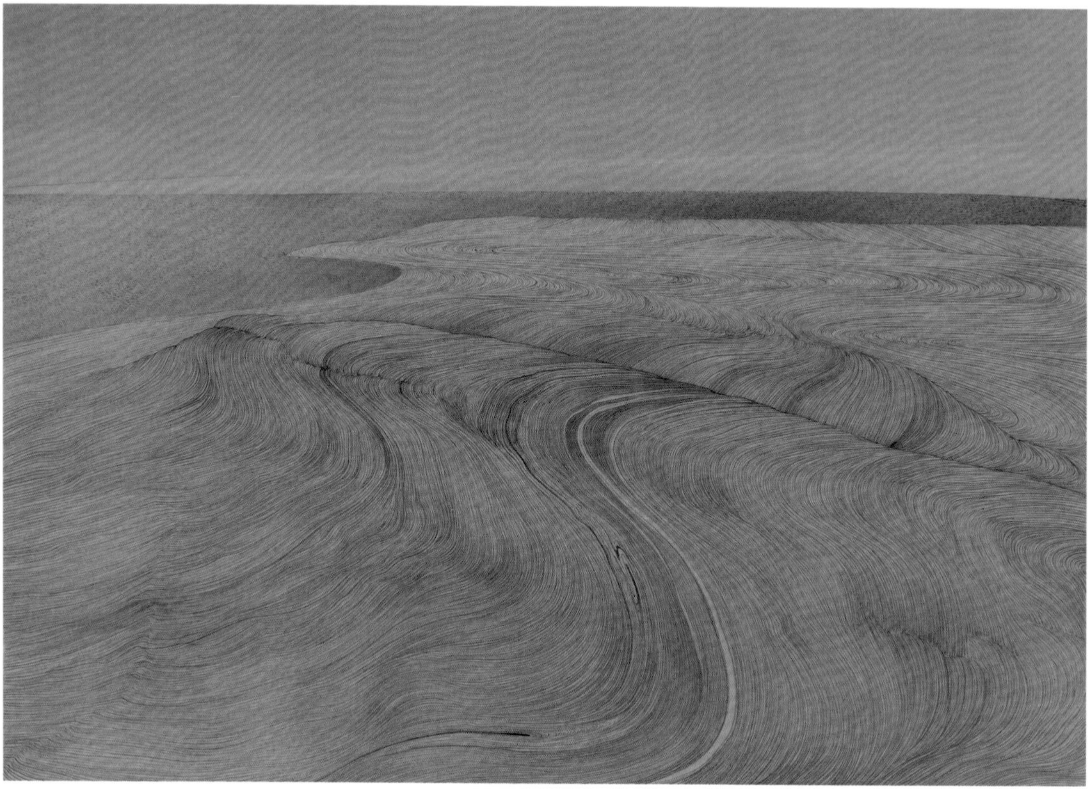

Contemplate #35

70×50 cm
Silk Mineral Pigment
2017

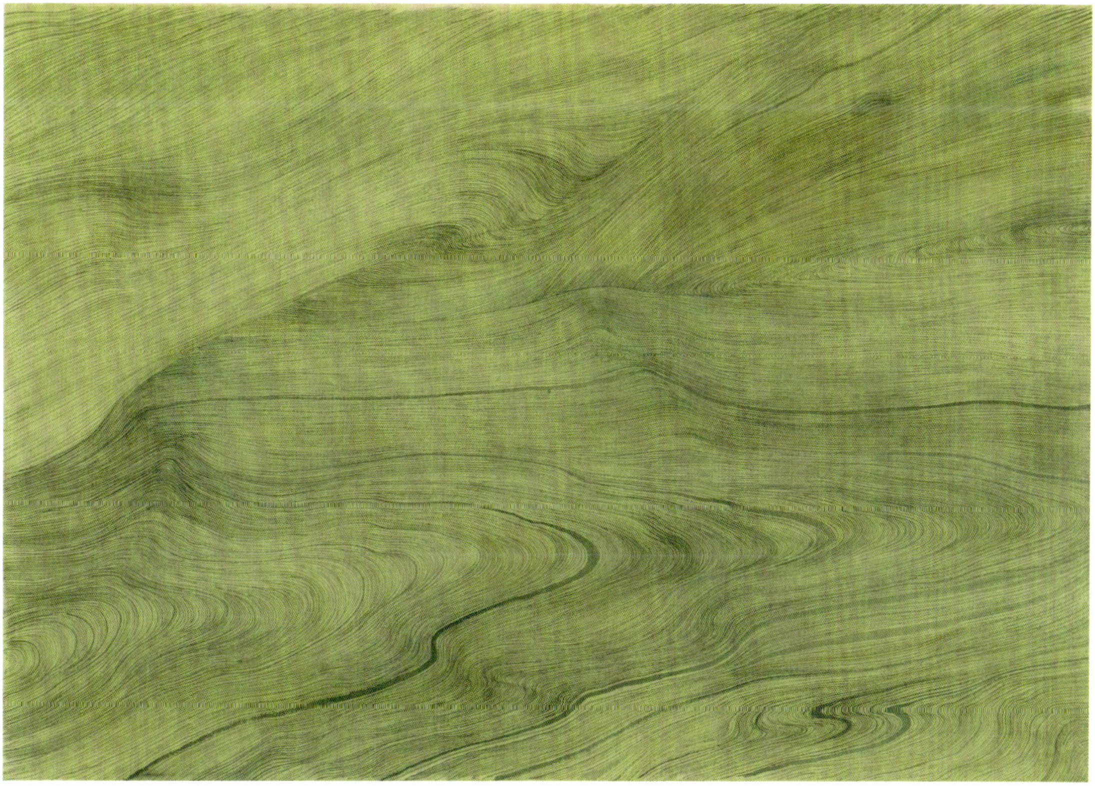

Contemplate#74

70×50 cm
Silk Mineral Pigment
2021

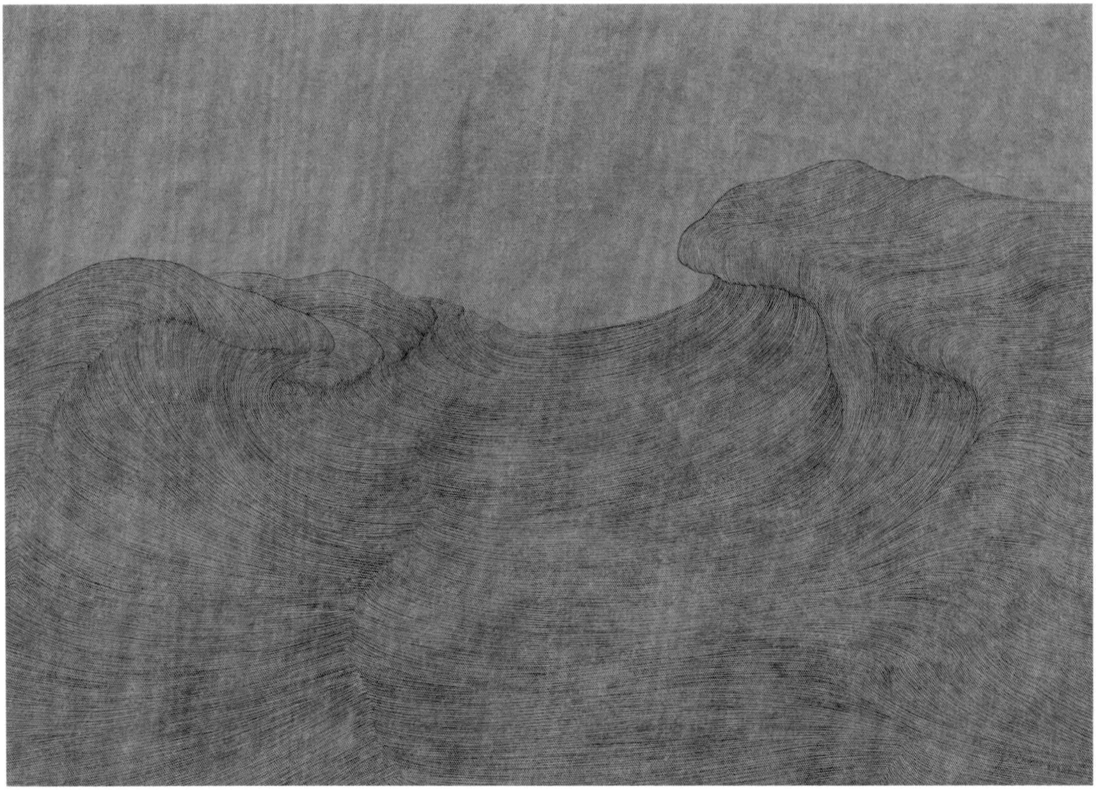

Contemplate #41

70×50 cm
Mineral Pigment on Paprer
2018

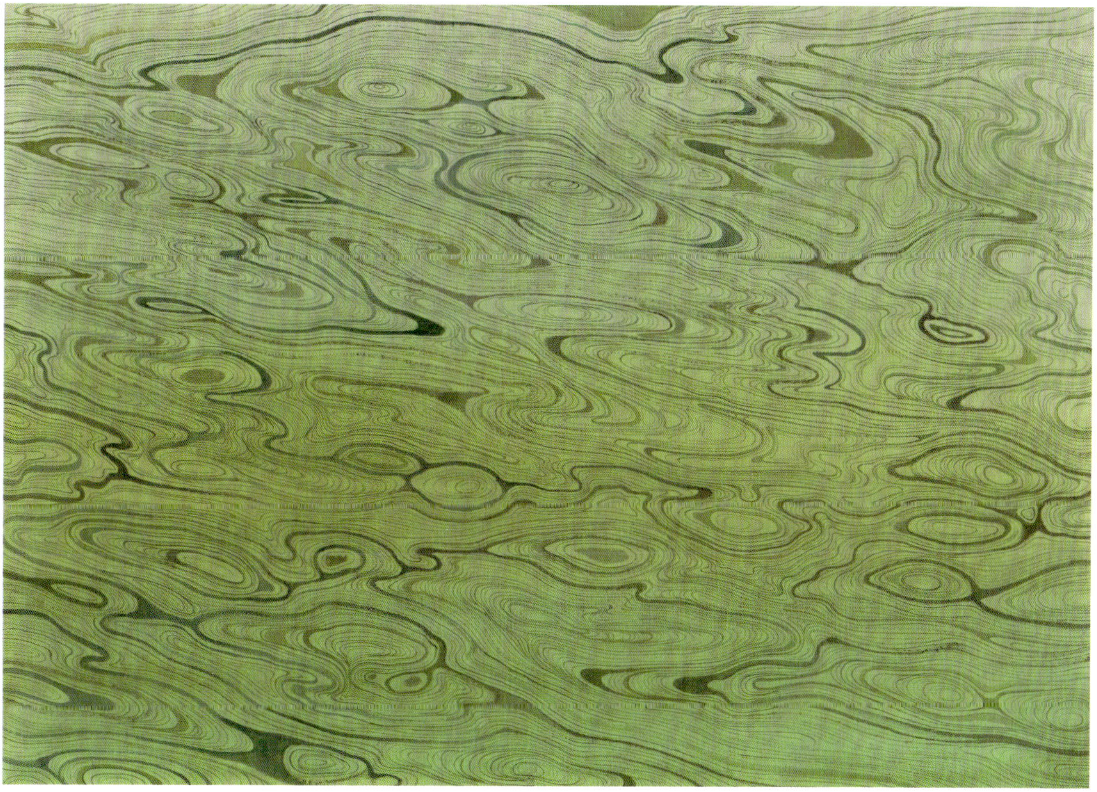

Contemplate #73

68×47 cm
Silk Mineral Pigment
2022

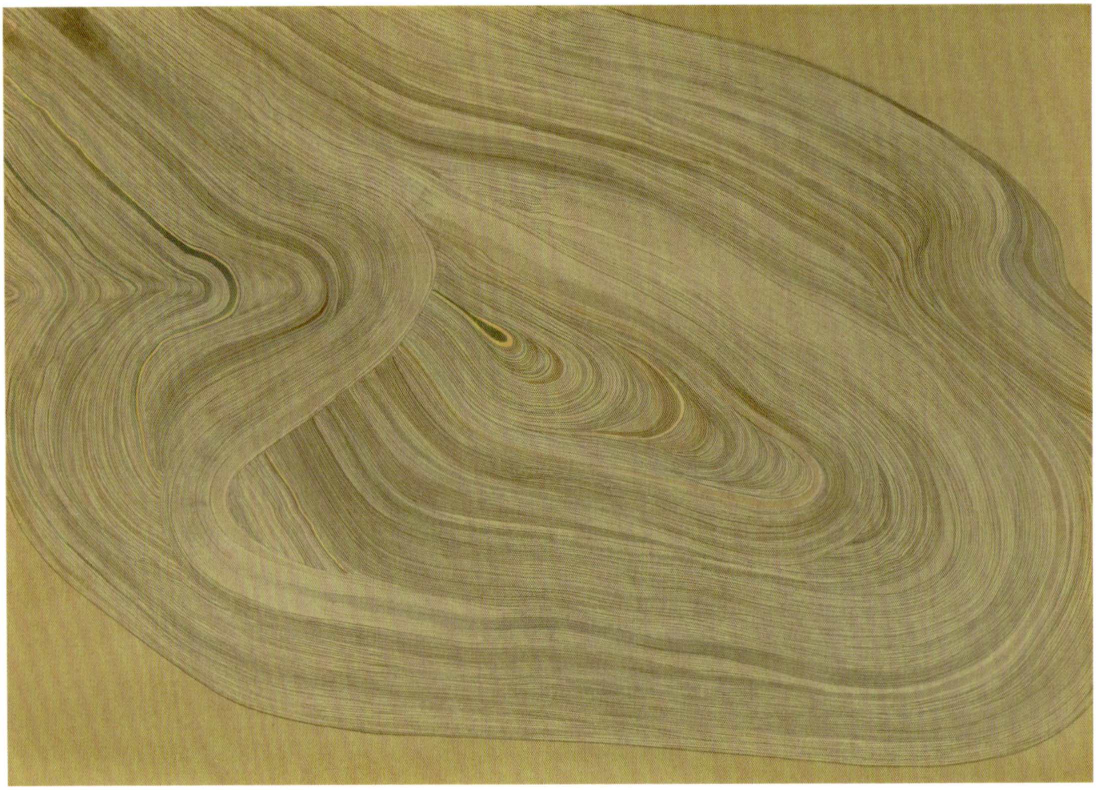

Contemplate #63

70×50 cm
Silk Mineral Pigment
2021

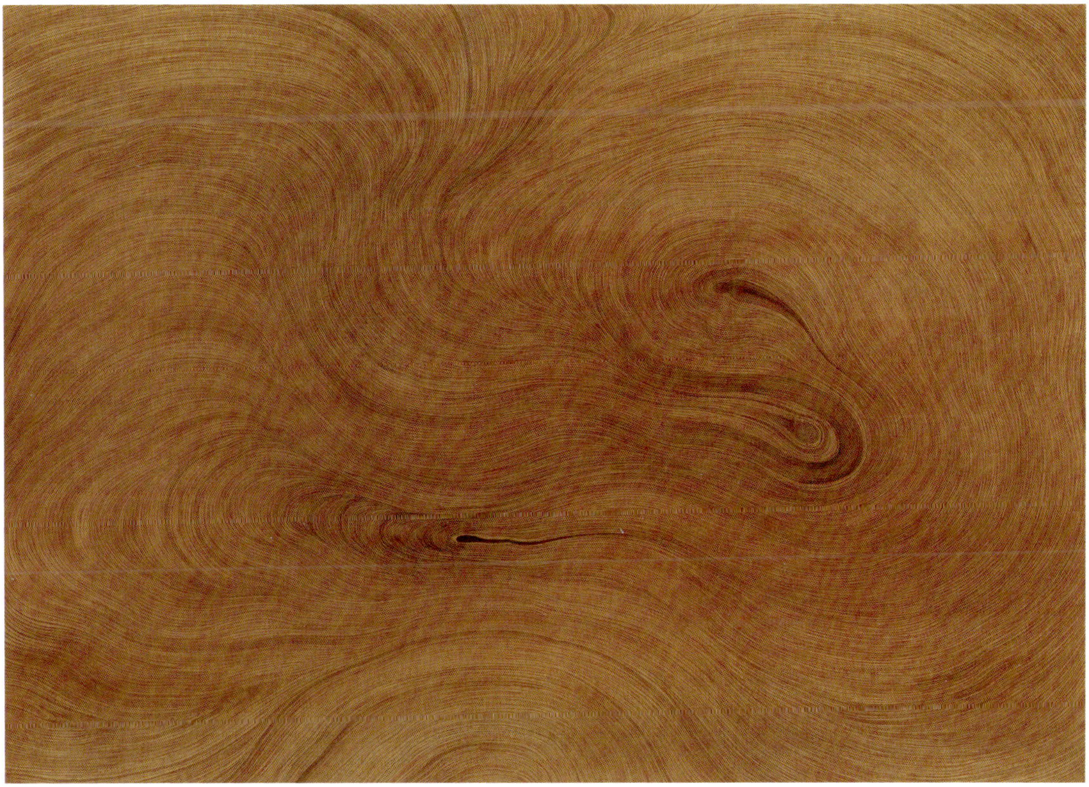

Contemplate #46

70×50 cm
Silk Mineral Pigment
2019

Contemplate #26

70×50 cm
Mineral Pigment on Paper
2018

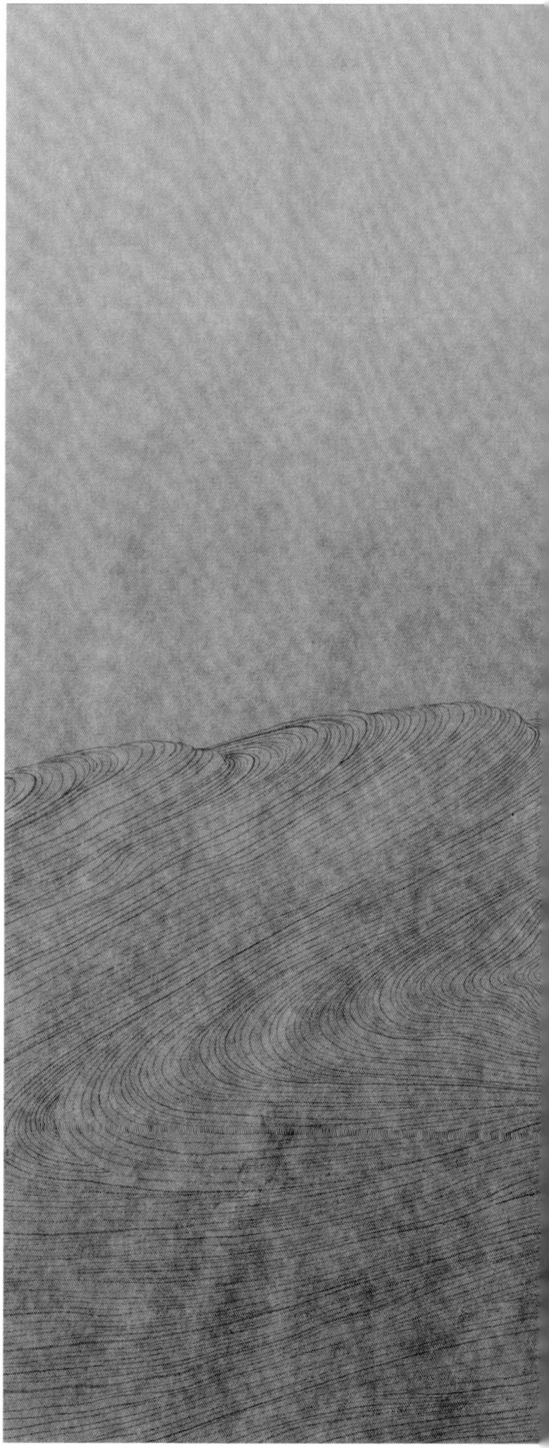

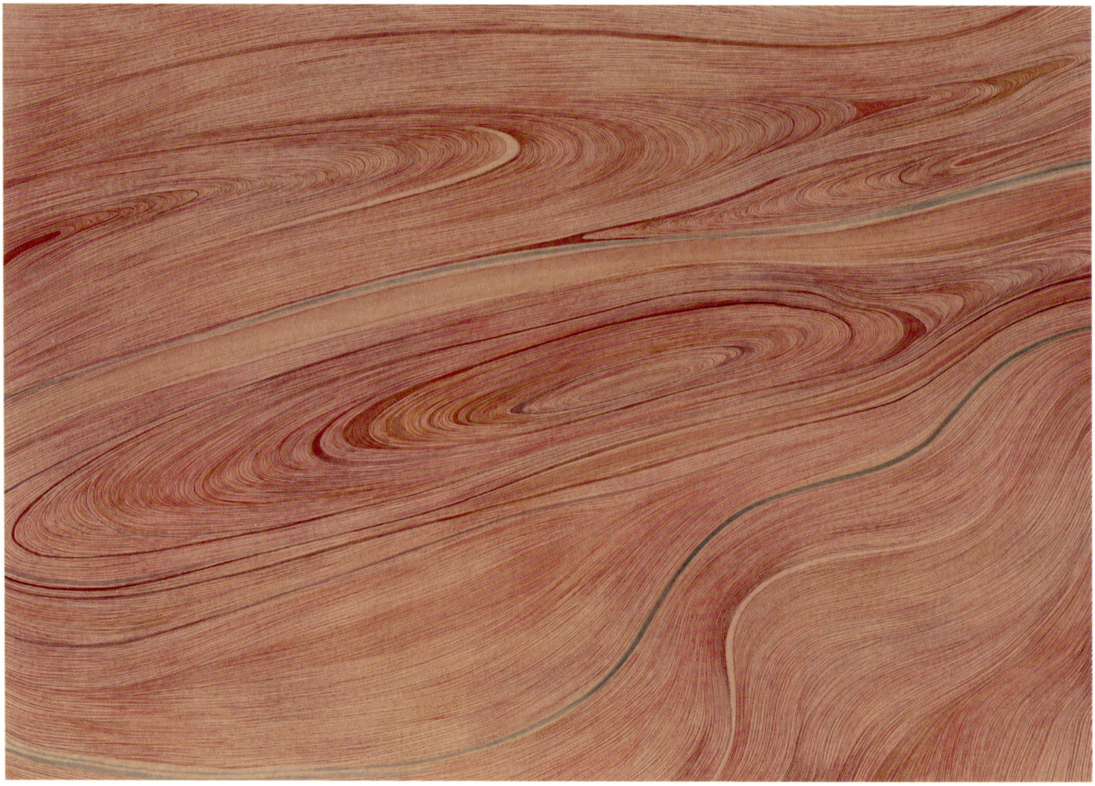

Contemplate #45

70×50 cm
Silk Mineral Pigment
2019

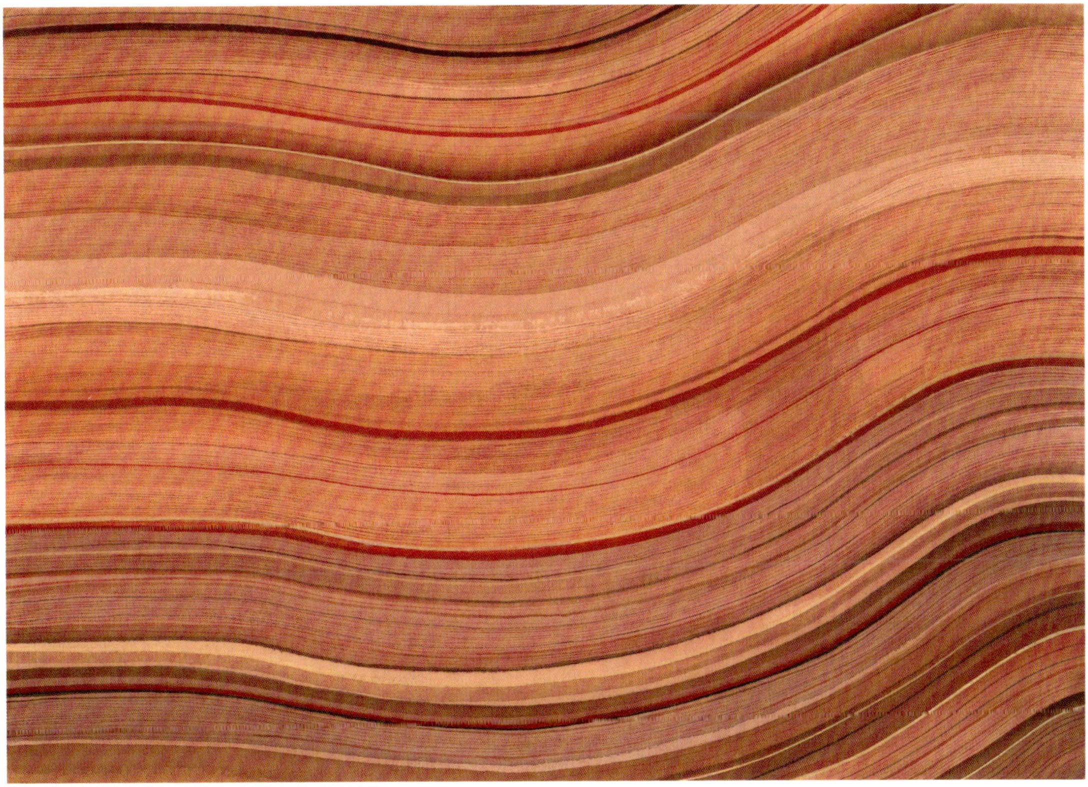

Contemplate #75

67×47 cm
Silk Mineral Pigment
2021

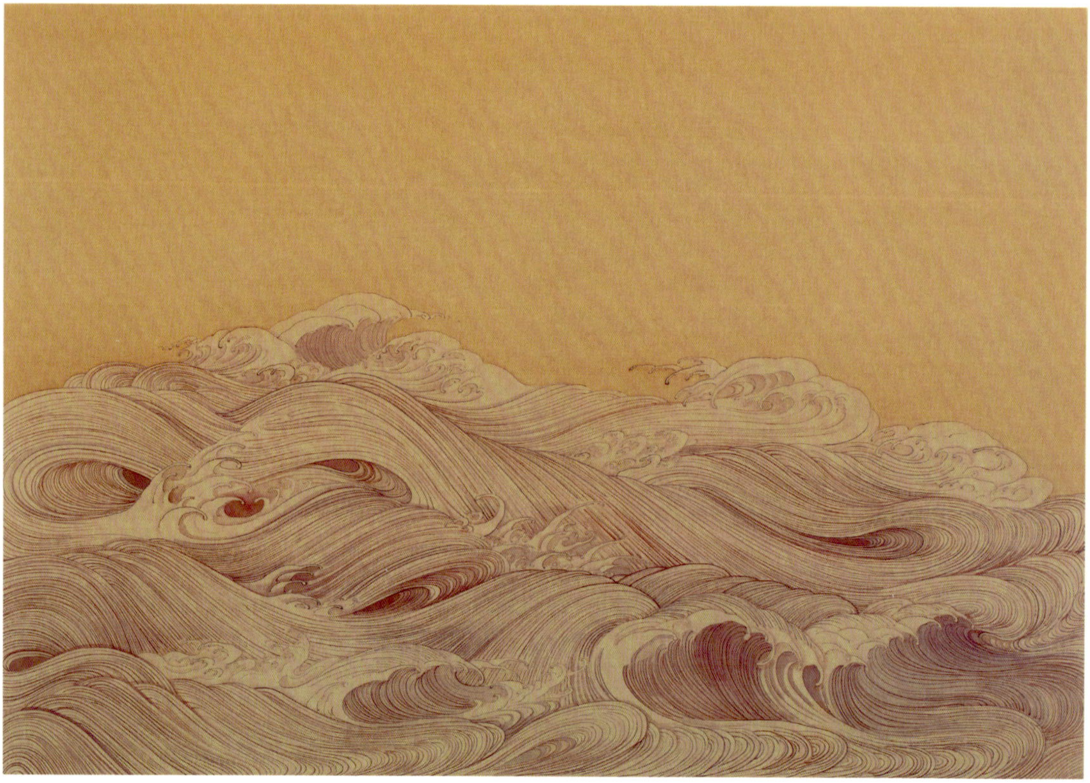

Contemplate #42

70×50 cm
Silk Mineral Pigment
2019

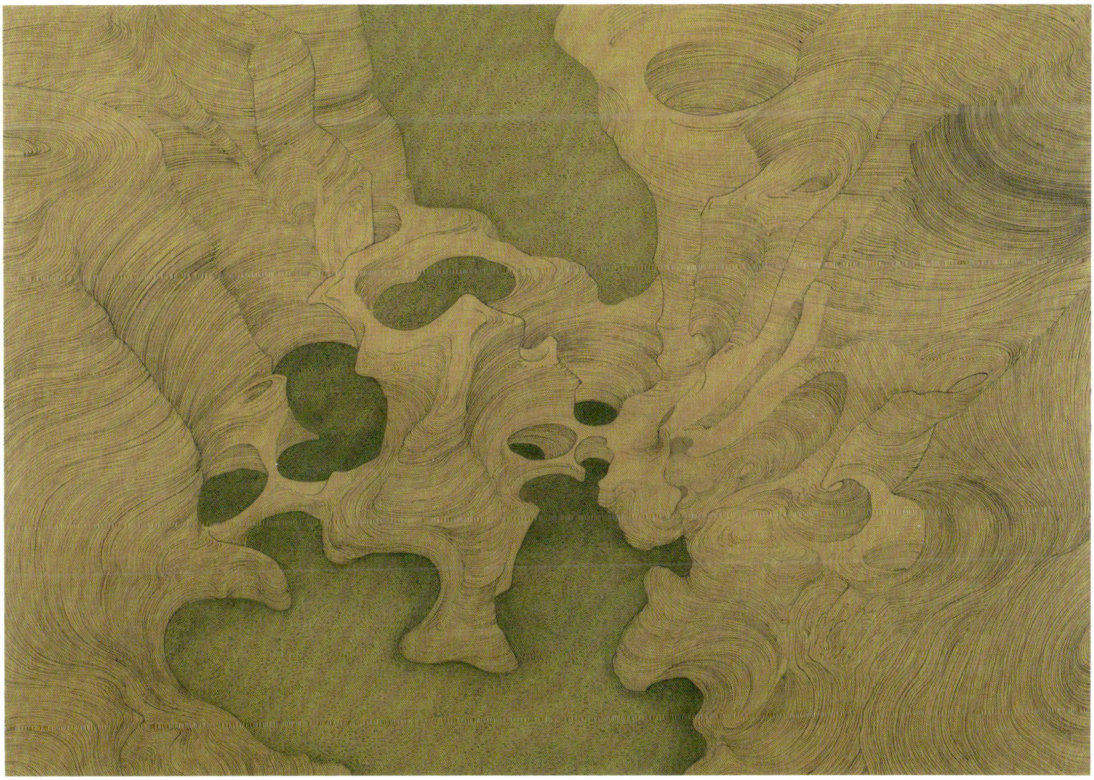

Contemplate #43

70×50 cm
Silk Mineral Pigment
2019

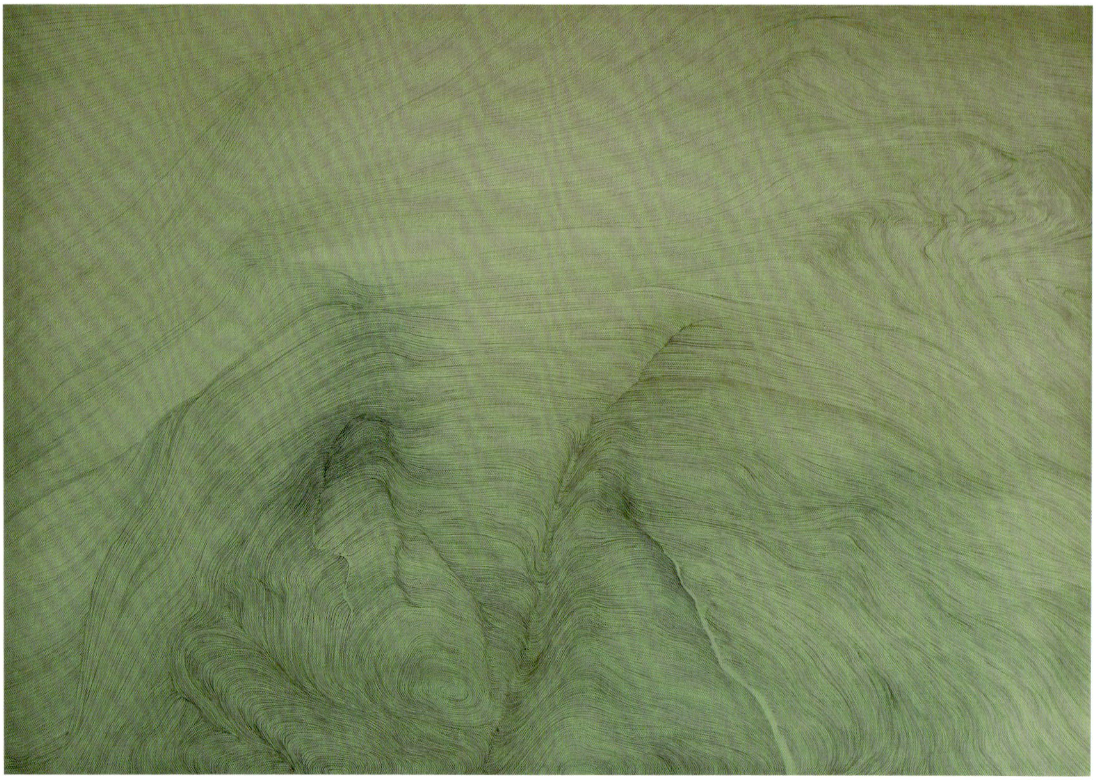

Contemplate #50

70×50 cm
Silk Mineral Pigment
2017

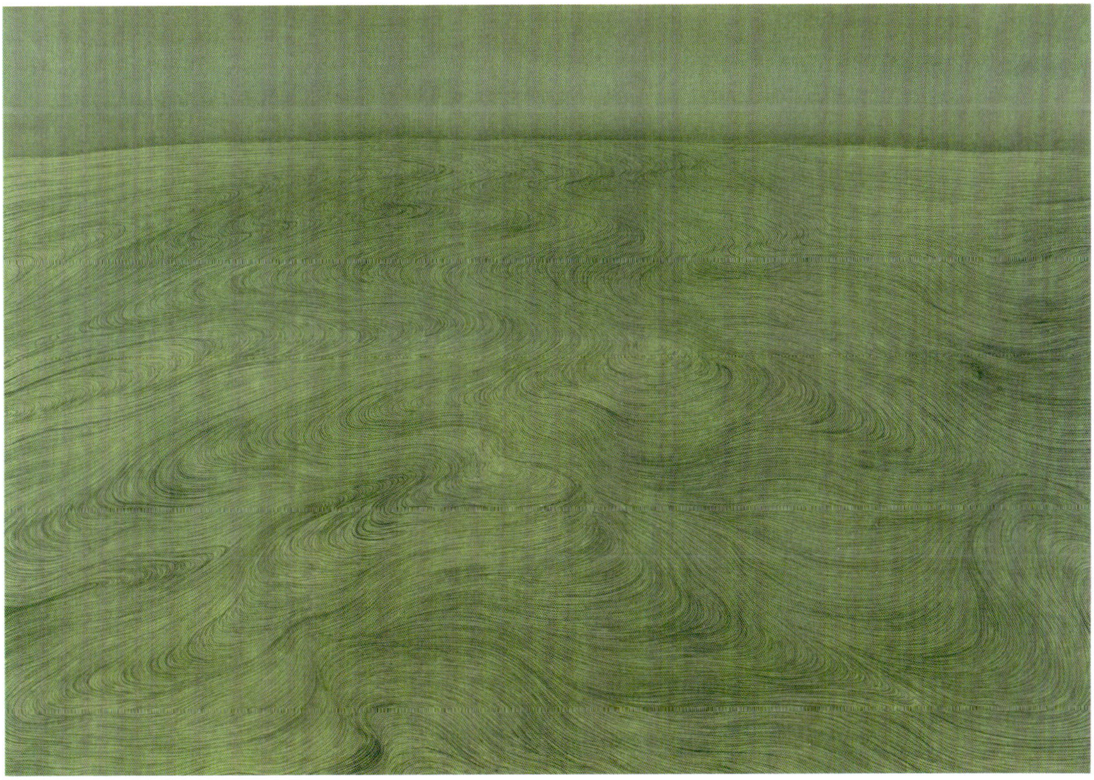

Contemplate #33

70×50 cm
Silk Mineral Pigment
2020

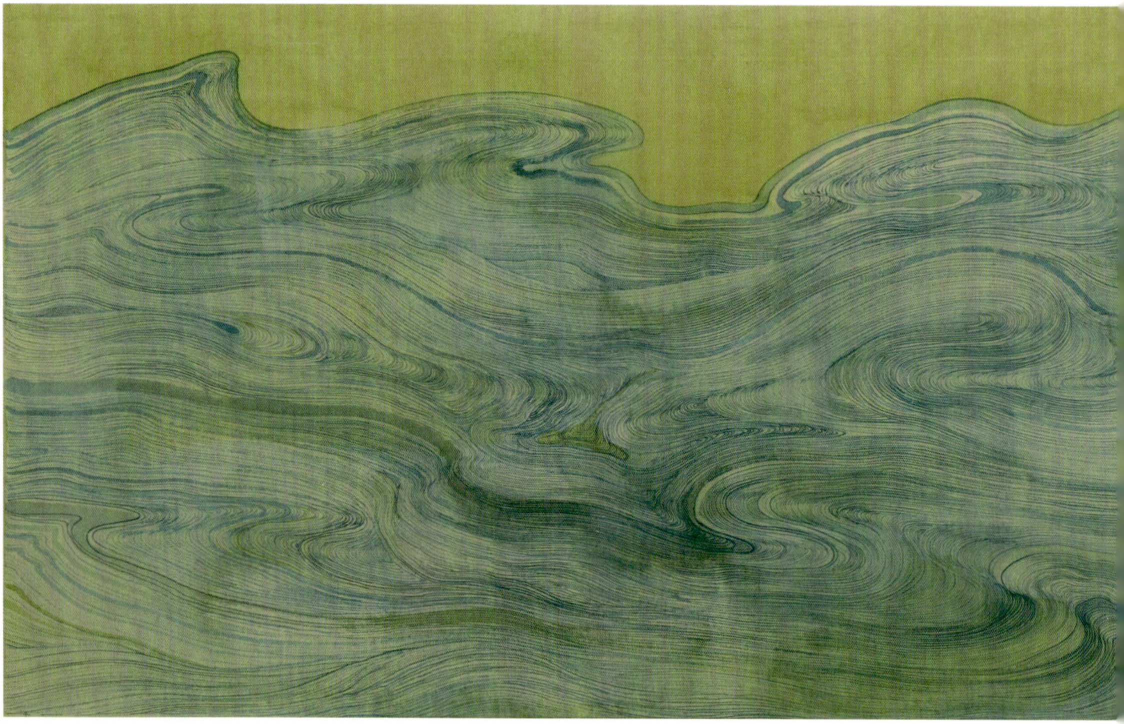

Contemplate #88

235x45 cm
Silk Mineral Pigment
2023

Contemplate #75

30×20 cm
Silk Mineral Pigment
2020

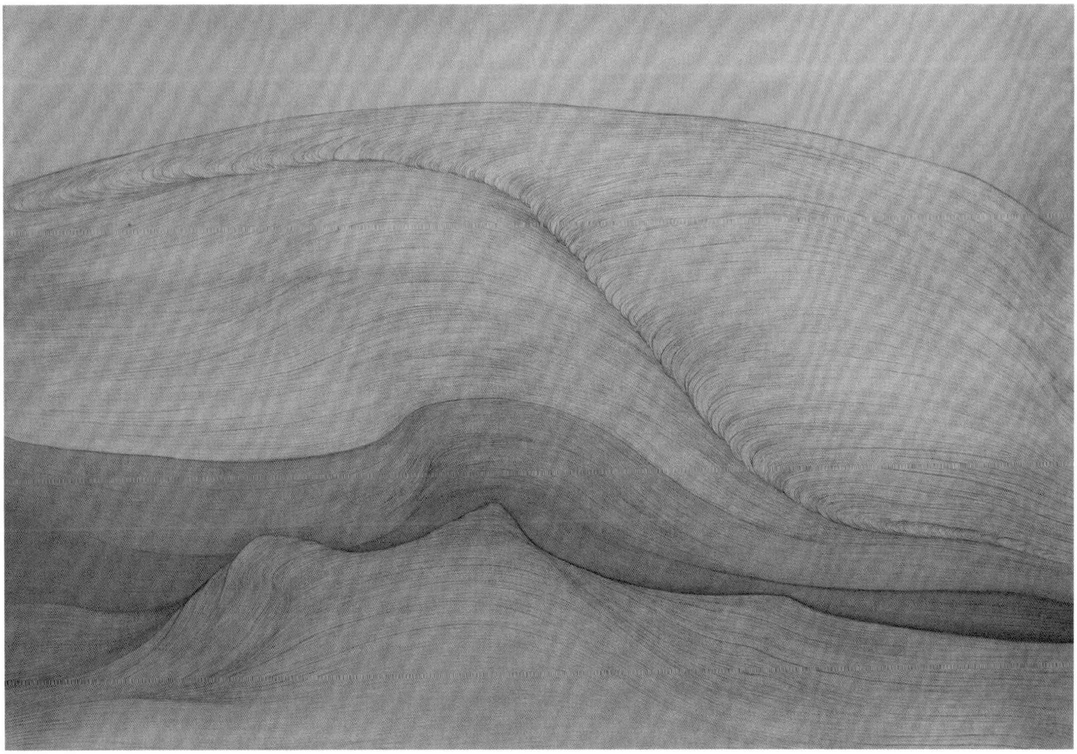

Contemplate #28

70×50 cm
Silk Mineral Pigment
2018

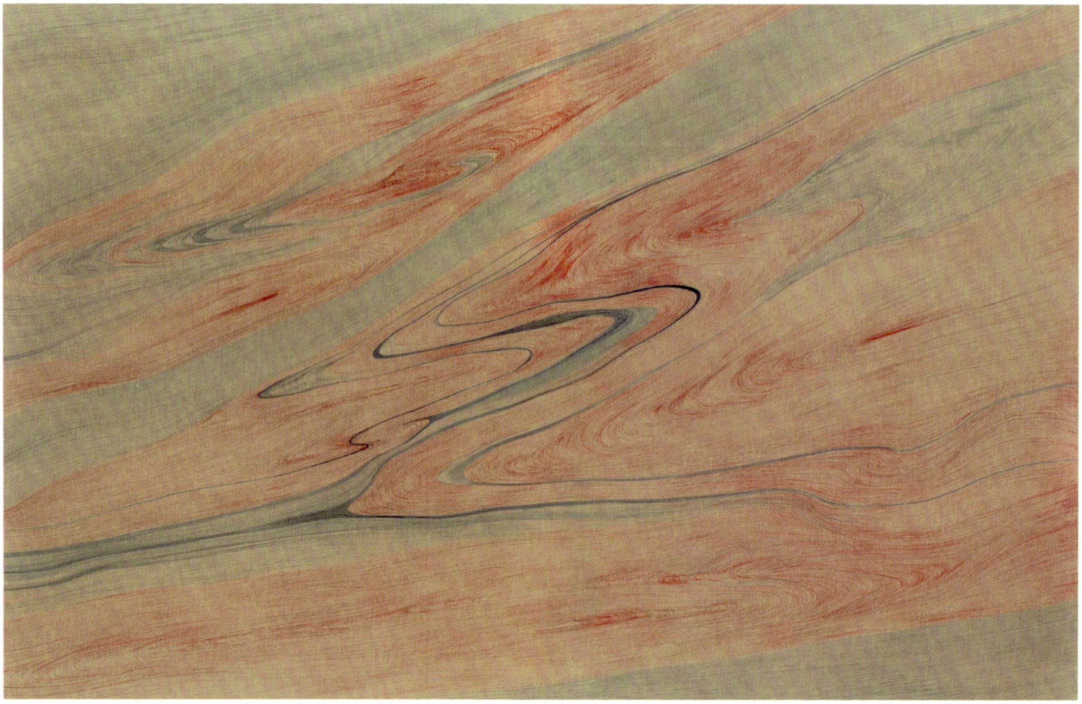

Contemplate #36

155×100 cm
Silk Mineral Pigment
2019

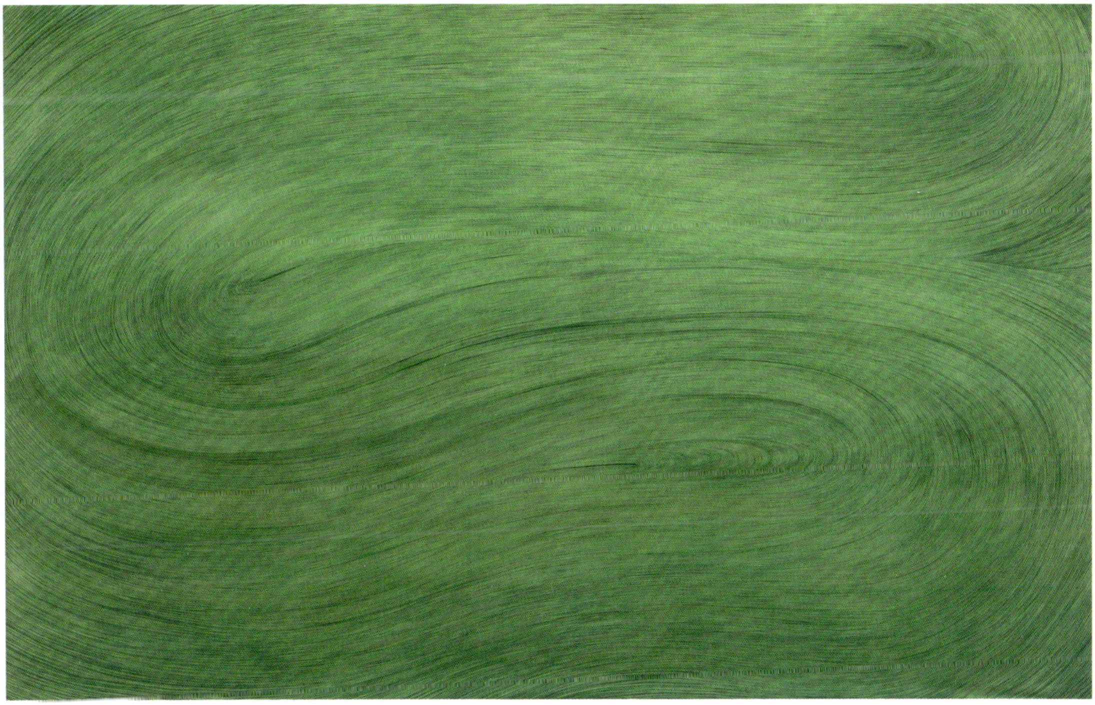

Contemplate #32

150×100 cm
Silk Mineral Pigment
2018

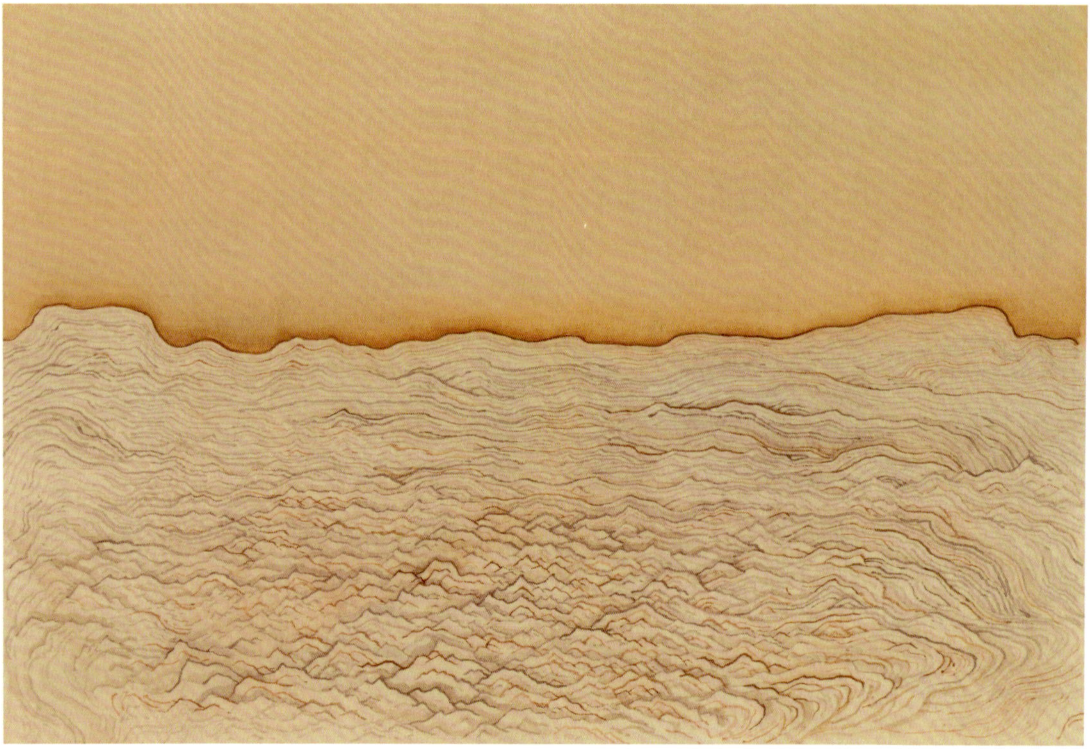

Contemplate #79

30×20 cm
Silk Mineral Pigment
2022

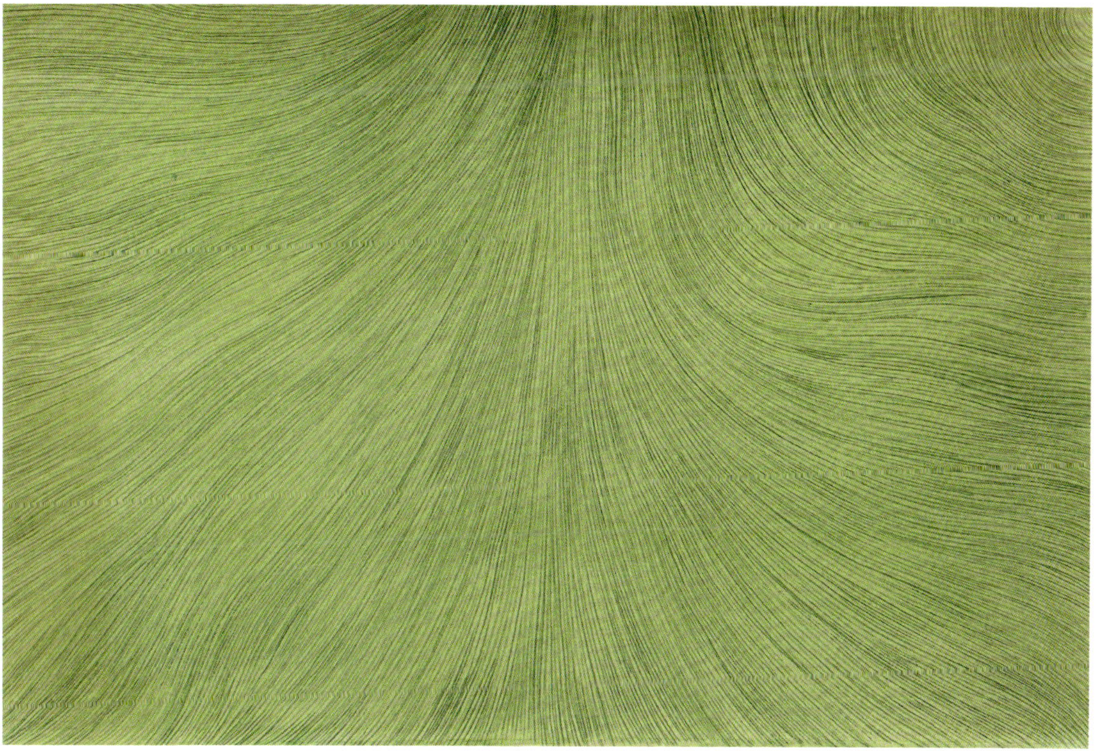

Contemplate #60

32×22 cm
Silk Mineral Pigment
2021

Contemplate #37

150×100 cm
Silk Mineral Pigment
2019

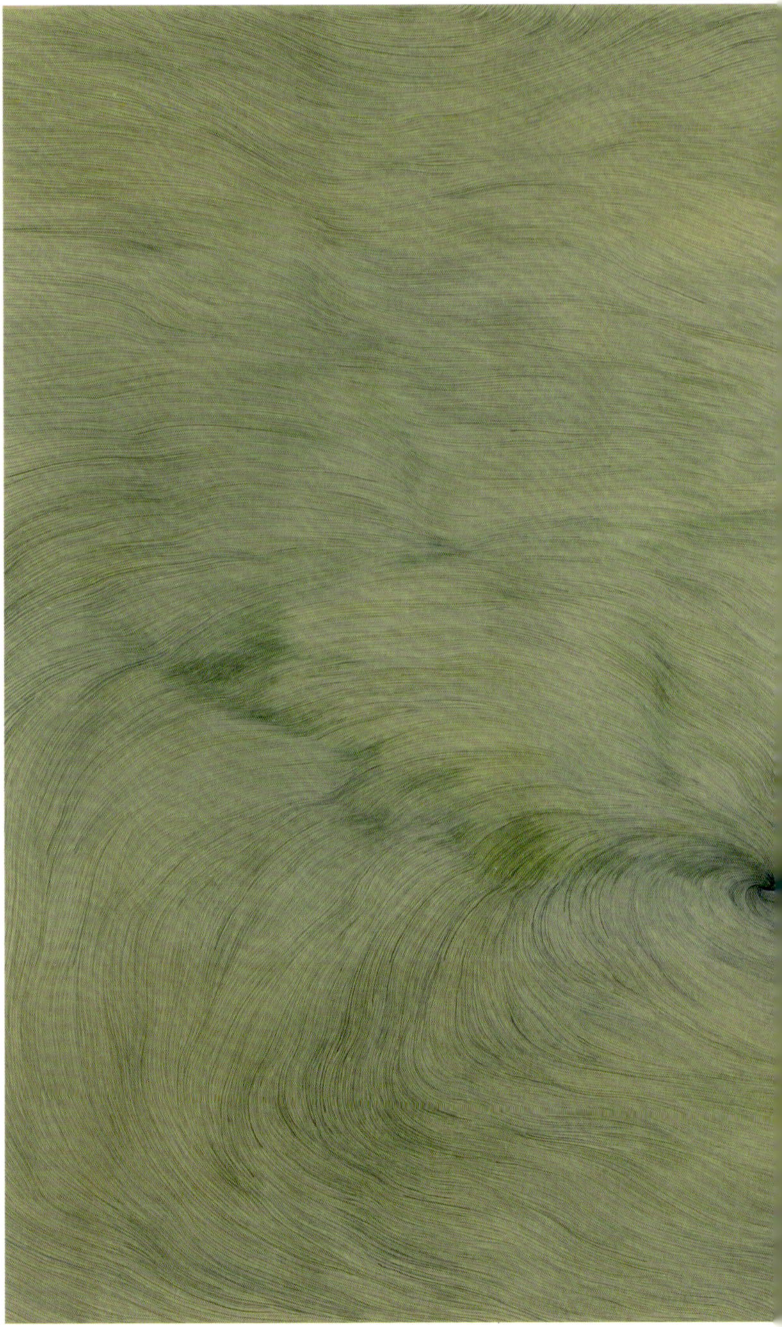

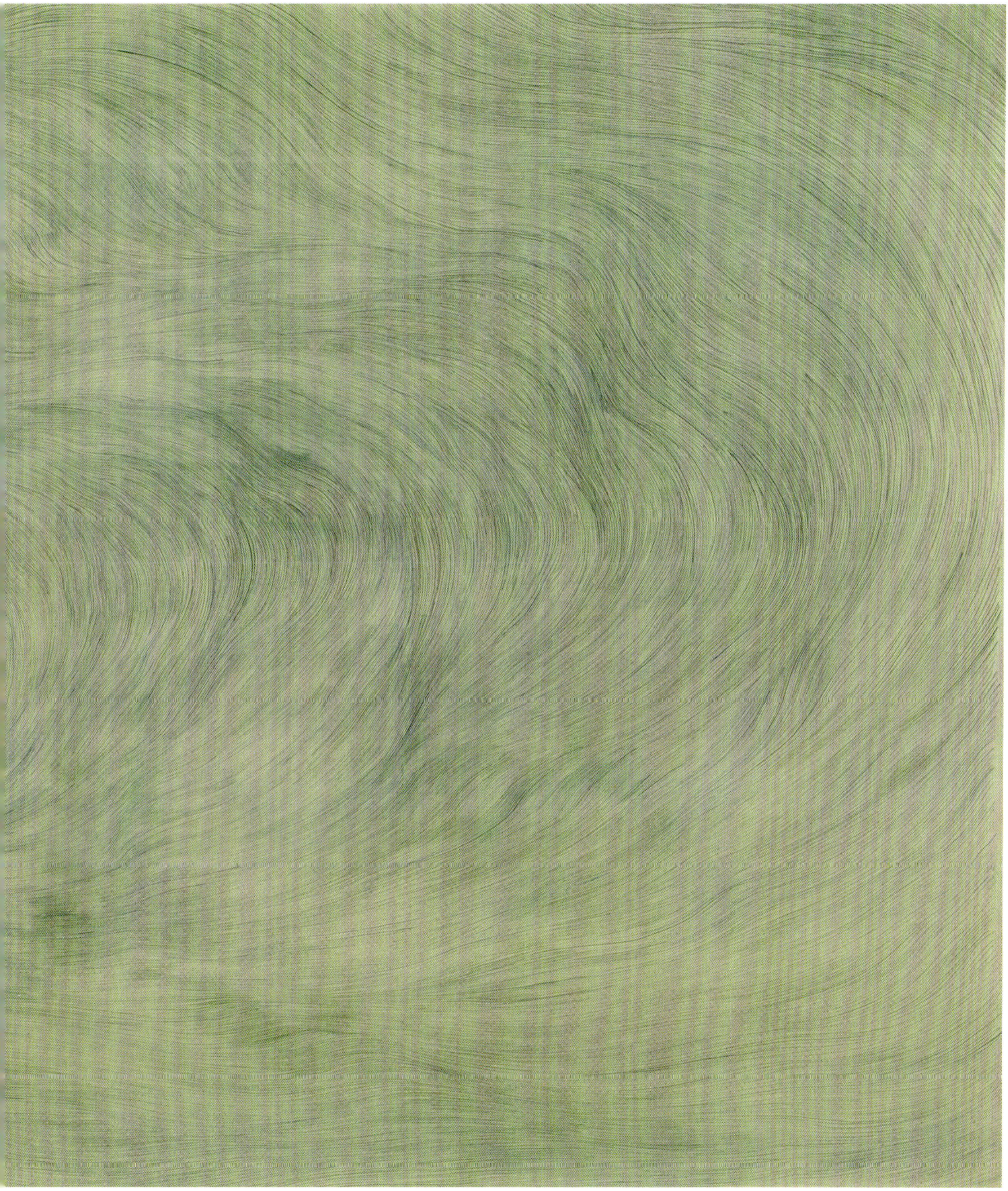

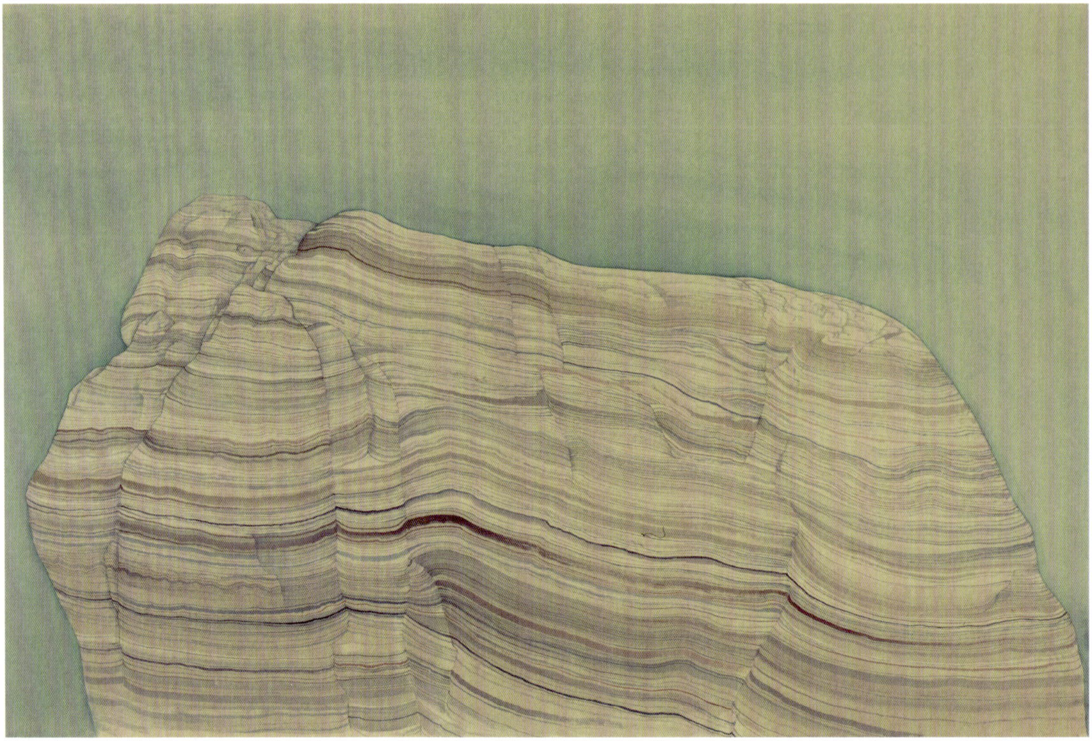

Contemplate #62

150×100 cm
Silk Mineral Pigment
2021

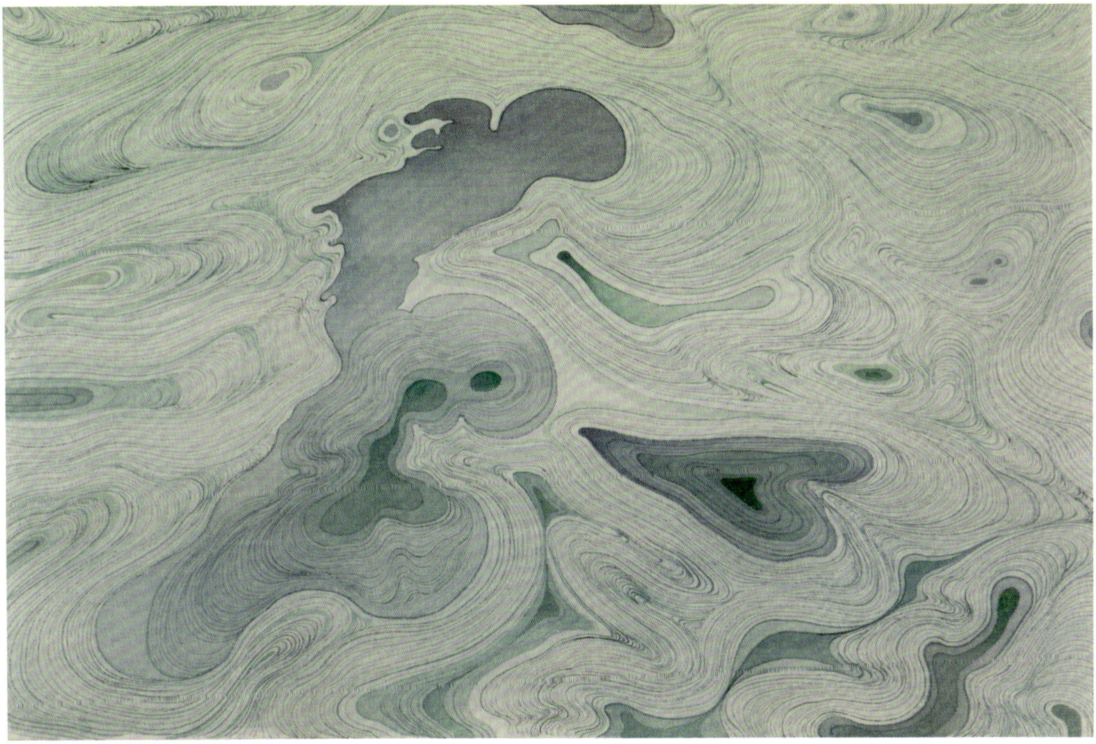

Contemplate #76

47 × 33 cm
Silk Mineral Pigment
2021

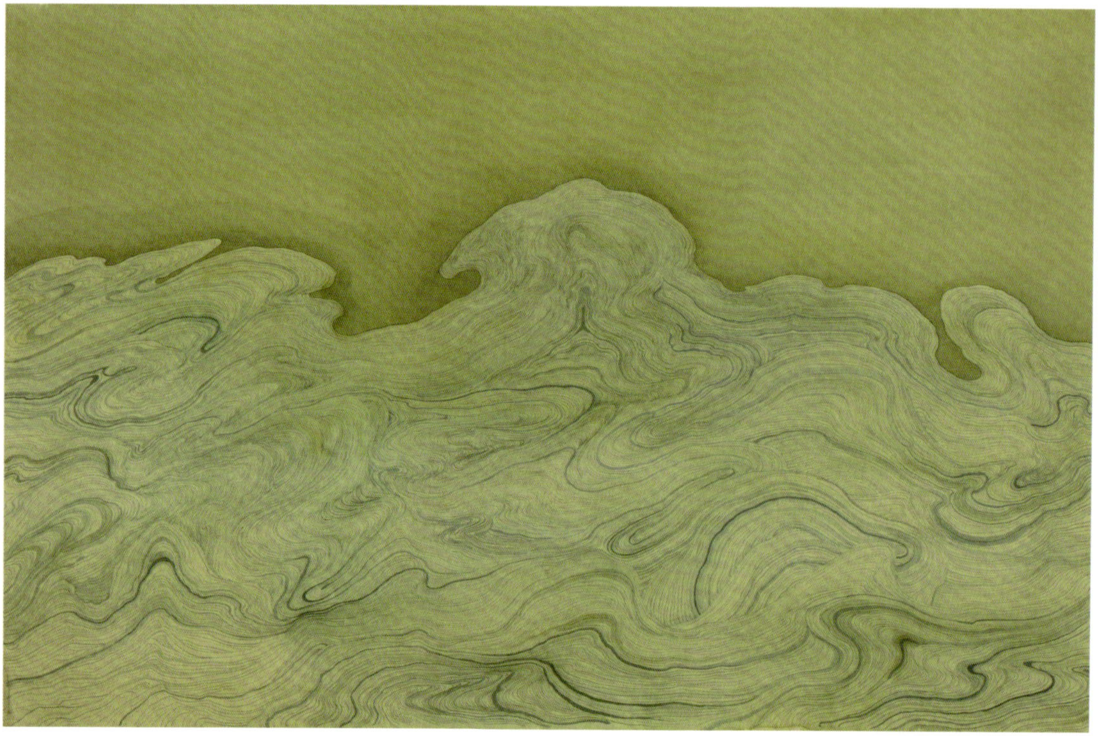

Contemplate #61

150×100 cm
Silk Mineral Pigment
2021

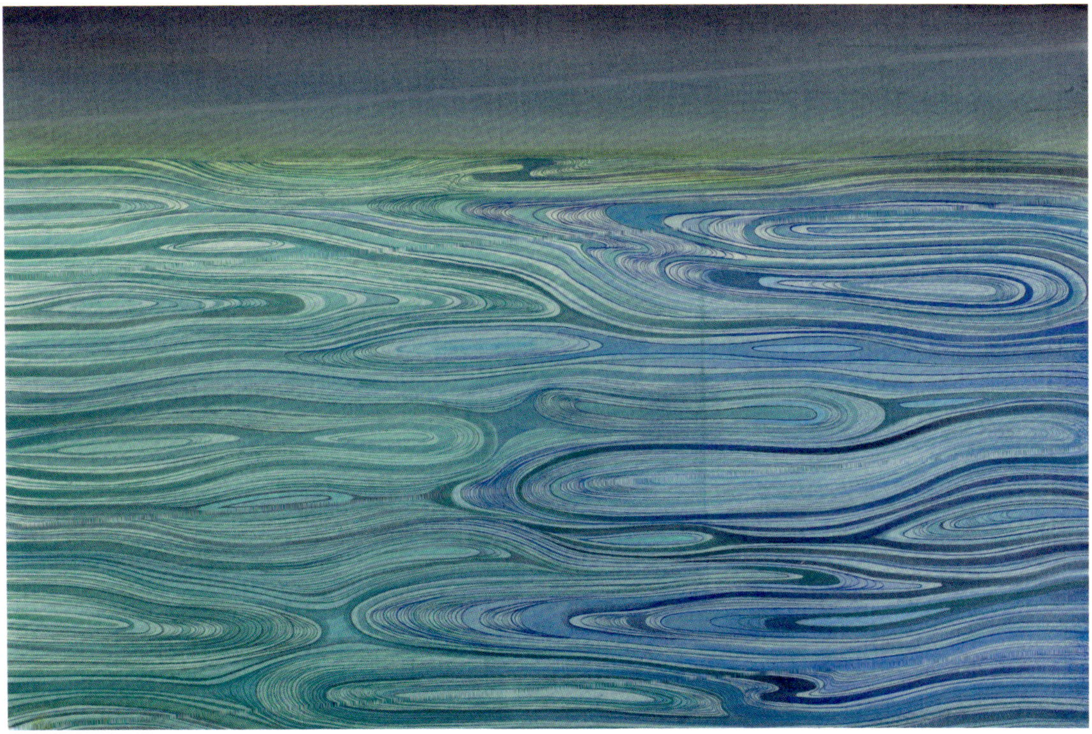

Contemplate-Mine #86

86×55.5 cm
Silk Mineral Pigment
2023

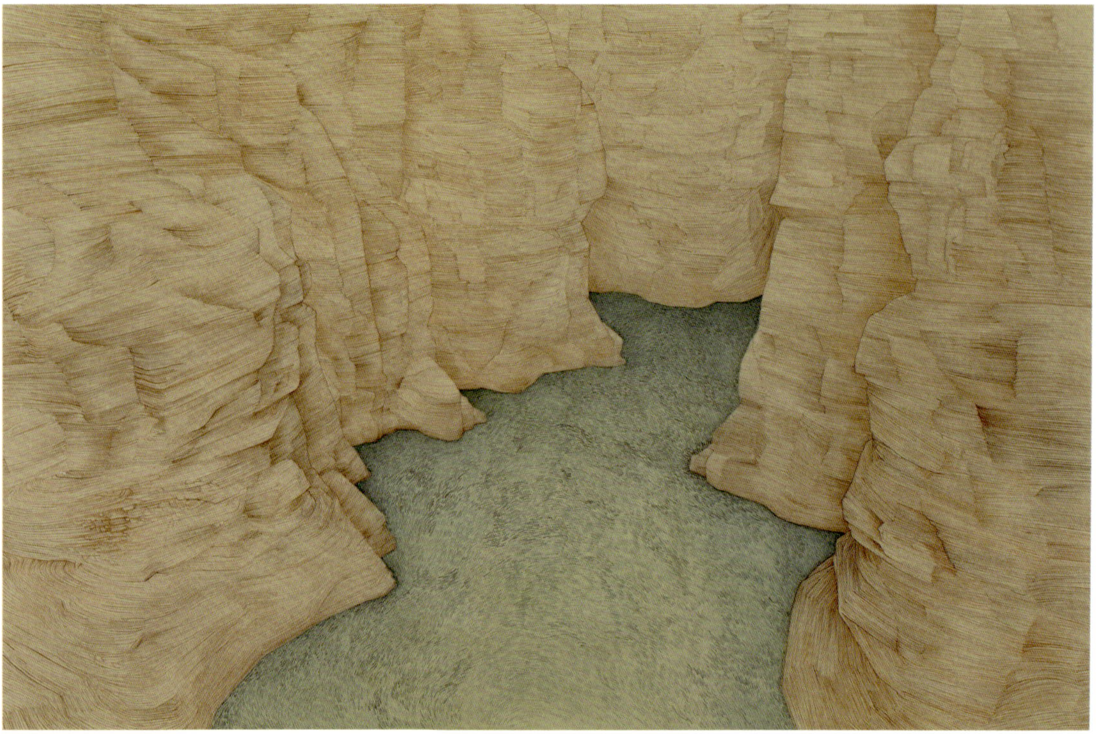

Contemplate #40

150×100 cm
Silk Mineral Pigment
2019

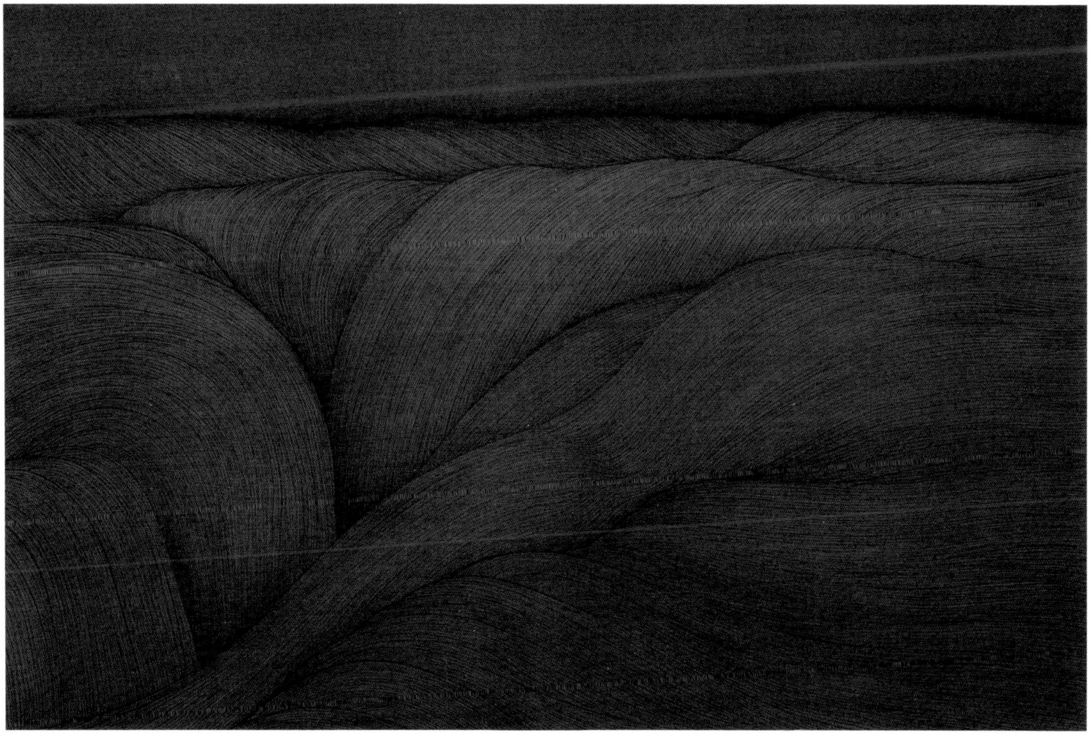

Contemplate #12

55×35 cm
Silk Mineral Pigment
2016

Contemplate #14

500×180 cm
Silk Mineral Pigment
2015

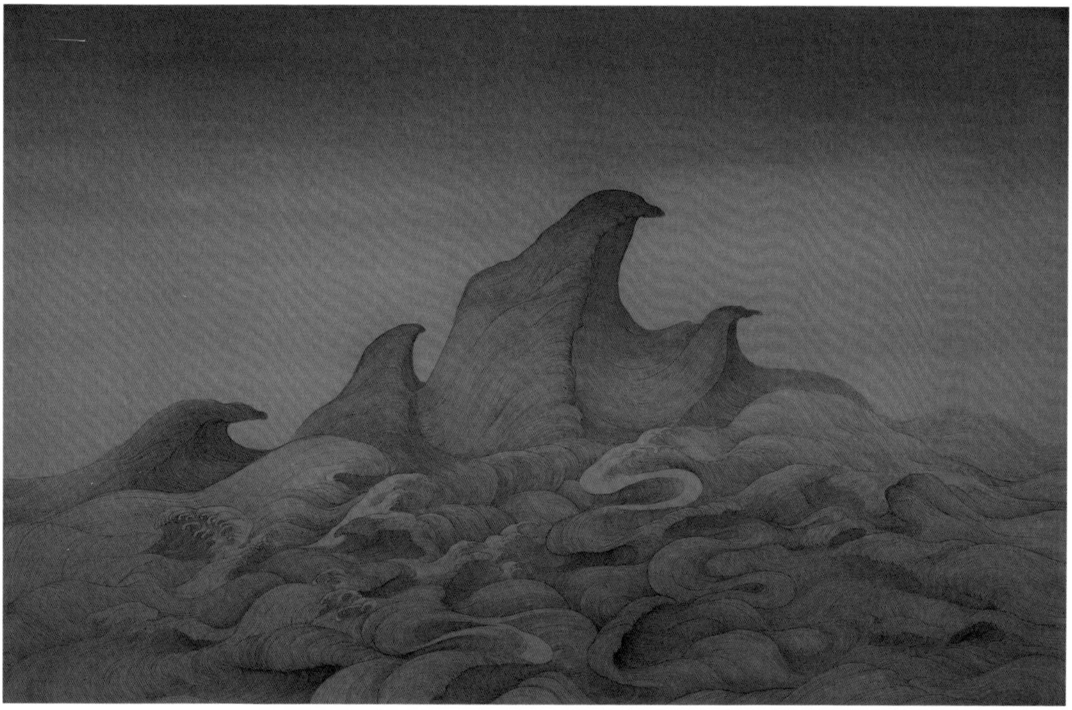

Contemplate #22

100×50 cm
Silk Mineral Pigment
2016

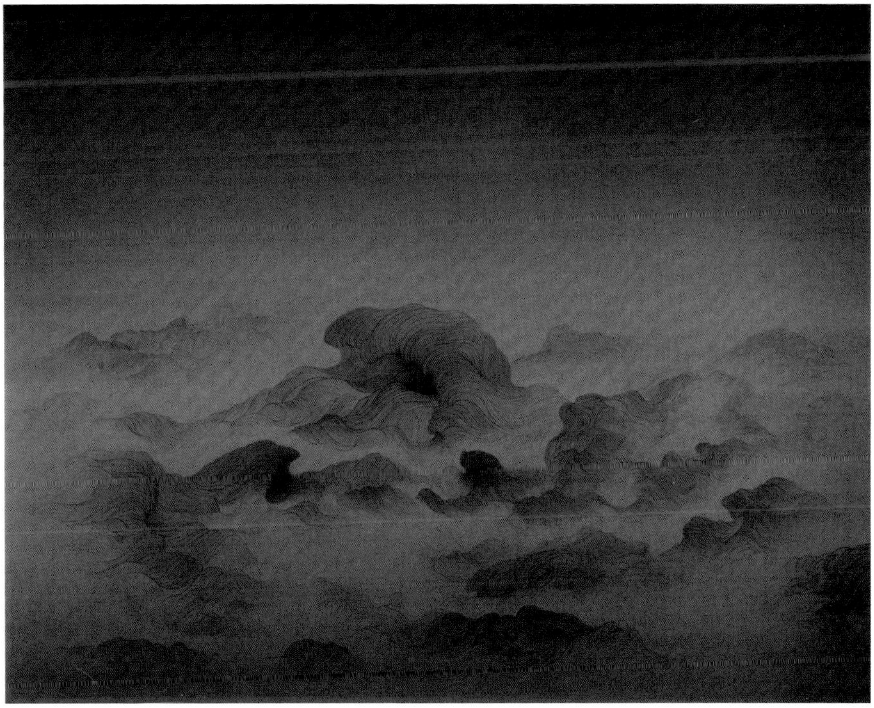

Contemplate #11

75×55 cm
Silk Mineral Pigment
2015

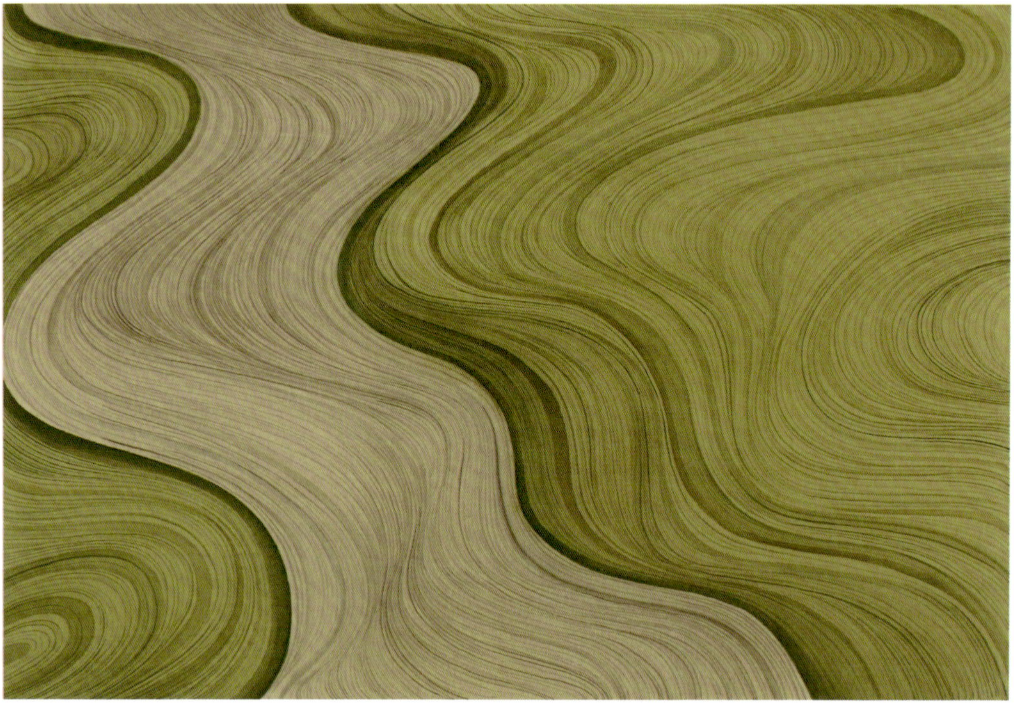

Contemplate #49

32×22 cm
Silk Mineral Pigment
2021

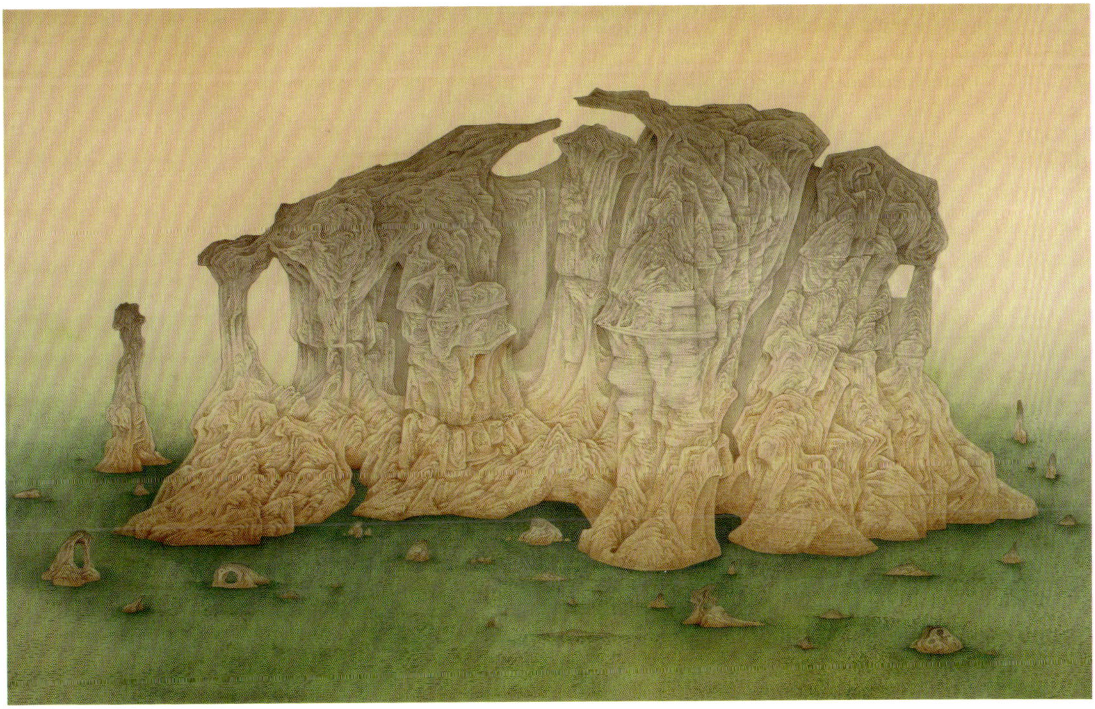

Contemplate #39

150×100 cm
Silk Mineral Pigment
2019

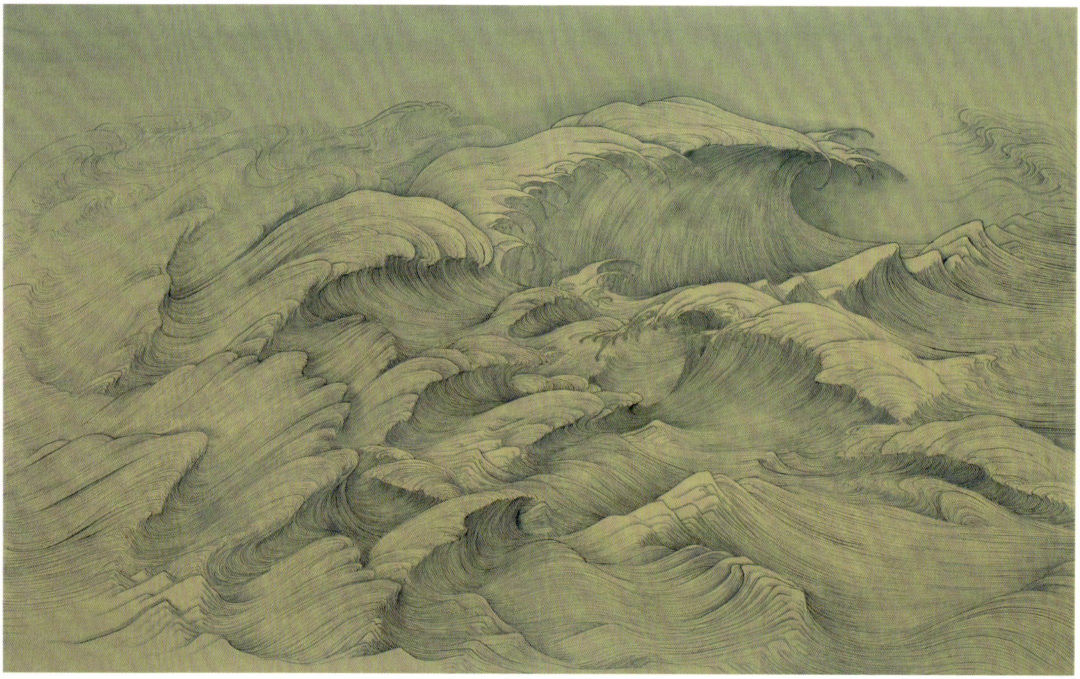

Contemplate #38

150×100 cm
Silk Mineral Pigment
2019

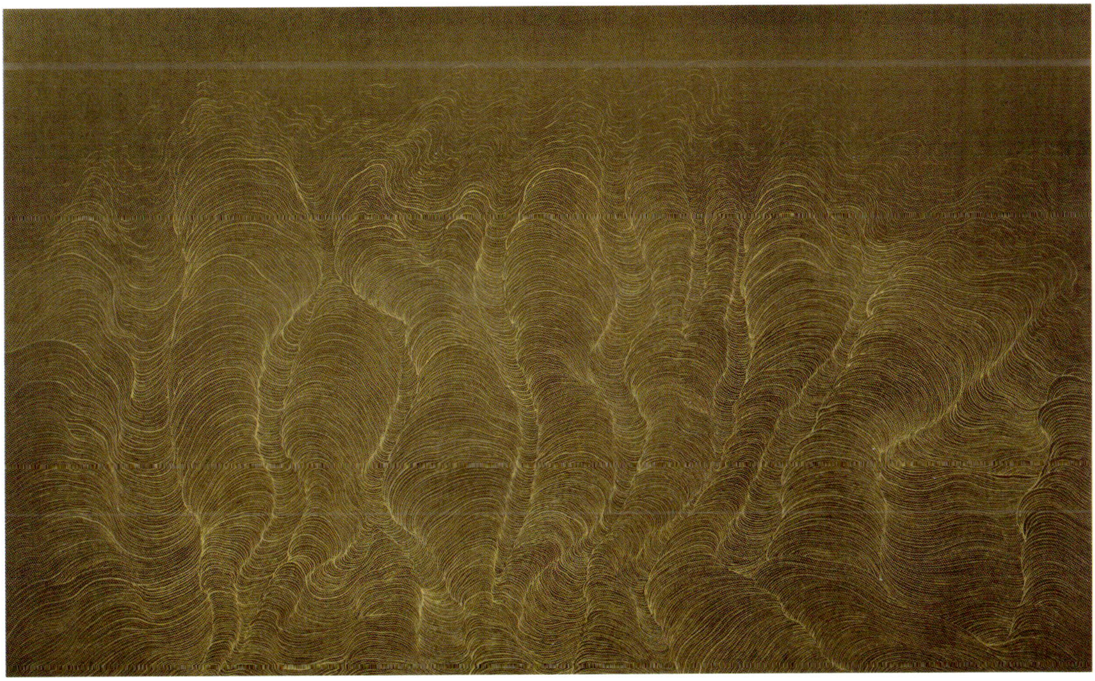

Contemplate #15

100×60 cm
Silk Mineral Pigment
2016

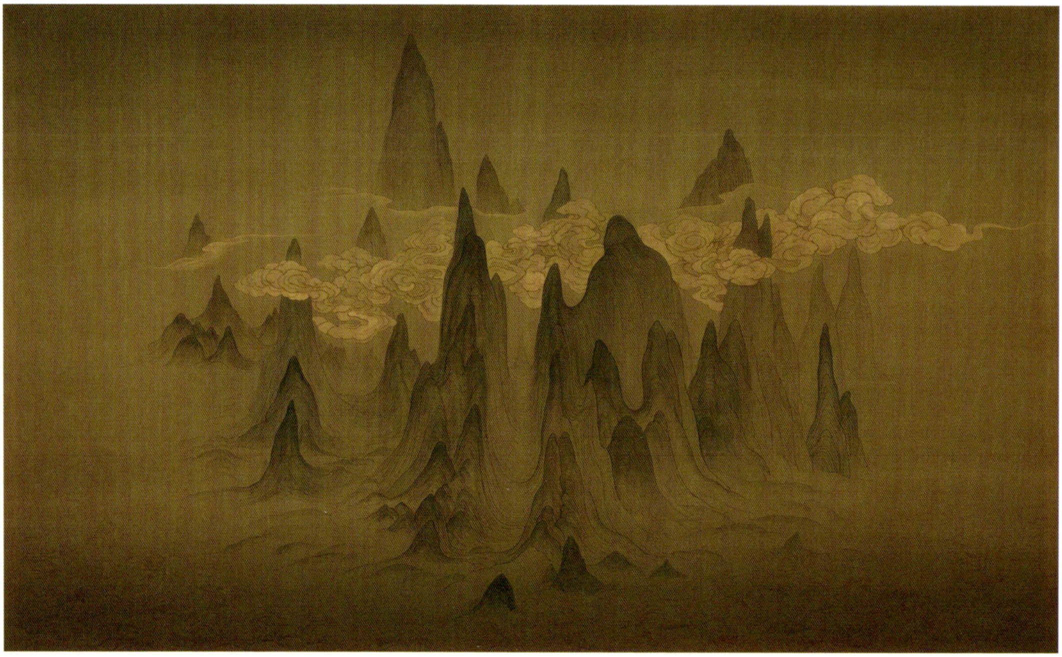

The Three Gorges

90×60 cm
Silk Mineral Pigment
2016

Contemplate #20

100×60 cm
Silk Mineral Pigment
2015

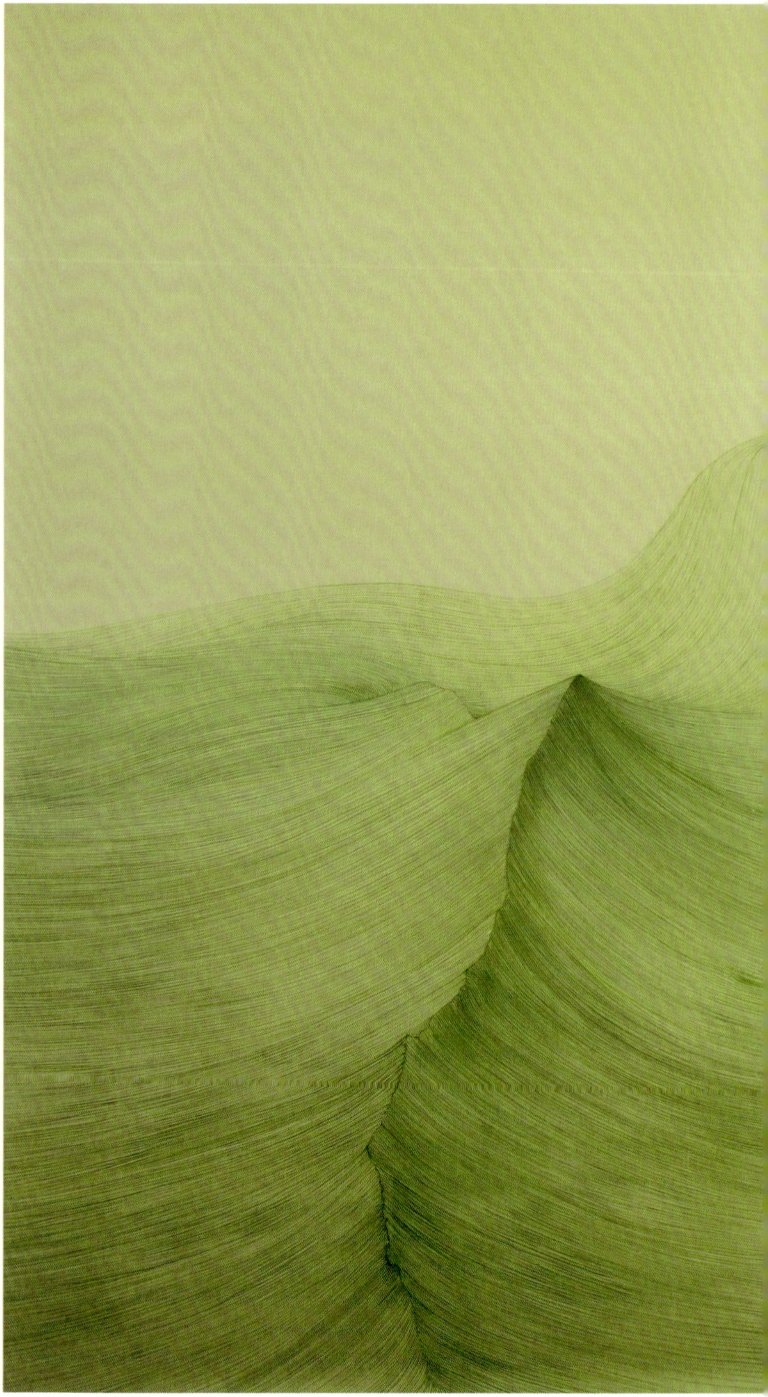

Contemplate #47

150×100 cm
Silk Mineral Pigment
2019

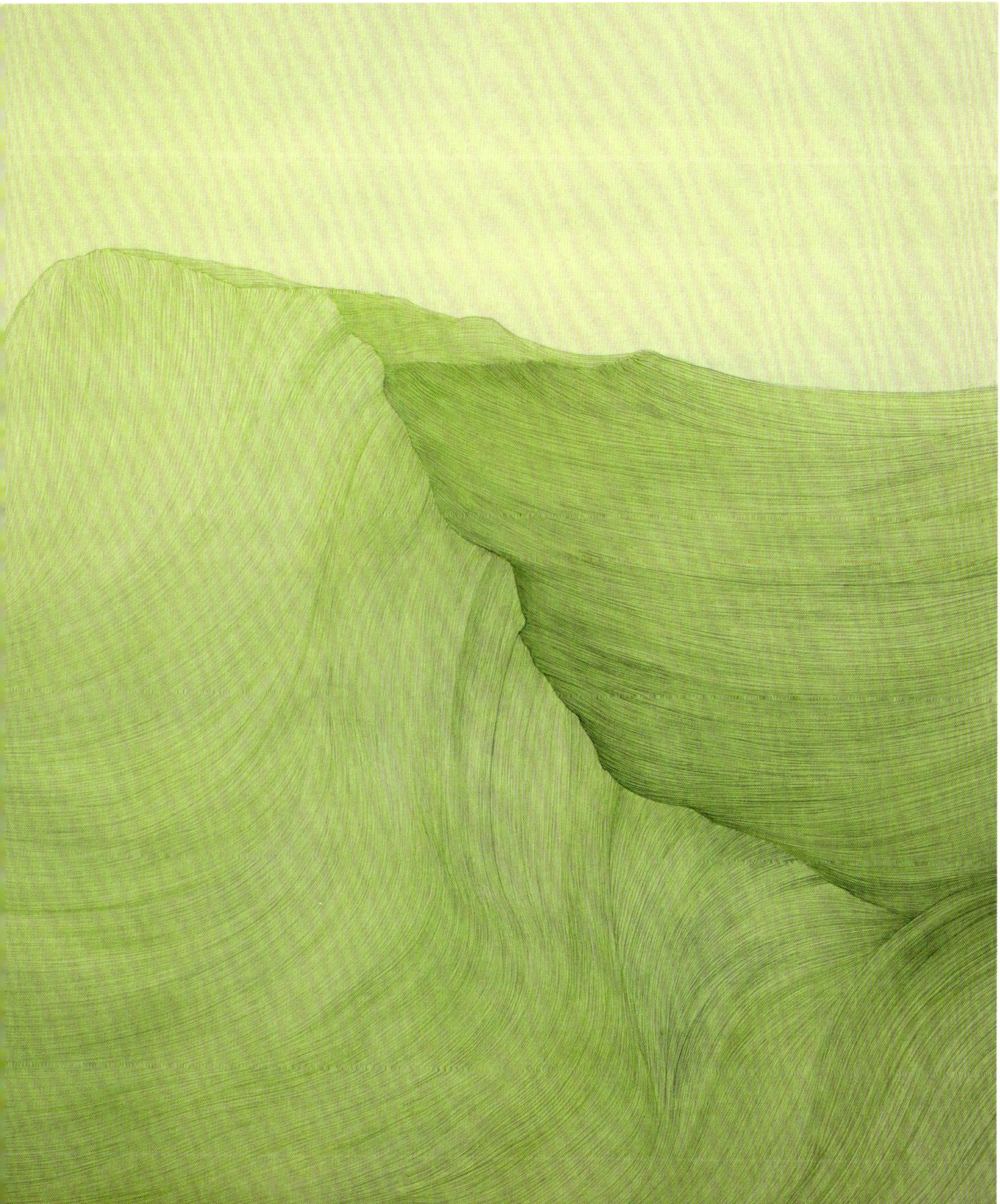

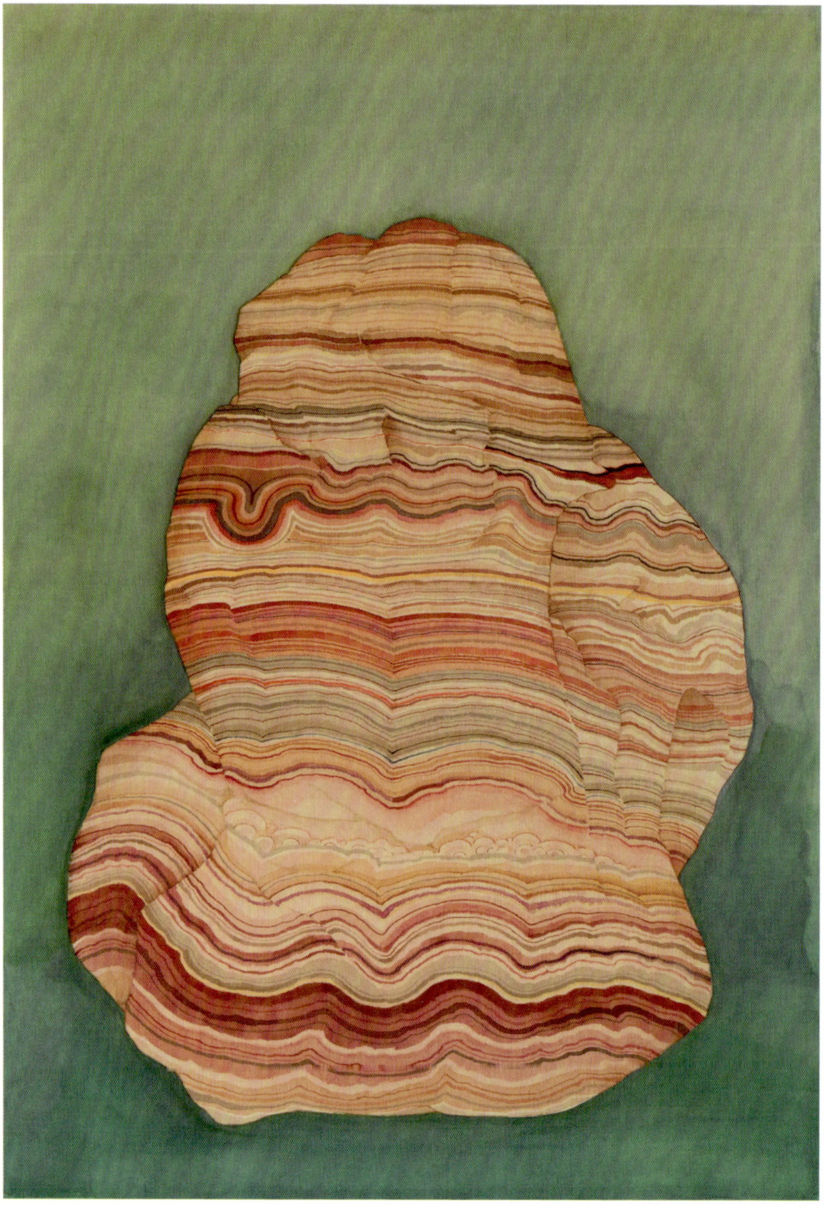

Cloud #4

47×67 cm
Silk Mineral Pigment
2021

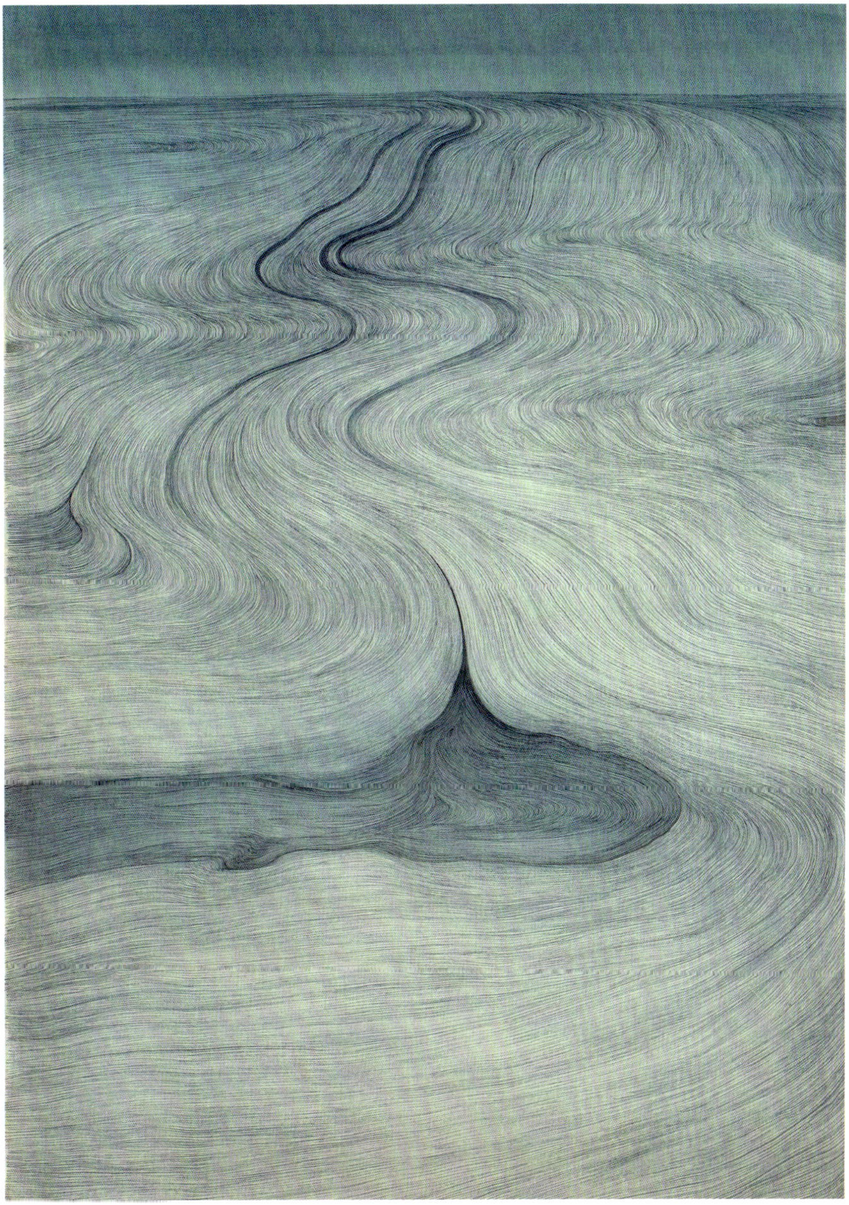

Contemplate #21

50×70 cm
Silk Mineral Pigment
2016

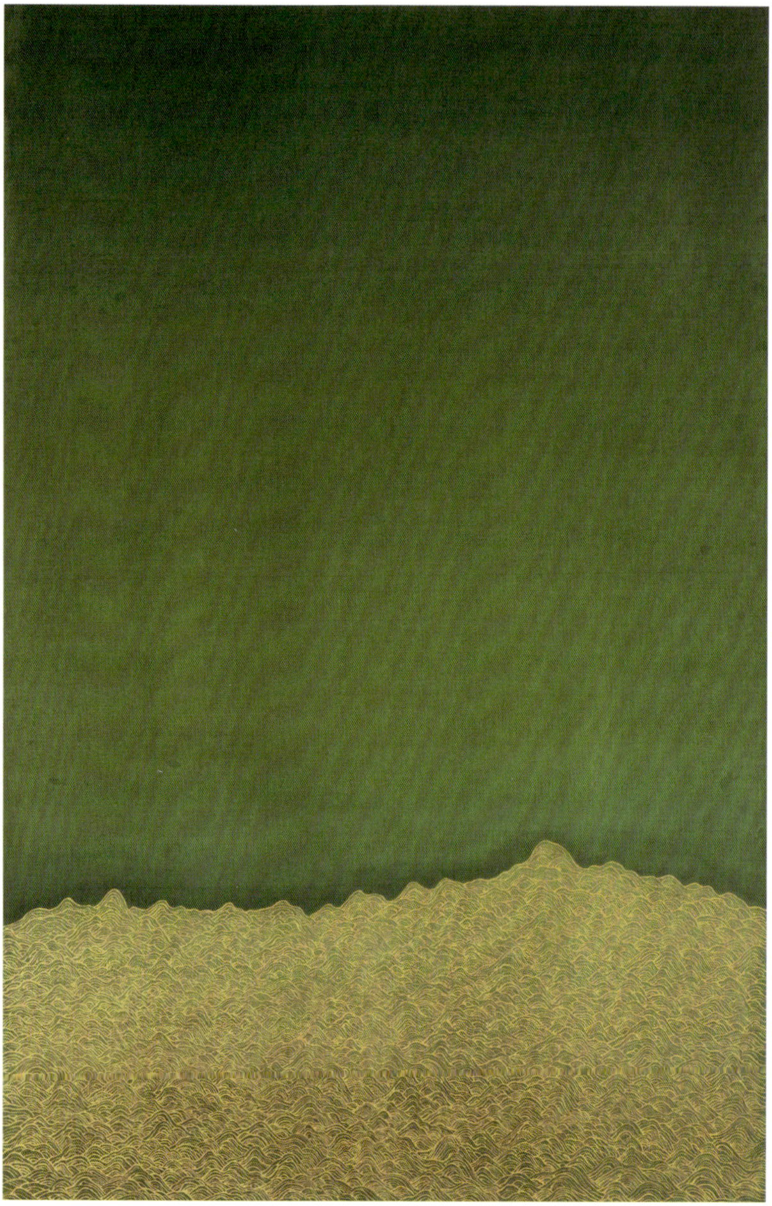

Contemplate-Mine#3

56.5×86.5 cm
Silk Mineral Pigment
2023

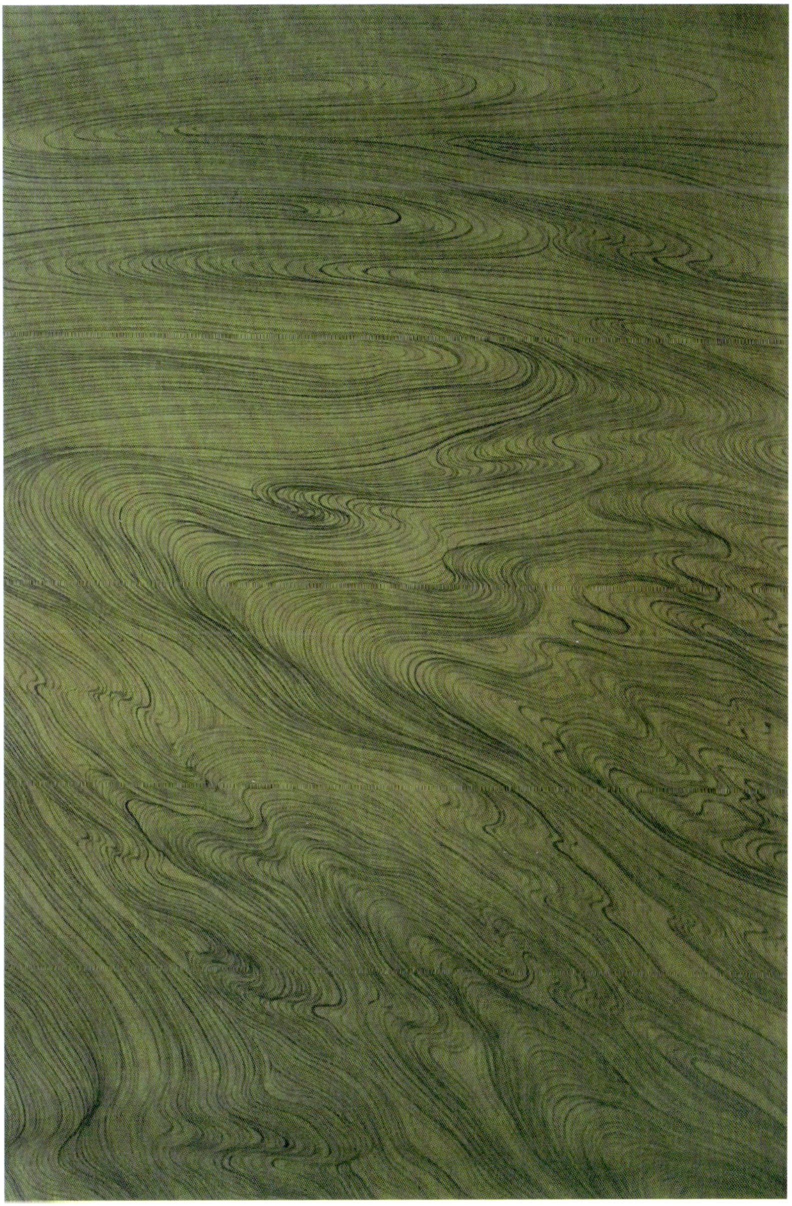

Contemplate #17

22×33 cm
Silk Mineral Pigment
2016

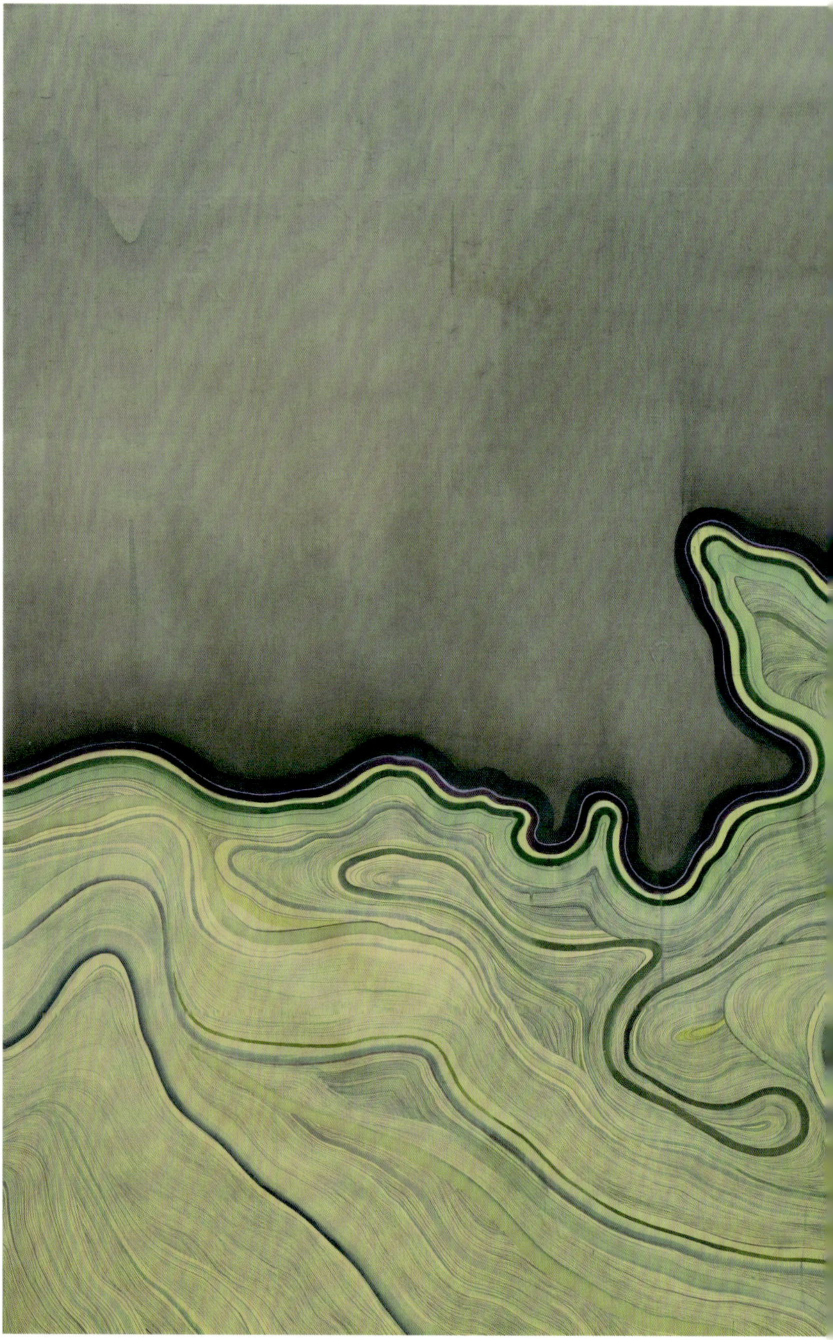

Hadean

700×300 cm
Silk Mineral Pigment
2023

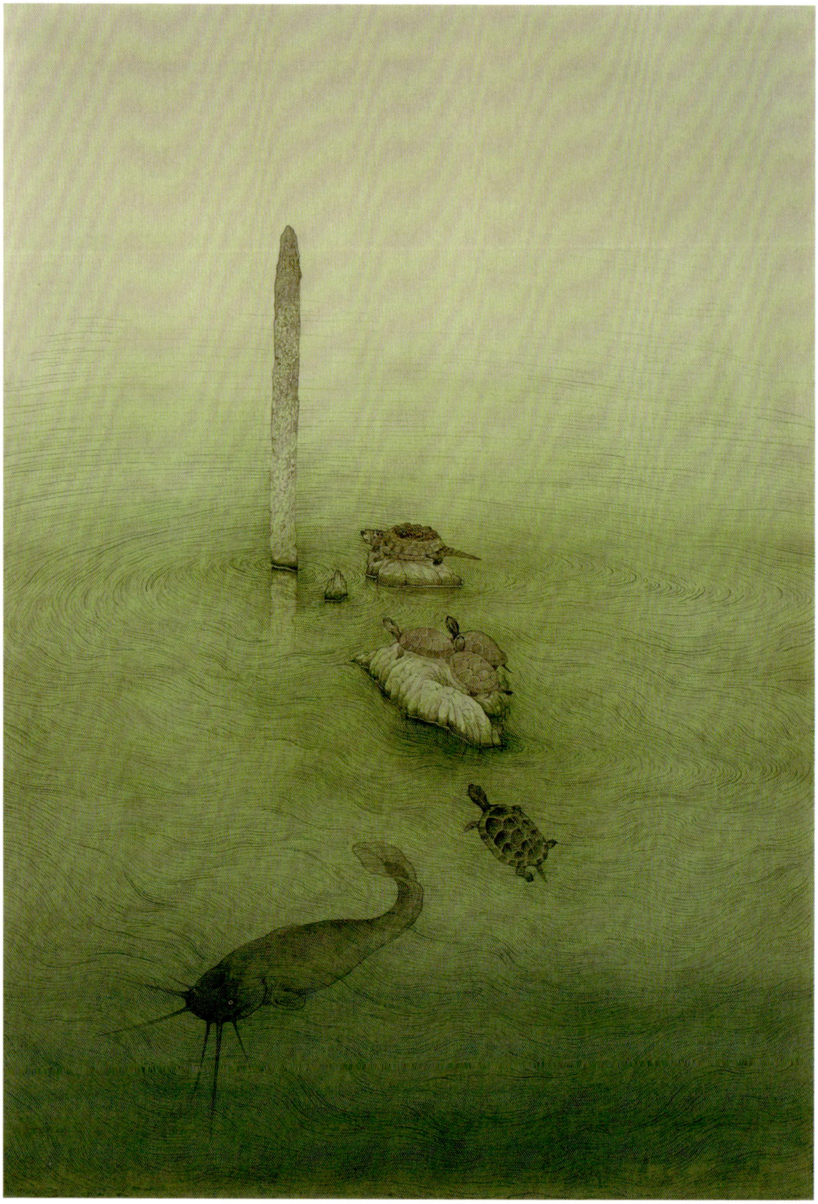

Kaiyuantempie

50×70 cm
Silk Mineral Pigment
2017

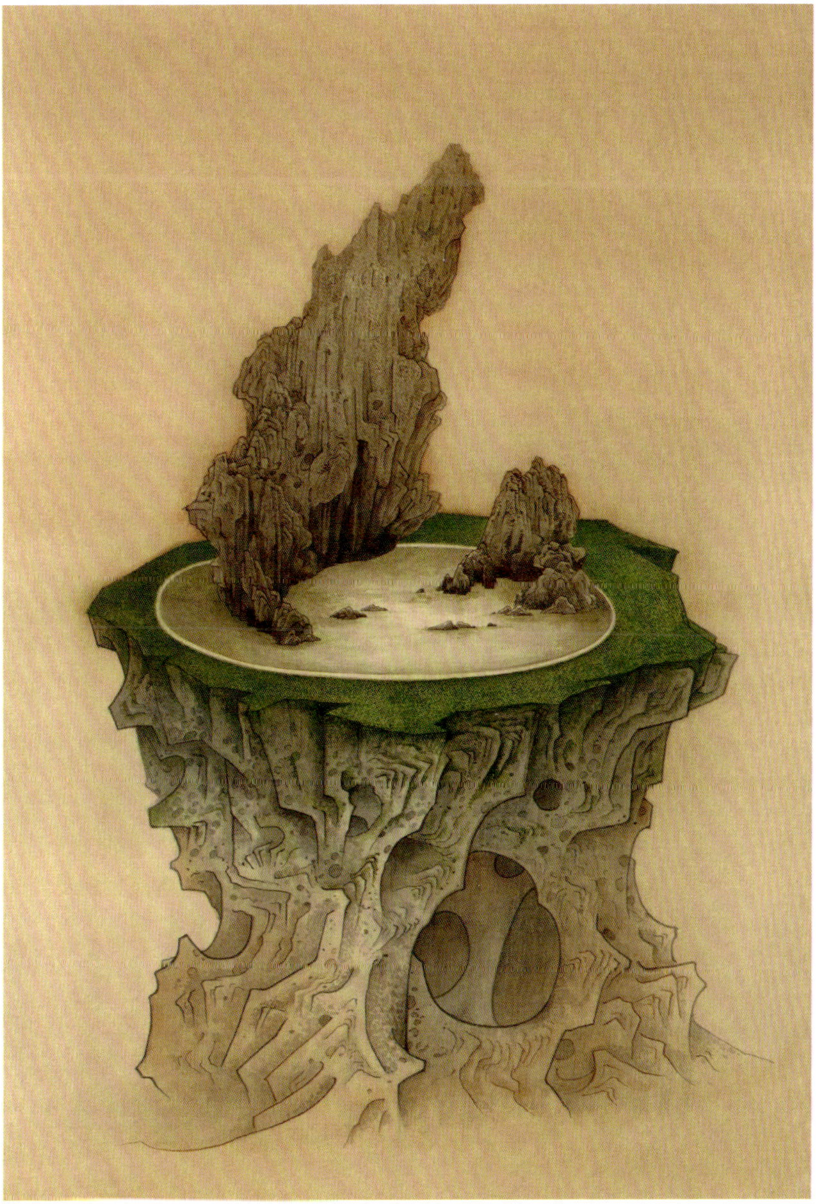

Garden

50×70 cm
Silk Mineral Pigment
2018

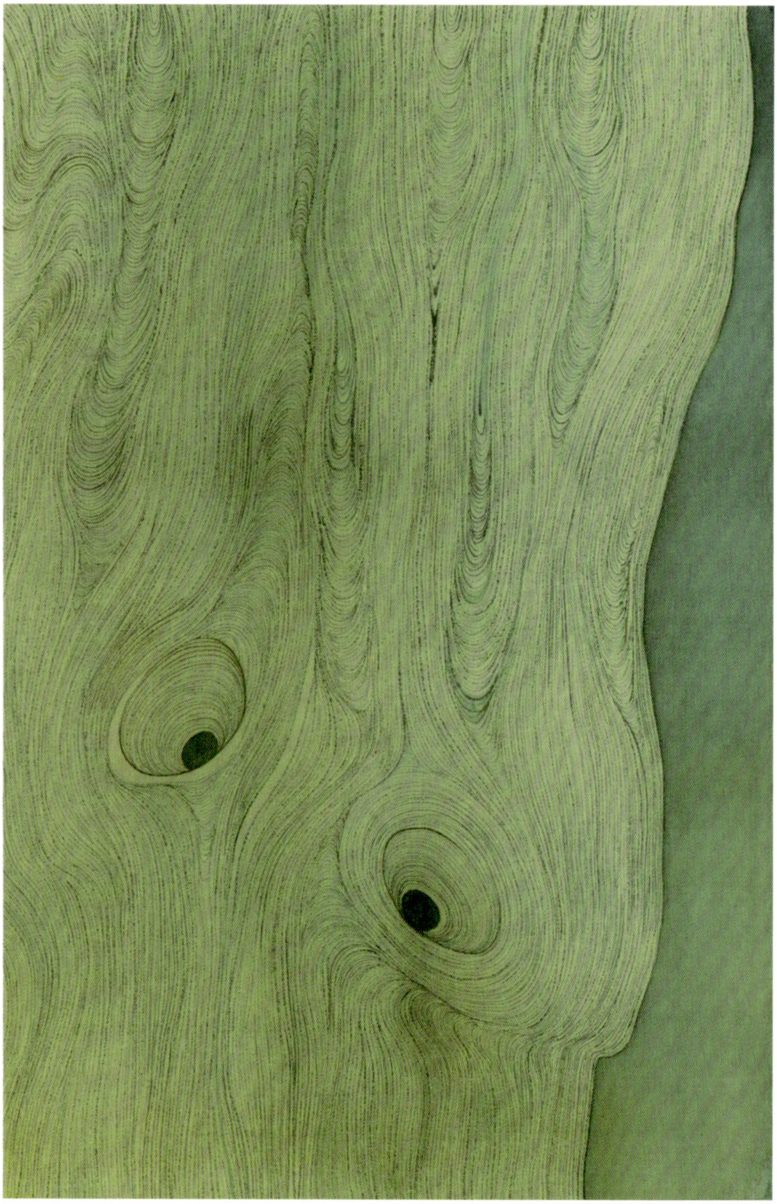

Contemplate #72

47×31 cm
Silk Mineral Pigment
2022

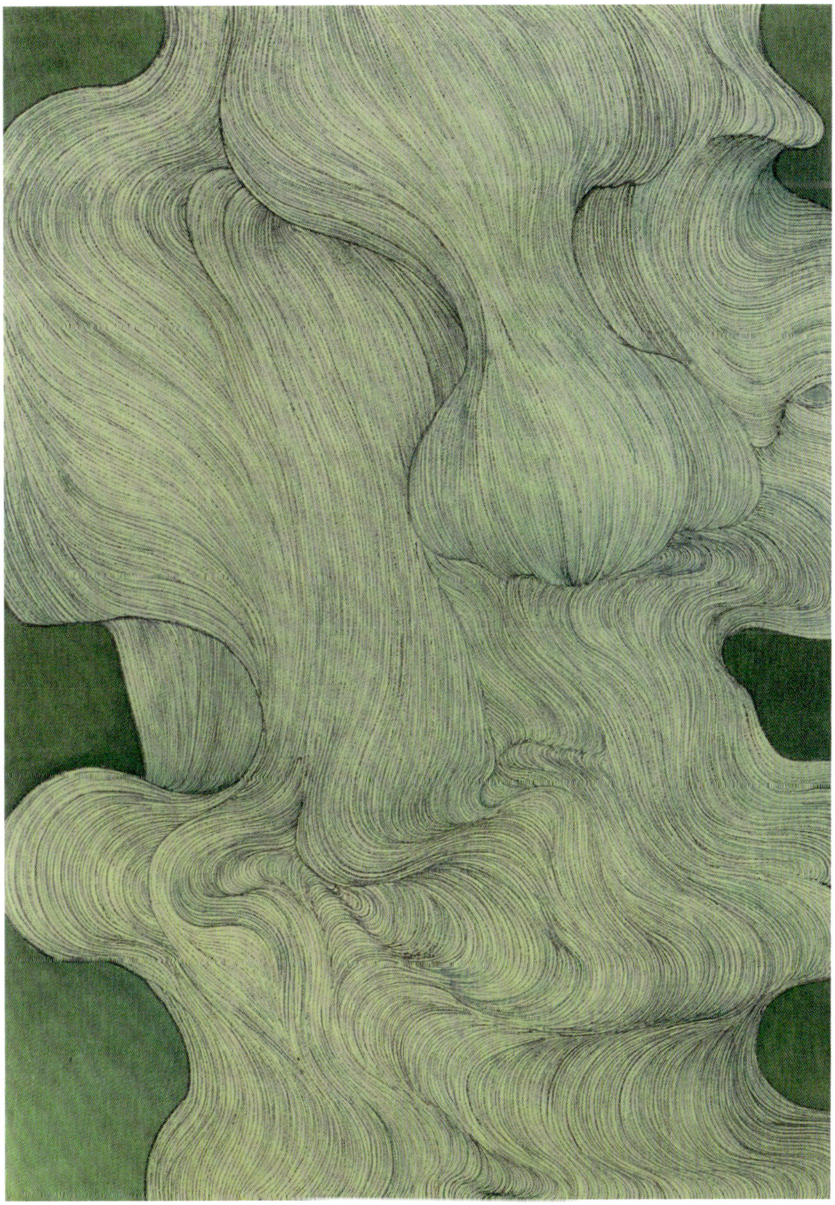

Contemplate #69

47×34 cm
Silk Mineral Migment
2022

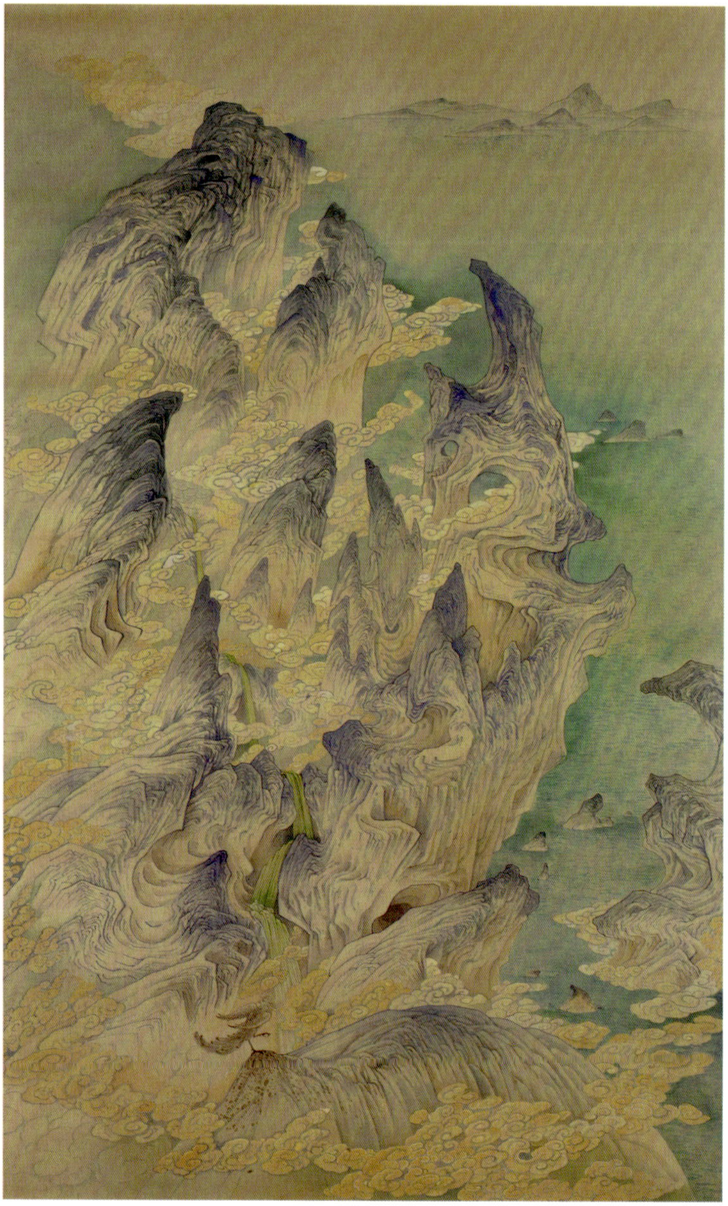

Cavern

80×120 cm
Silk Mineral Pigment
2018

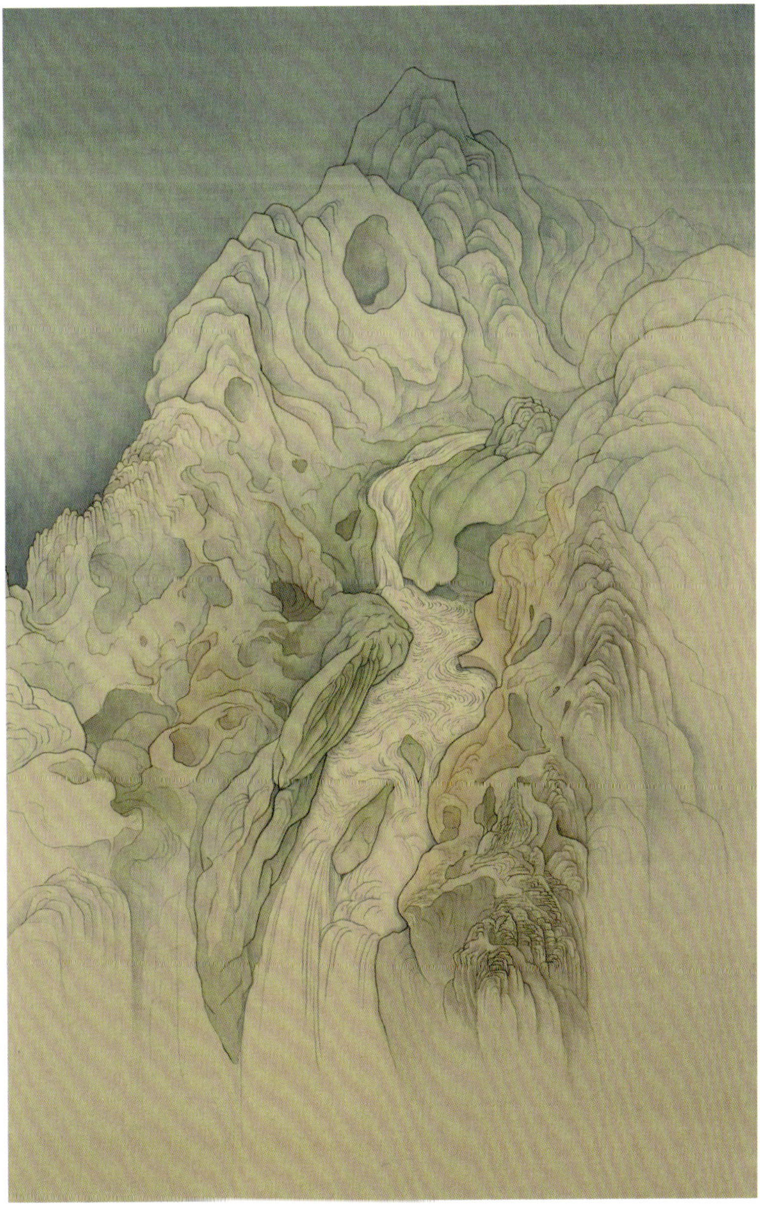

Contemplate #25

35×55 cm
Silk Mineral Pigment
2019

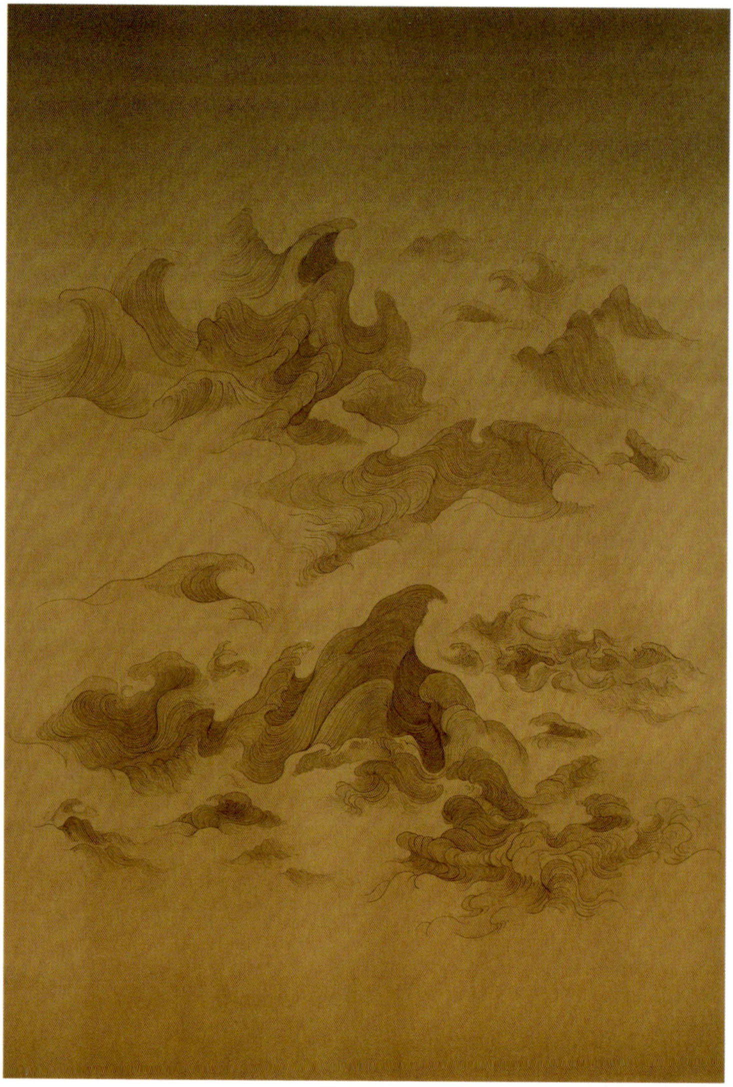

Contemplate #10

60×100 cm
Silk Mineral Pigment
2014

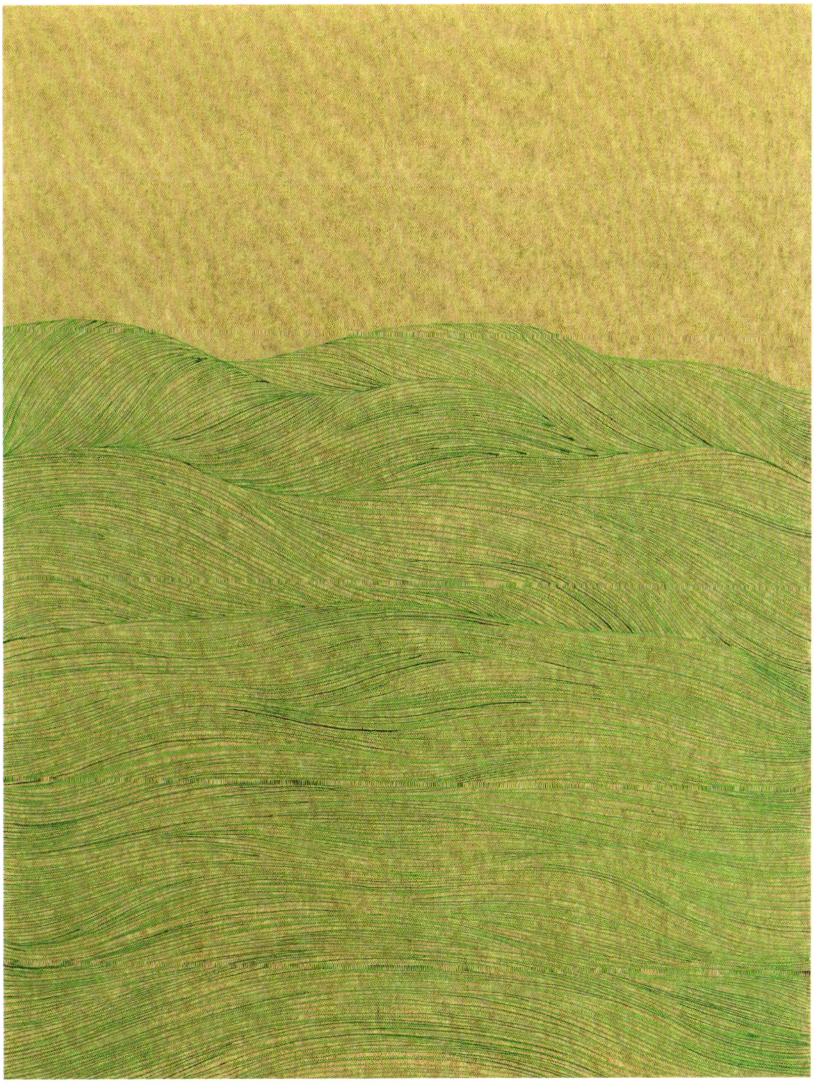

Contemplate-Mine #4

30×40 cm
Mineral Pigment on Paper
2023

Contemplate #23

38×40 cm
Silk Mineral Pigment
2016

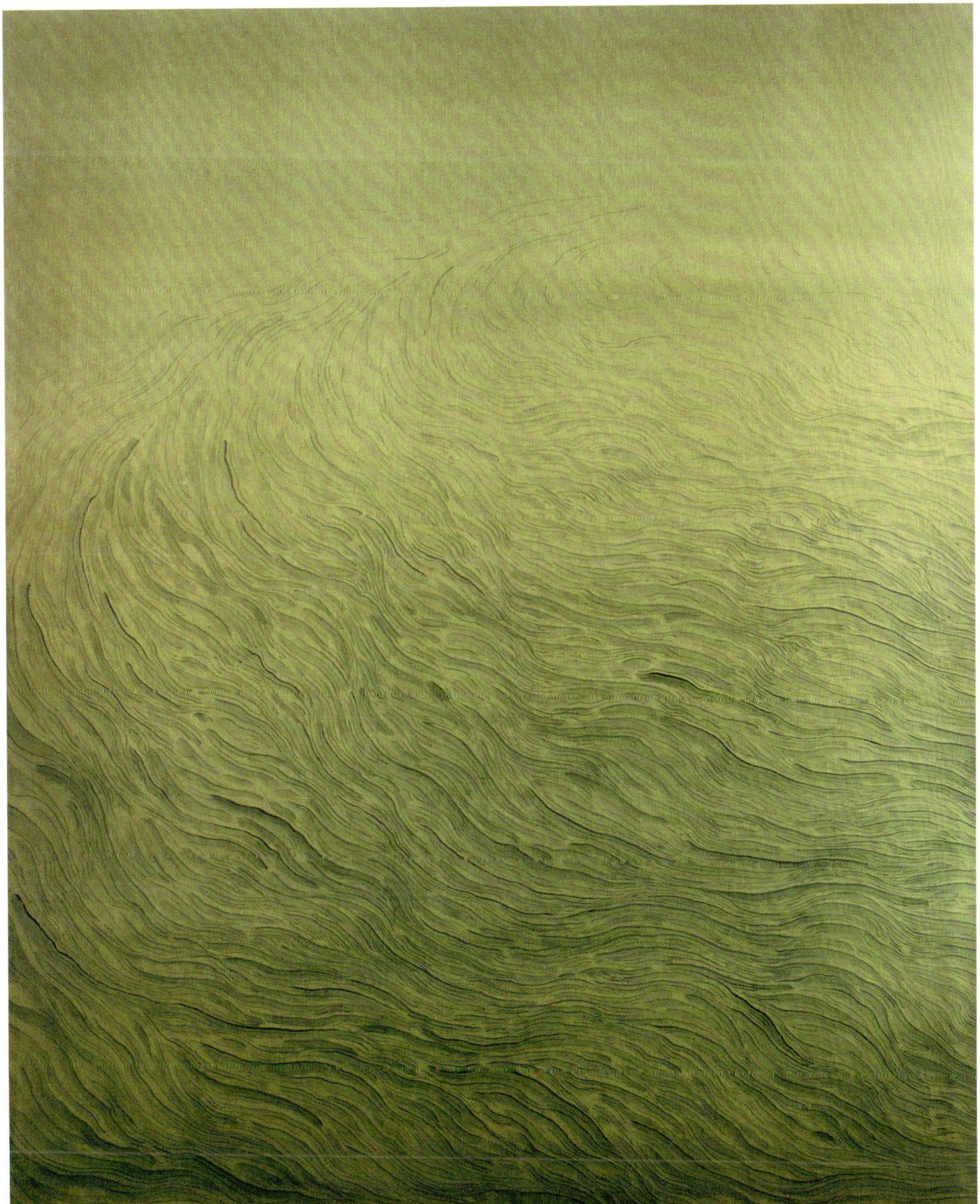

Contemplate #70 & 71

200×120 cm
Silk Mineral Pigment
2022

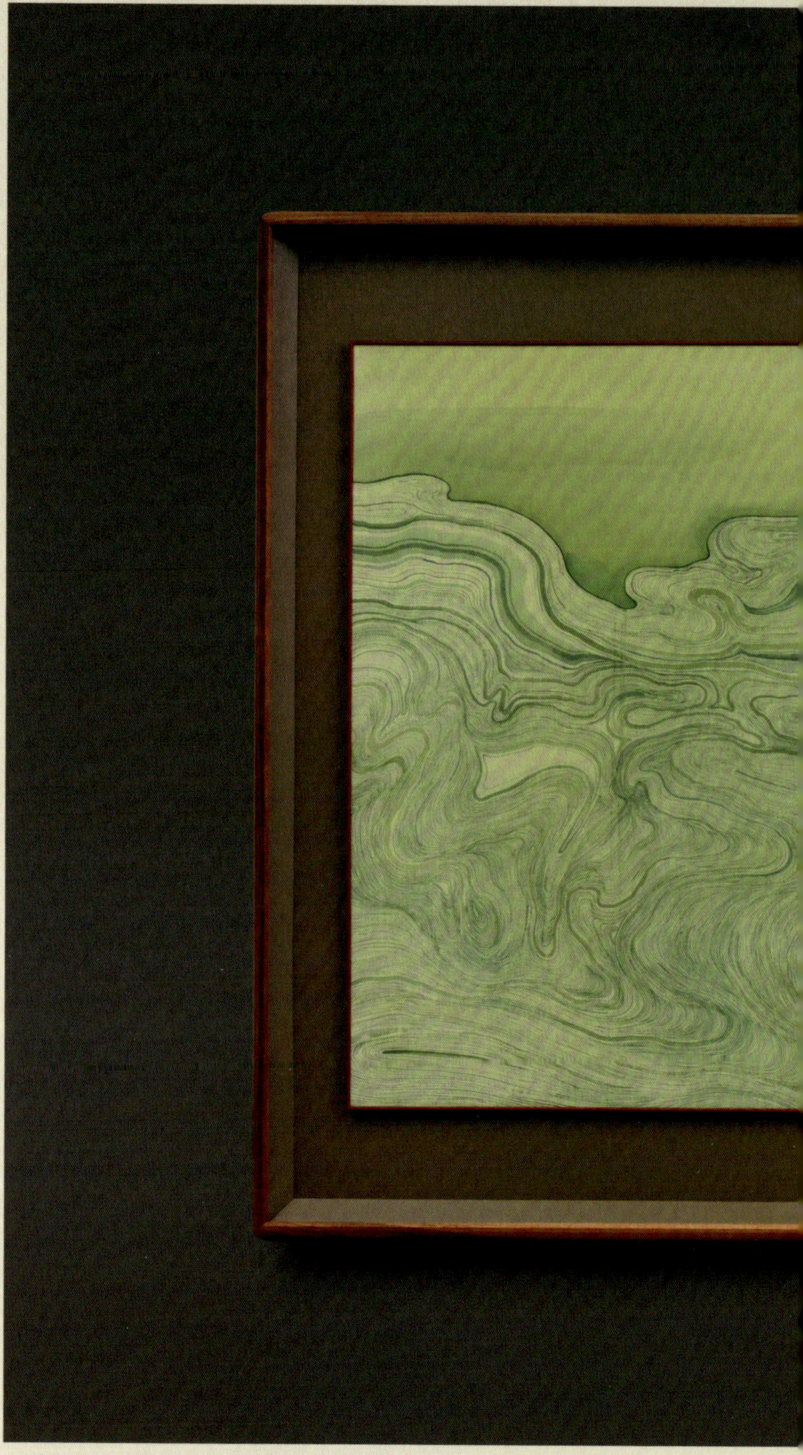

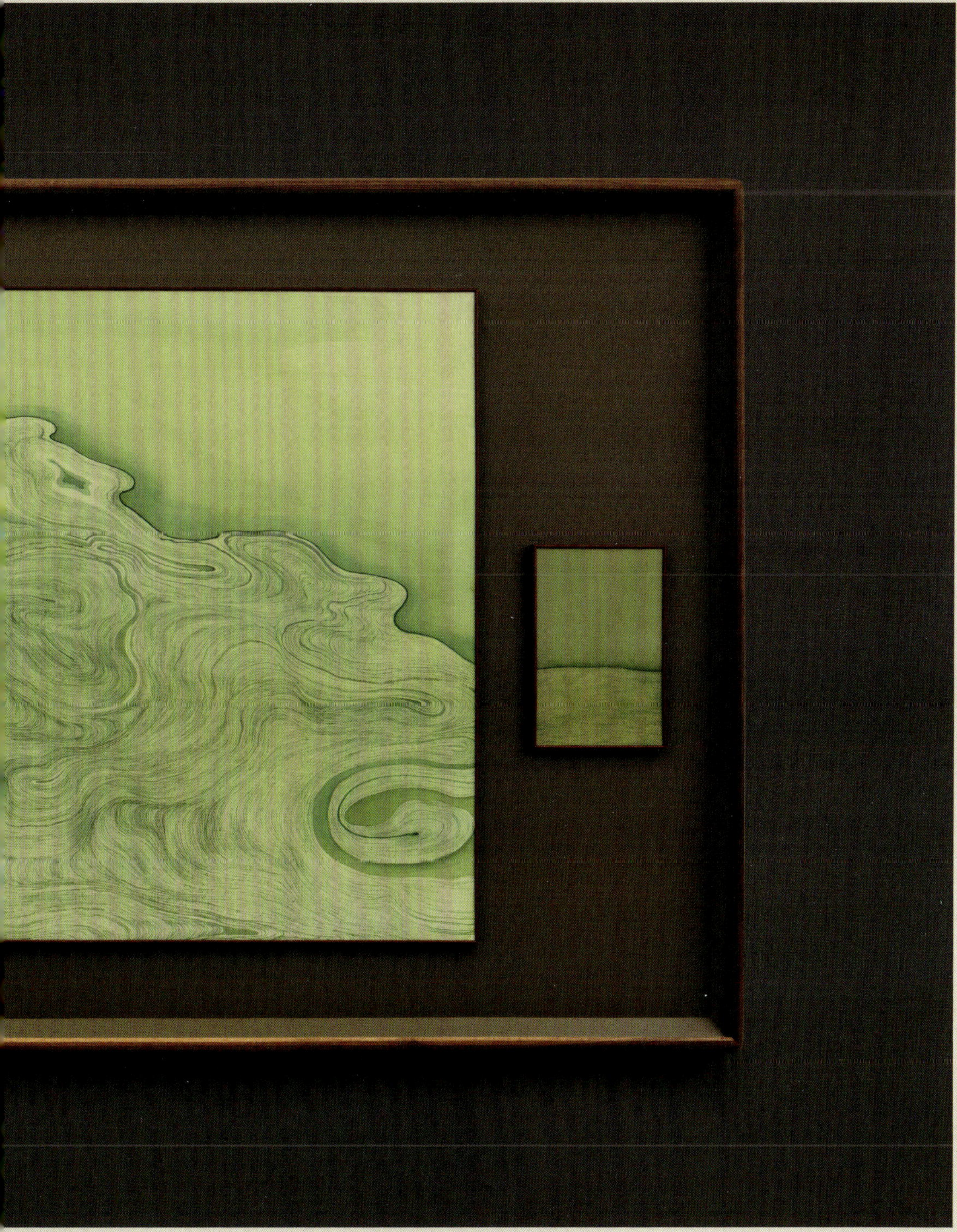

Contemplate #6

52×21 cm
Silk Mineral Pigment
2014

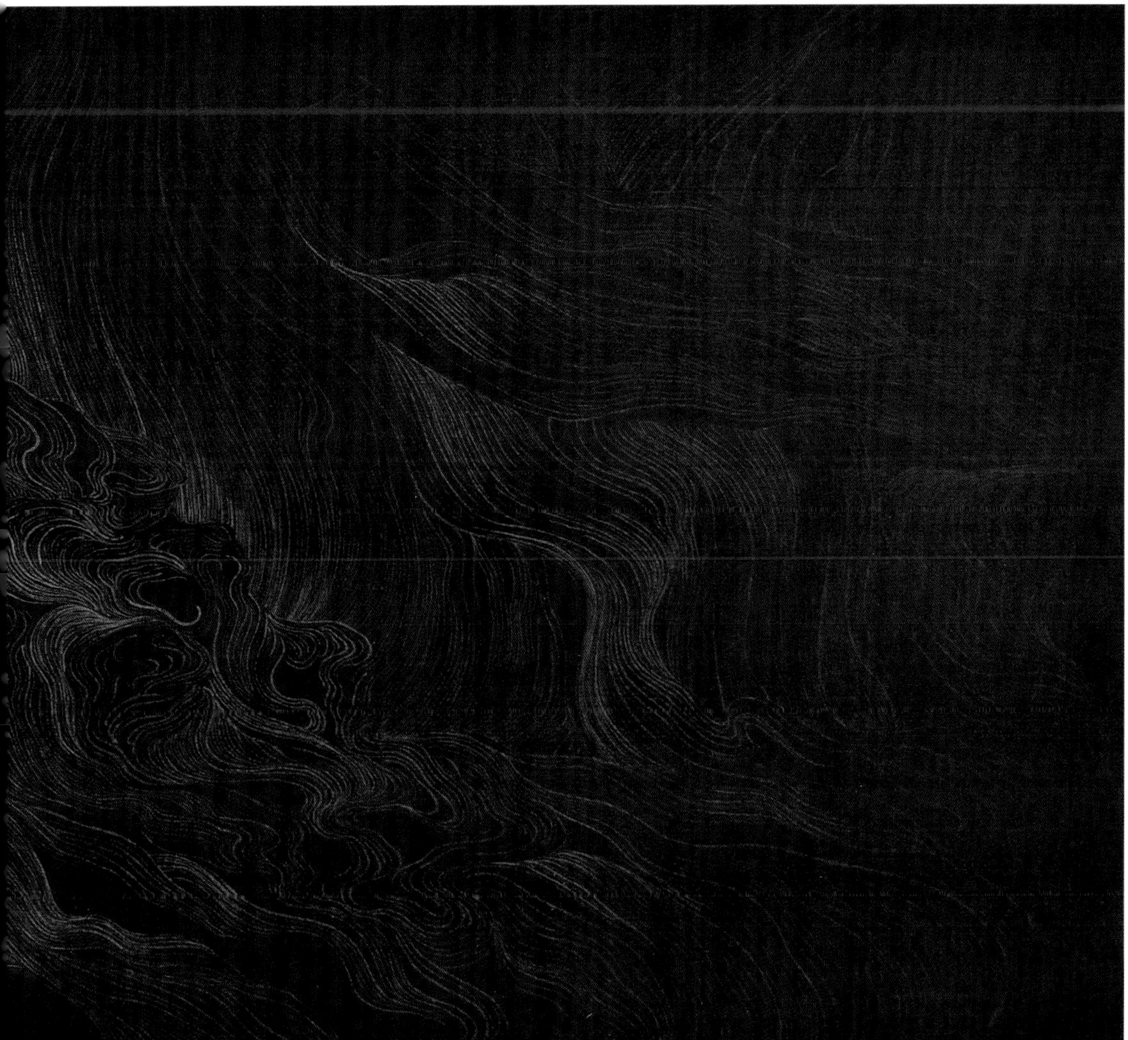

Sunrise on Huashan Mountain

260×100 cm
Silk Mineral Pigment
2017

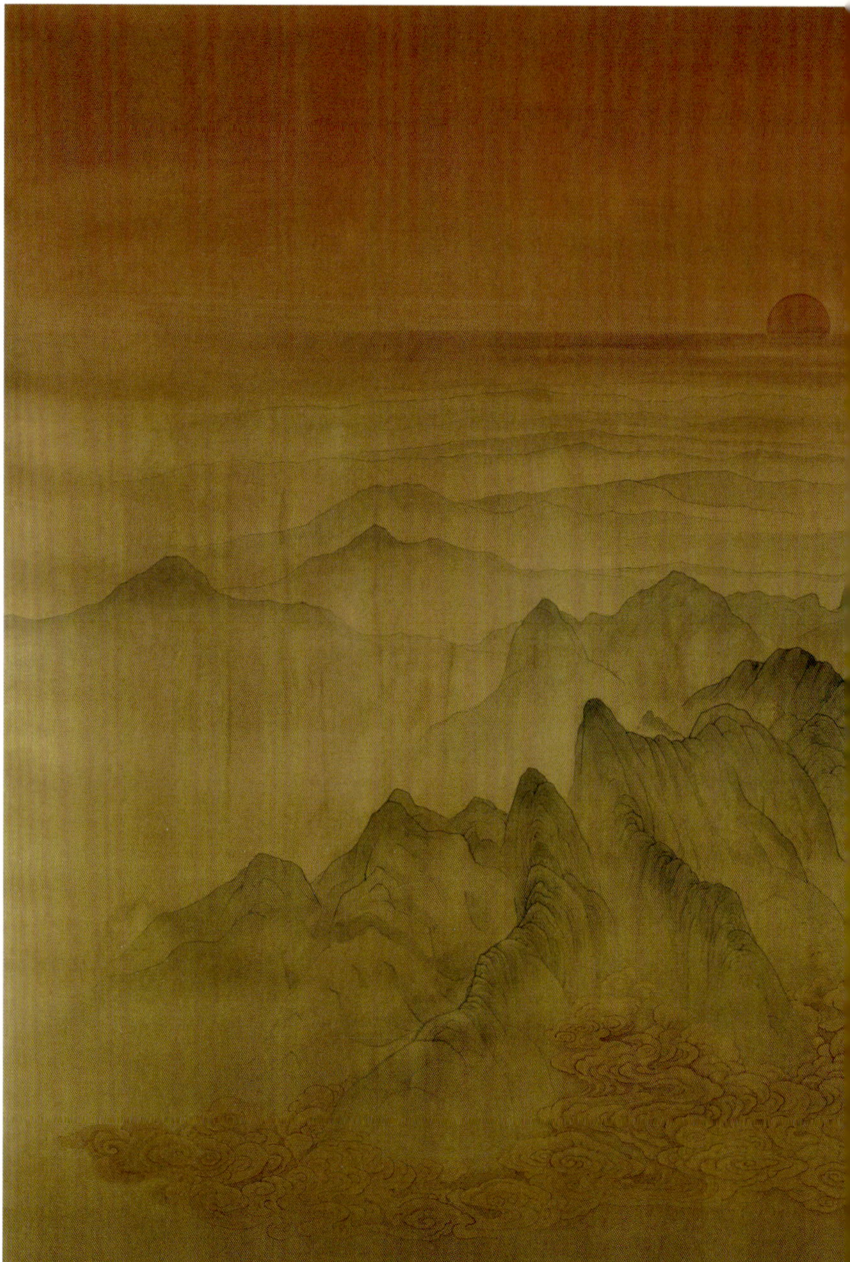

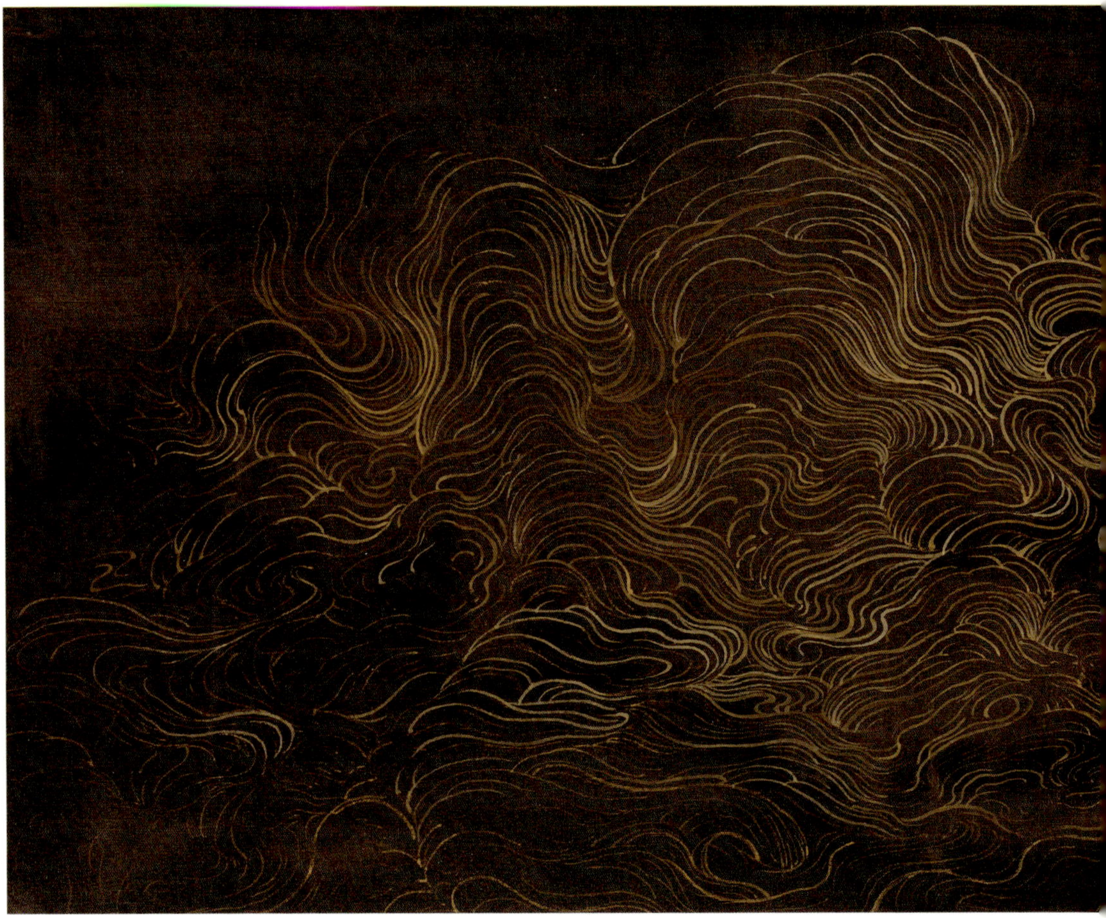

Contemplate #7

52×21 cm
Silk Mineral Pigment
2014

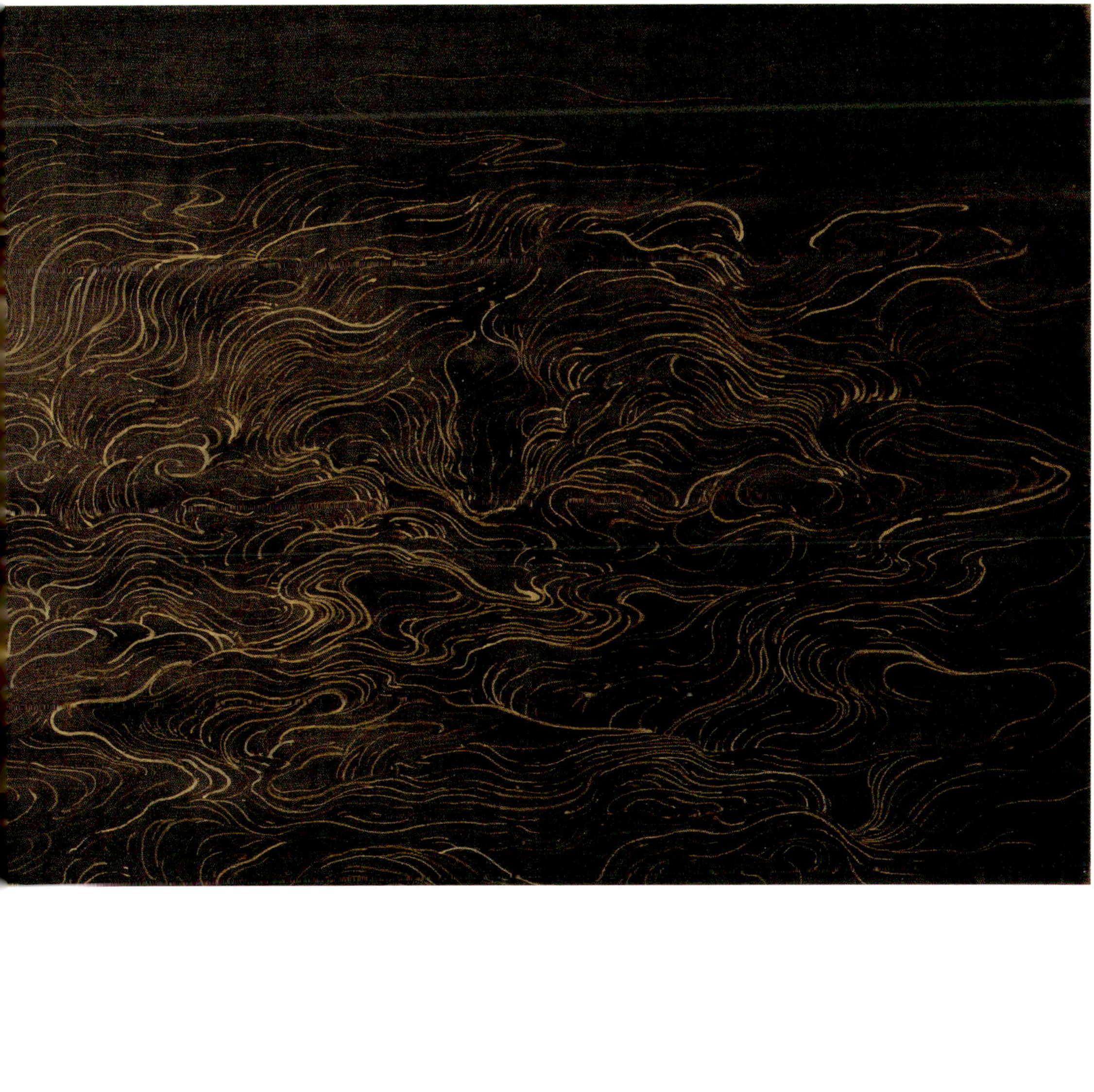

Contemplate #8

120×40 cm
Silk Mineral Pigment
2014

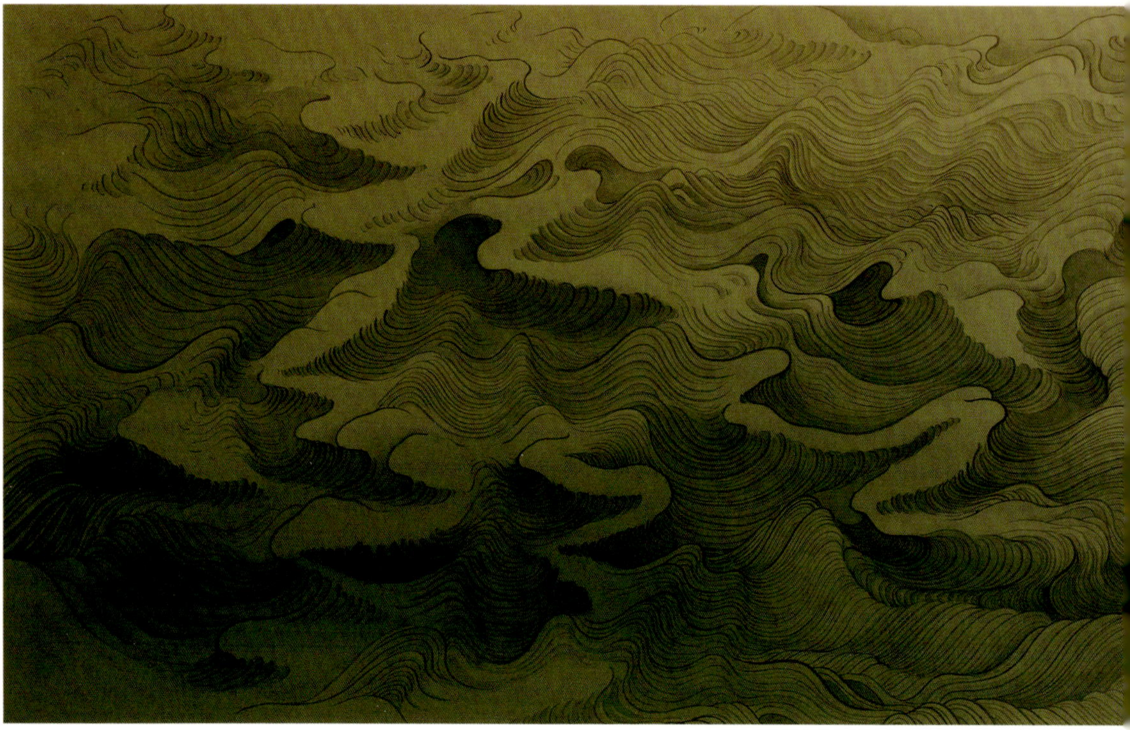

Contemplate #13

90×30 cm
Silk Mineral Pigment
2015

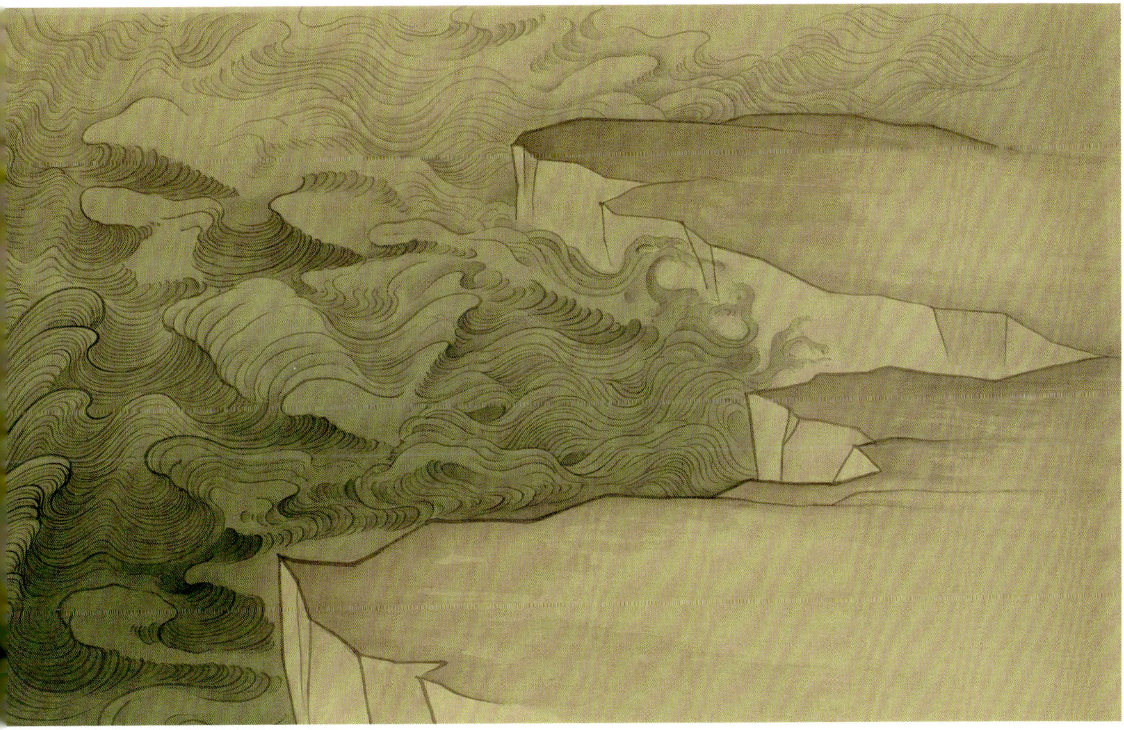

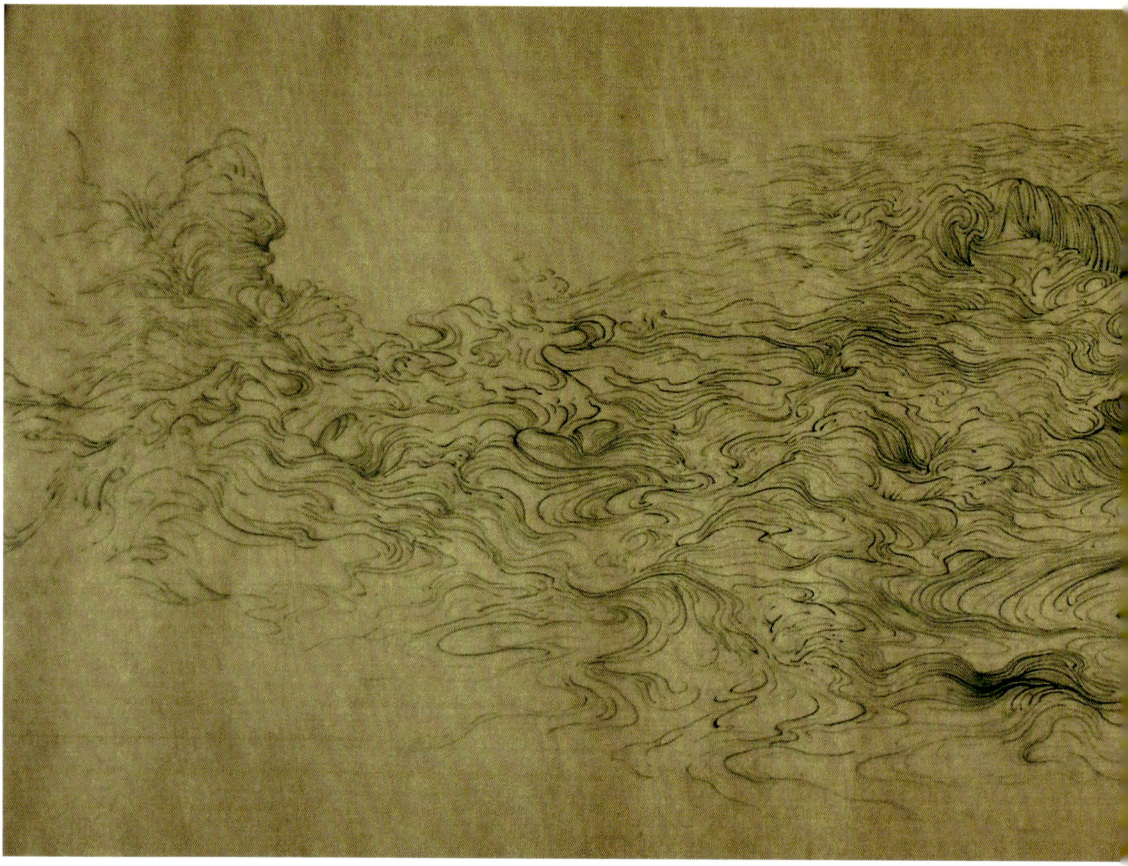

Contemplate #2

92×27 cm
Silk Mineral Pigment
2013

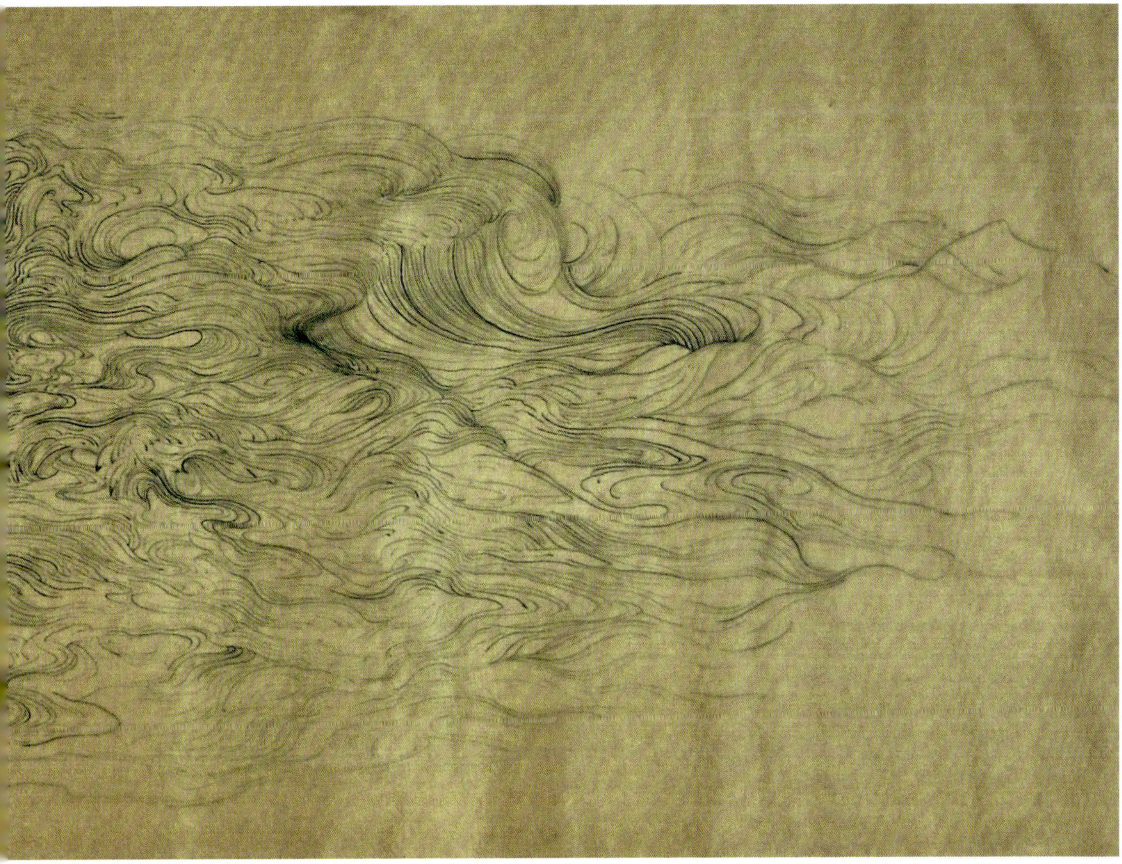

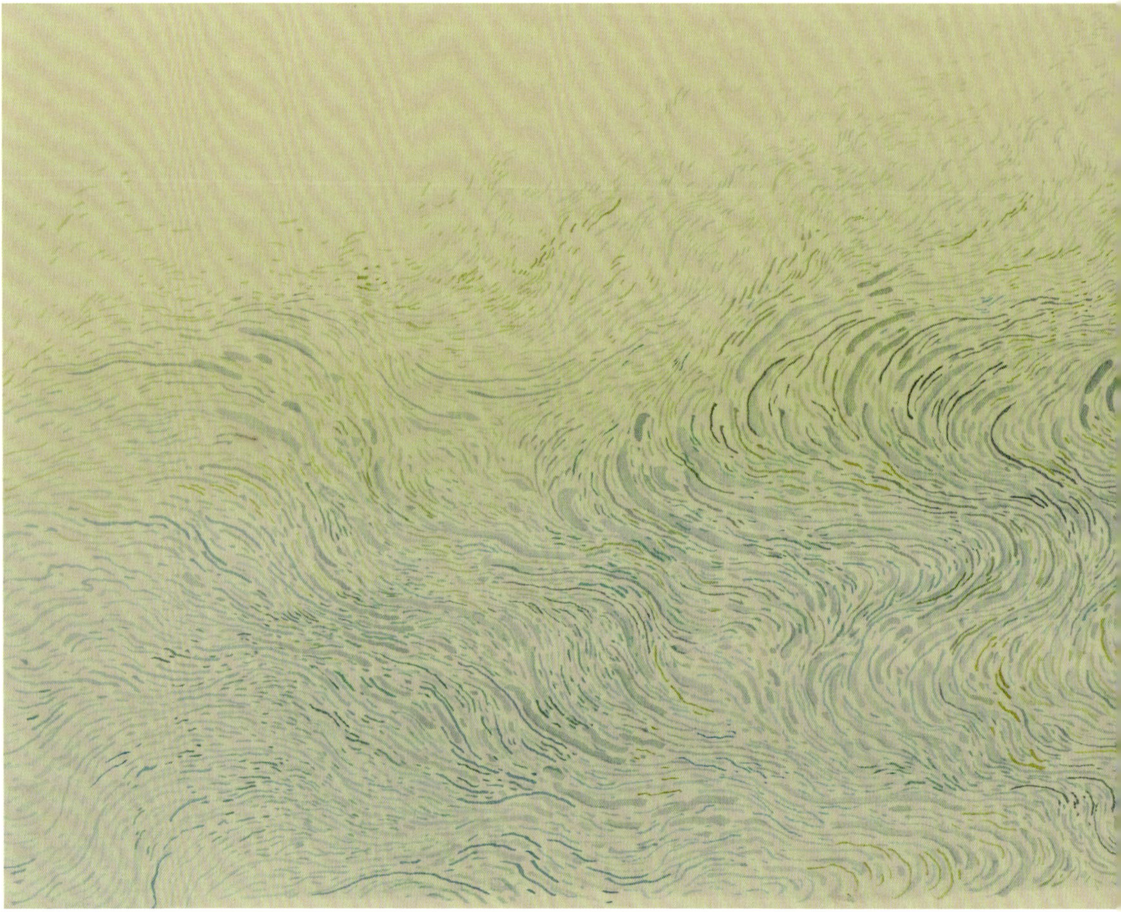

Contemplate #65

67×25 cm
Silk Mineral Pigment
2021

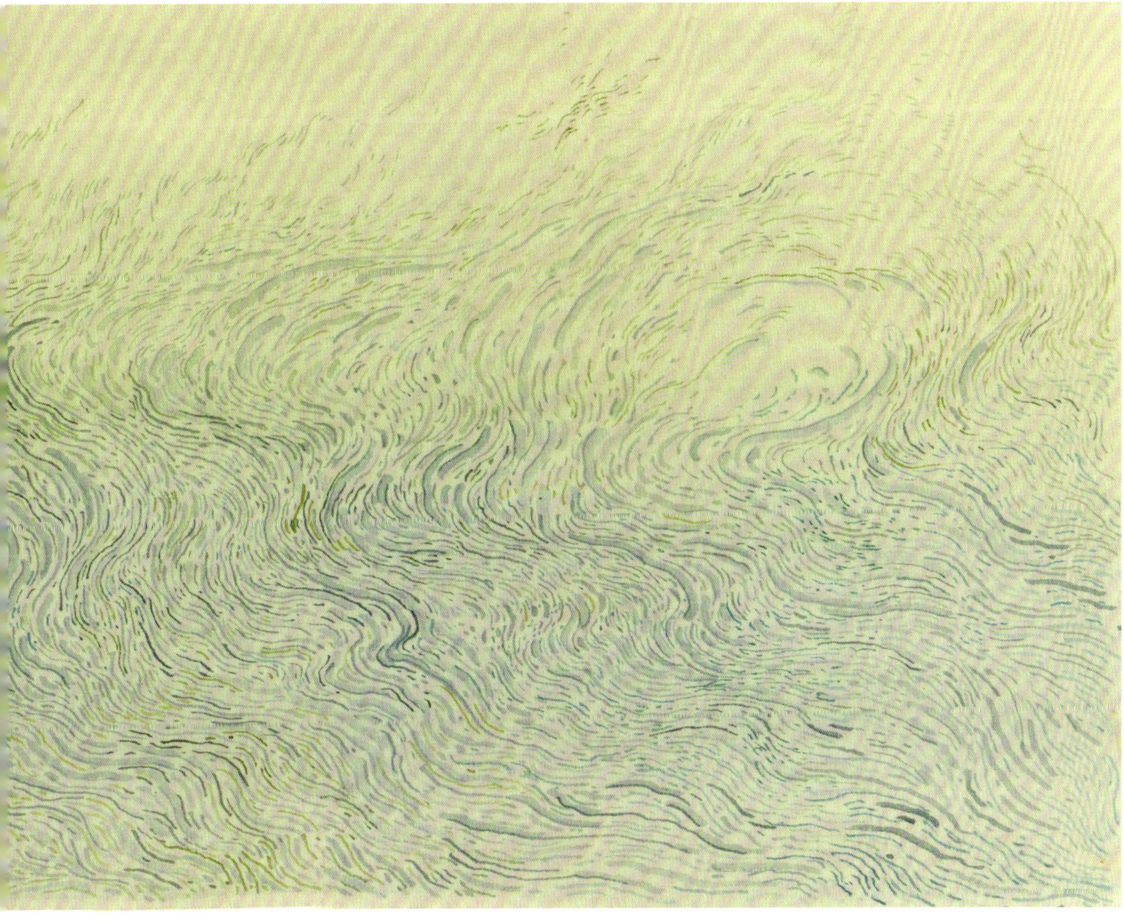

Contemplate #29

80×30 cm
Mineral Pigment on Paper
2018

Shell Drawing

120×20×20 cm
Shell Mineral Pigment

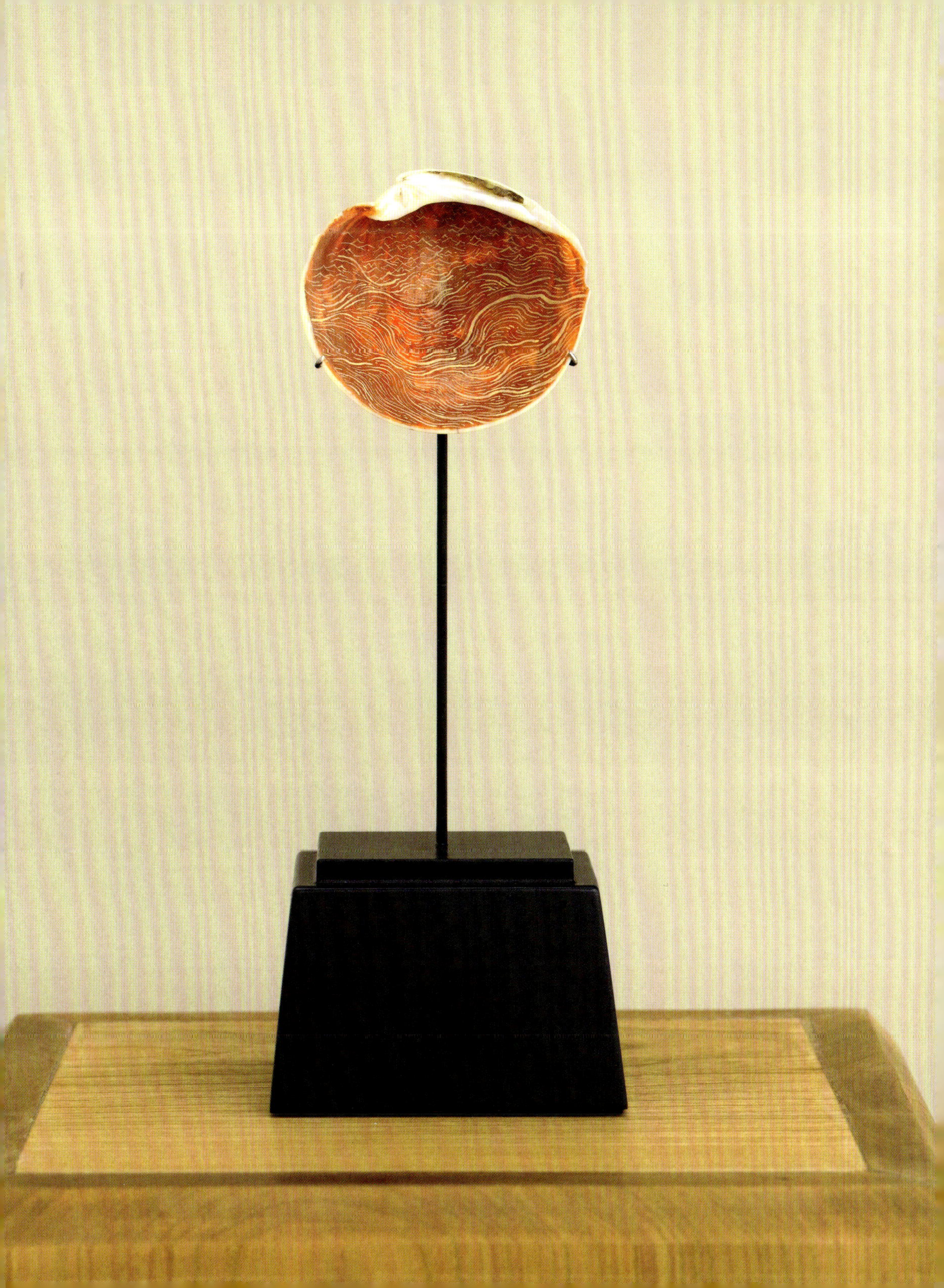

The Order of Body

生命的蜕变，是一次又一次的新生，伴随着阵痛与喜悦。色彩的直观与浓烈，是历史对生命的承诺，无论斑驳残缺，还是完美无暇，都不会影响它来过的决心。

The metamorphosis of life is rebirth, again and again, with moments of pain and joy. The intuitiveness and intensity of colors represent history's promises to each life. The colors may be mottled, incomplete, or flawless, but nevertheless they will not affect each life's determination to live colorfully as part of history.

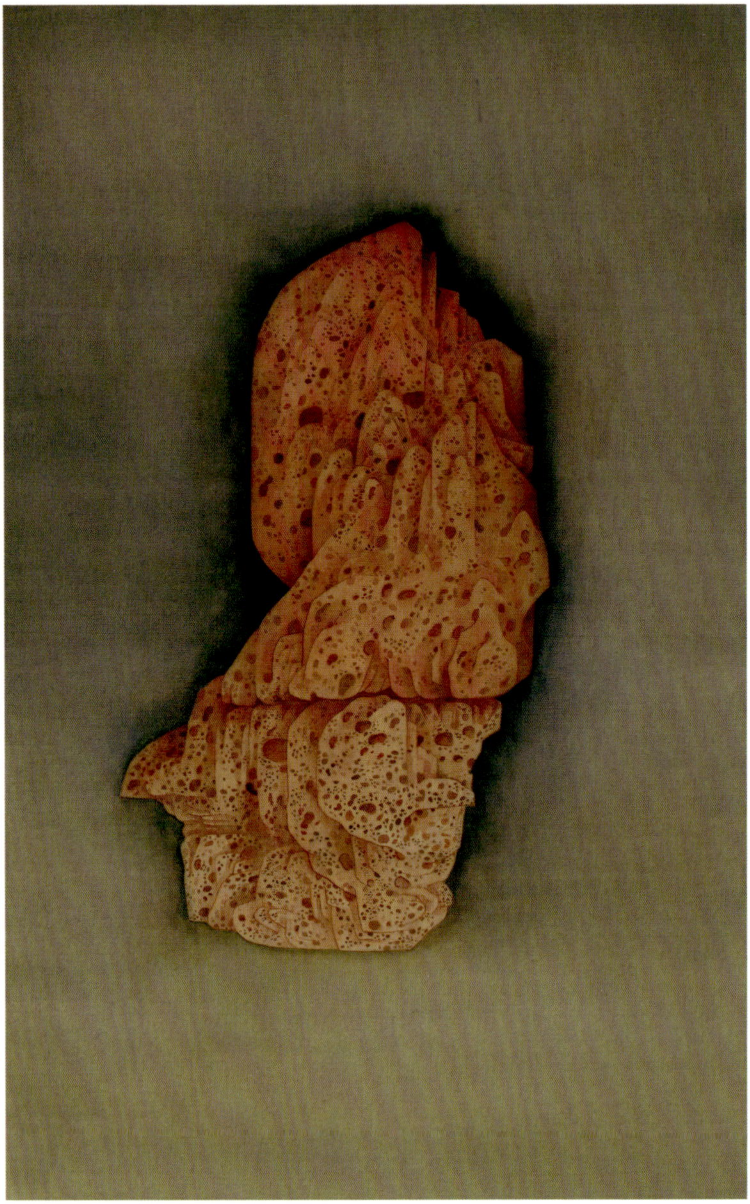

Cluod #1

50×70 cm
Silk Mineral Pigment
2020

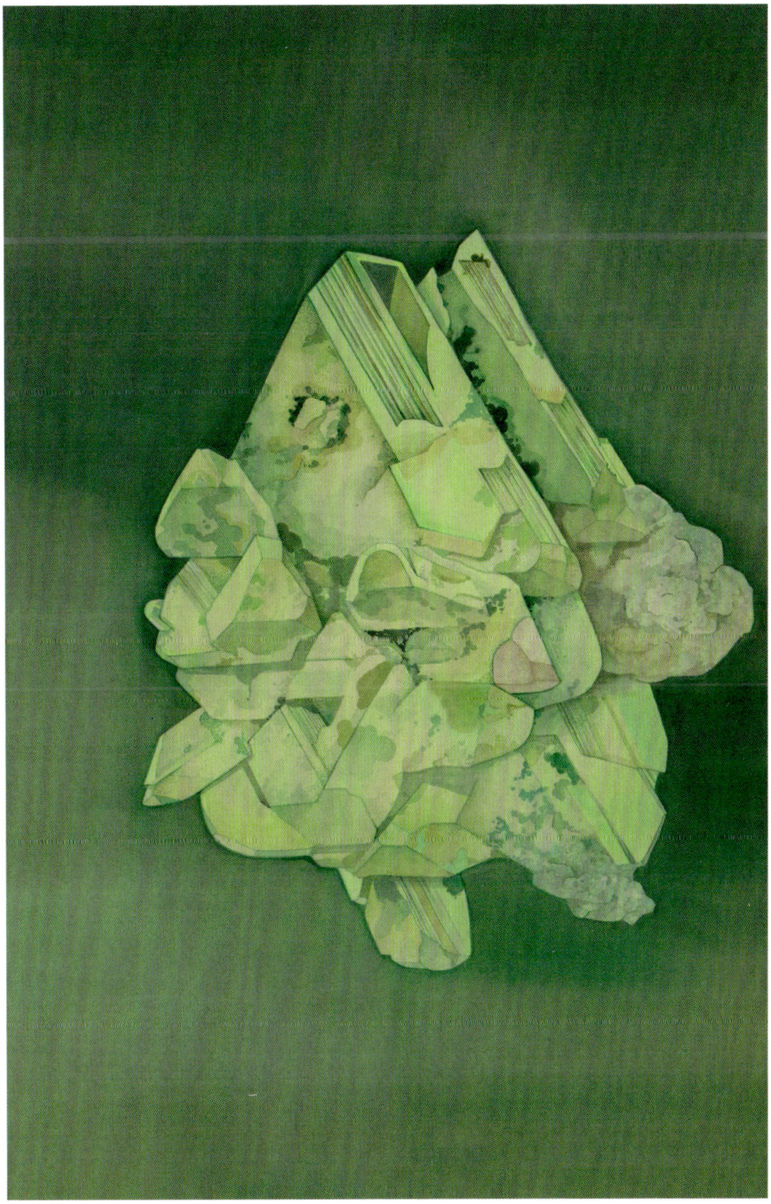

Panda Ore

50×70 cm
Silk Mineral Pigment
2022

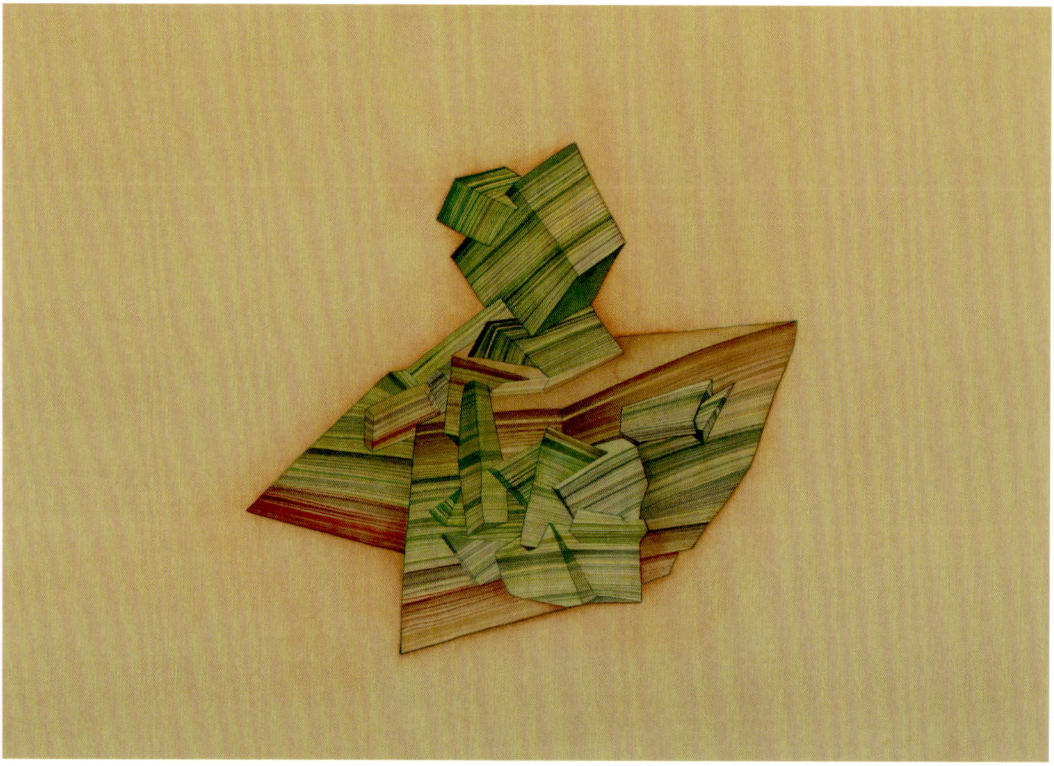

Cluod #3

70×50 cm
Silk Mineral Pigment
2021

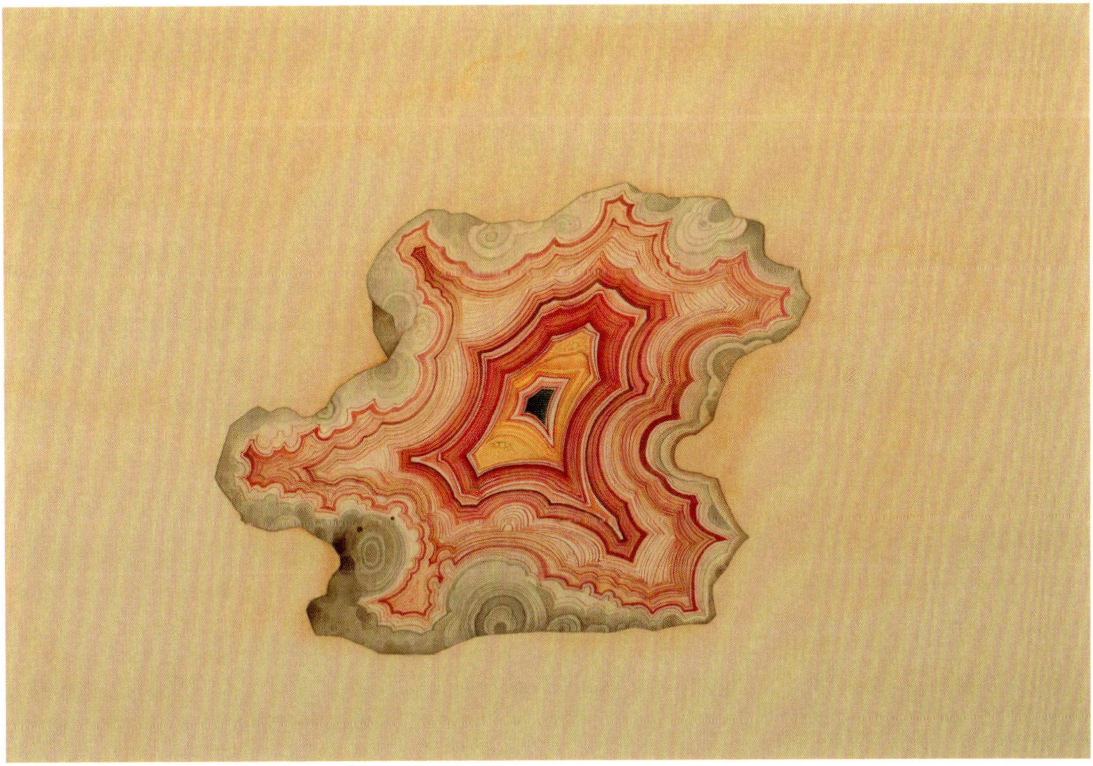

Cluod #2

70×50 cm
Silk Mineral Pigment
2021

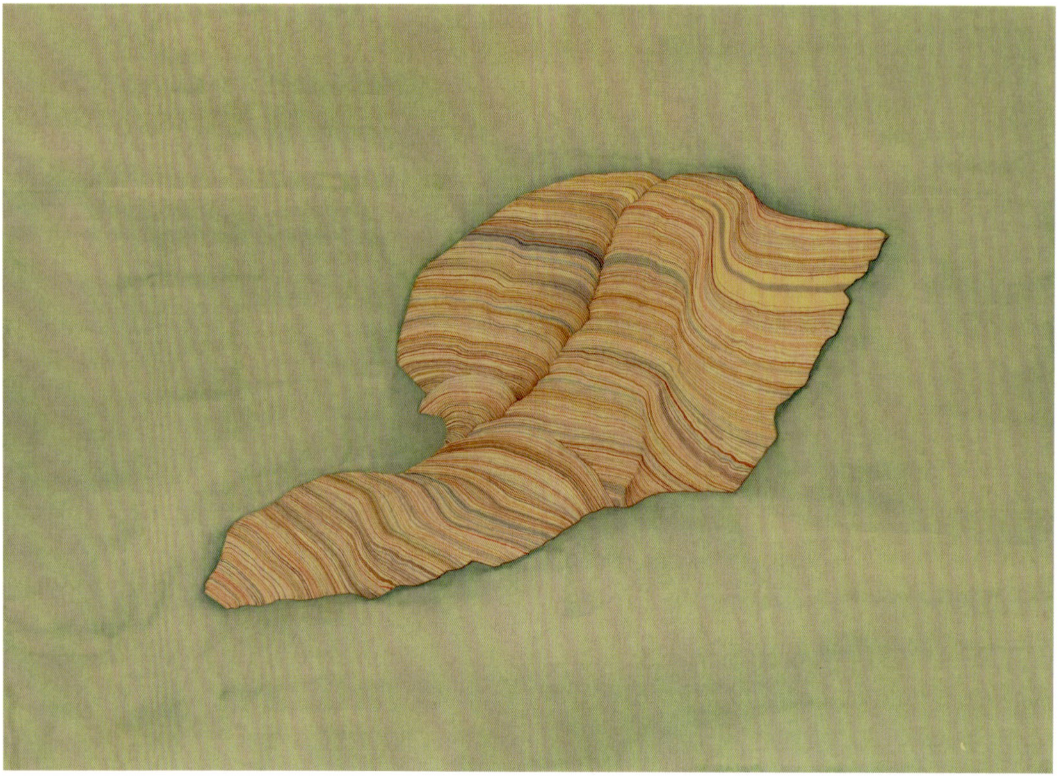

The Order of Body #9

70×50 cm
Silk Mineral Pigment
2022

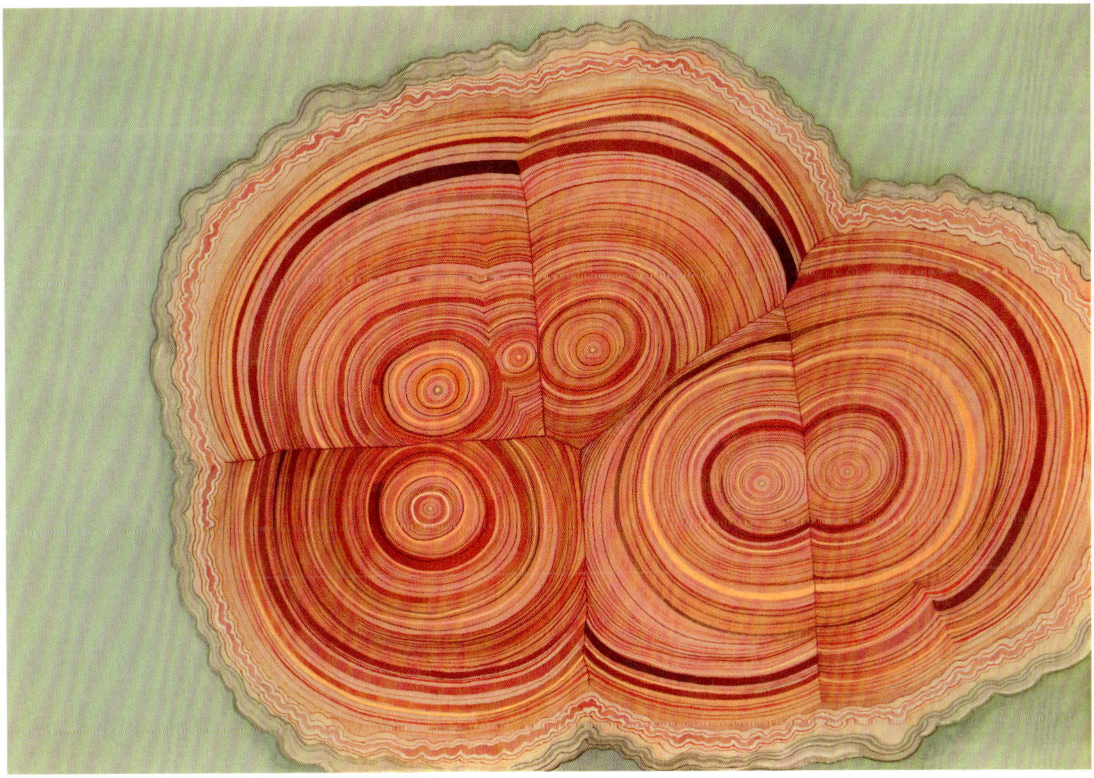

The Order of Body #10

70×50 cm
Silk Mineral Pigment
2022

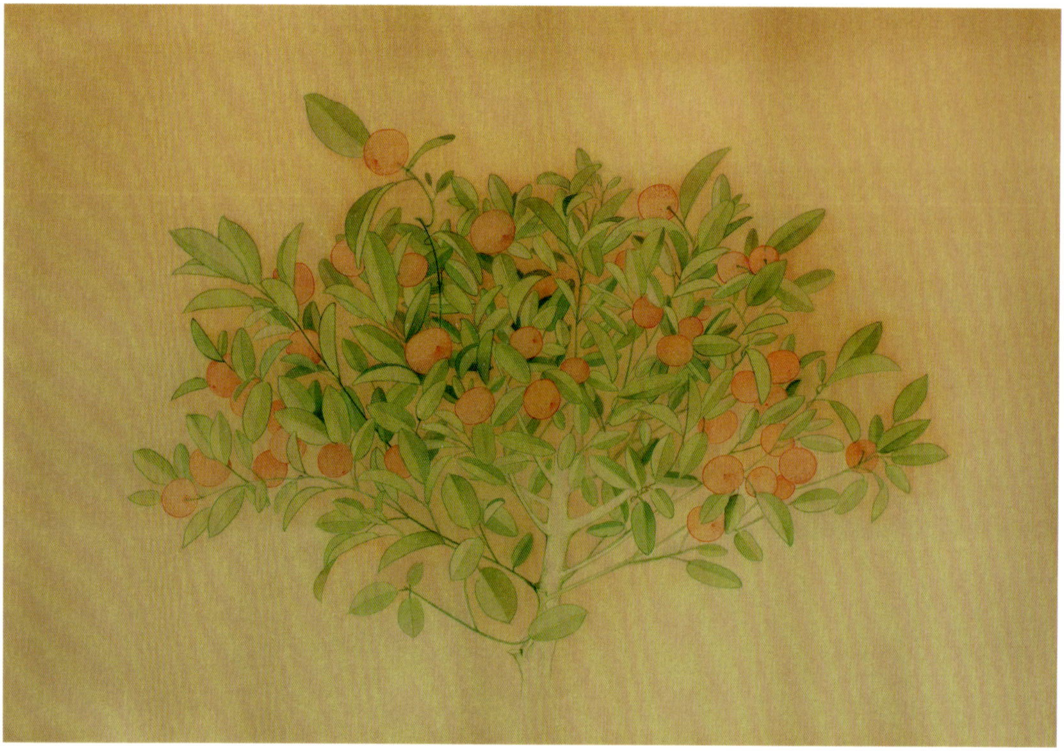

Orange Tree

70×50 cm
Silk Mineral Pigment
2020

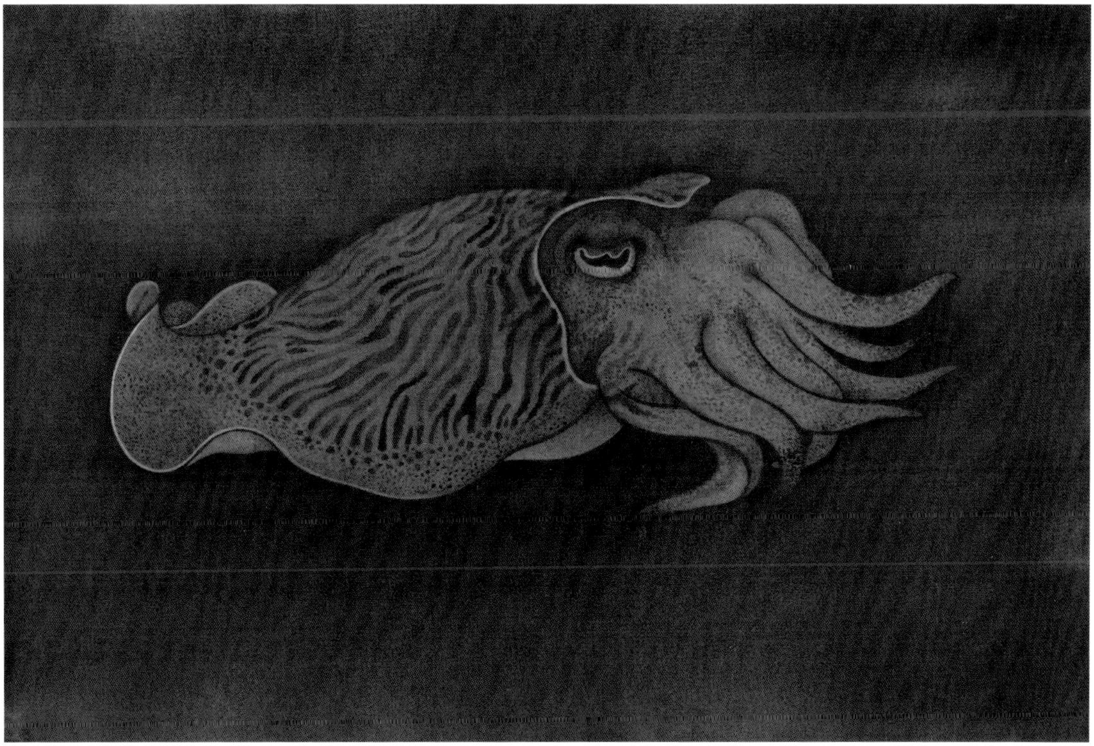

The Order of Body #8

22×21 cm
Silk Mineral Pigment
2020

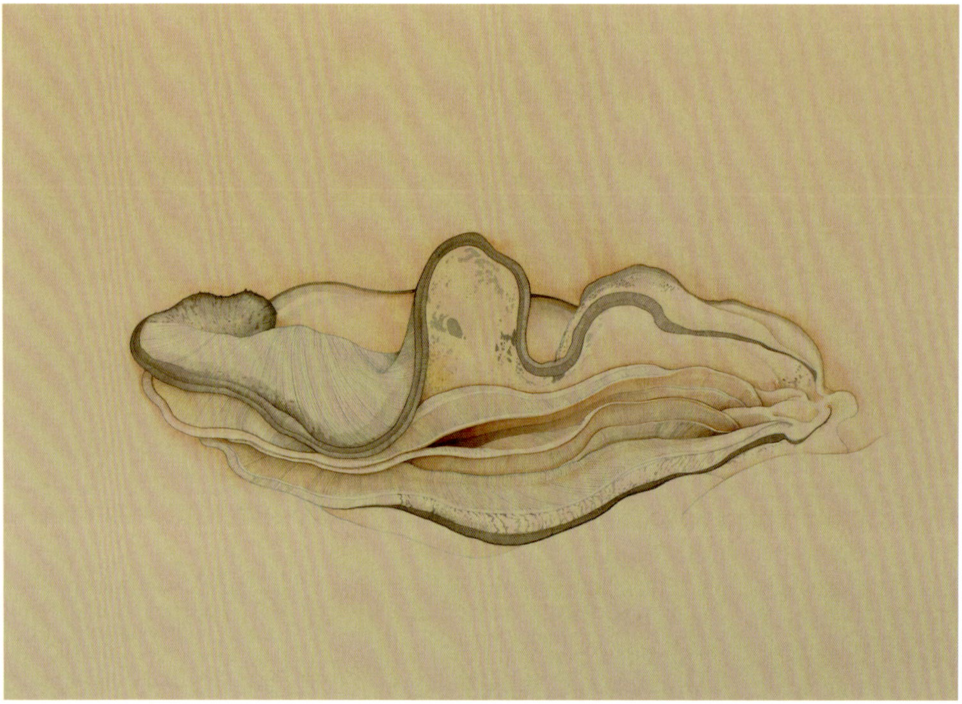

The Order of Body #11

90×60 cm
Silk Mineral Pigment
2021

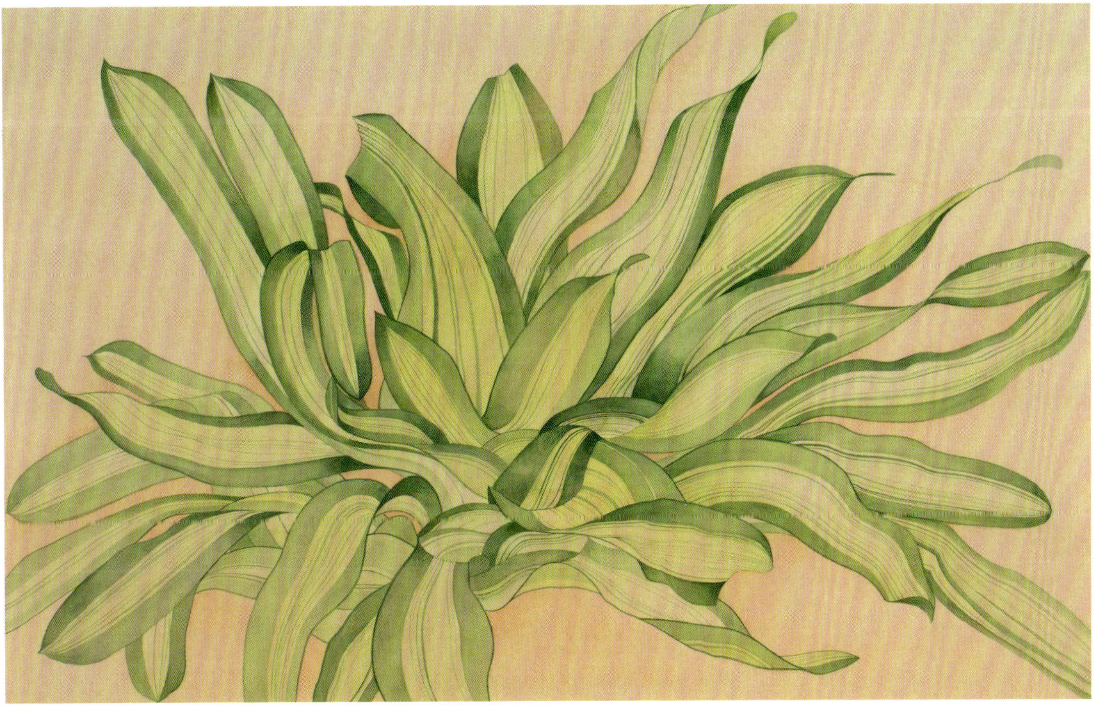

The Order of Body #1

150×100 cm
Silk Mineral Pigment
2020

Orchid

50×70 cm
Silk Mineral Pigment
2020

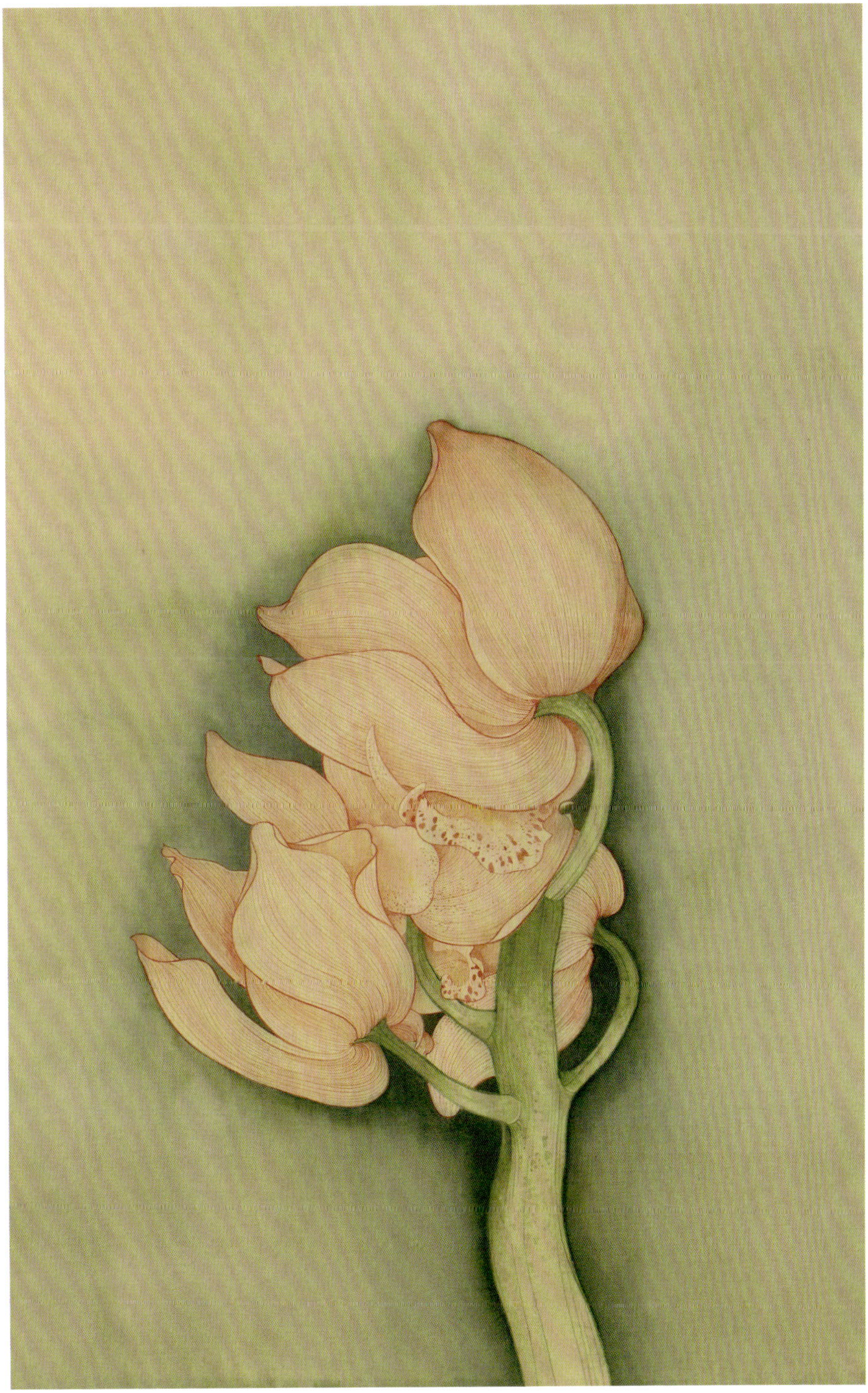

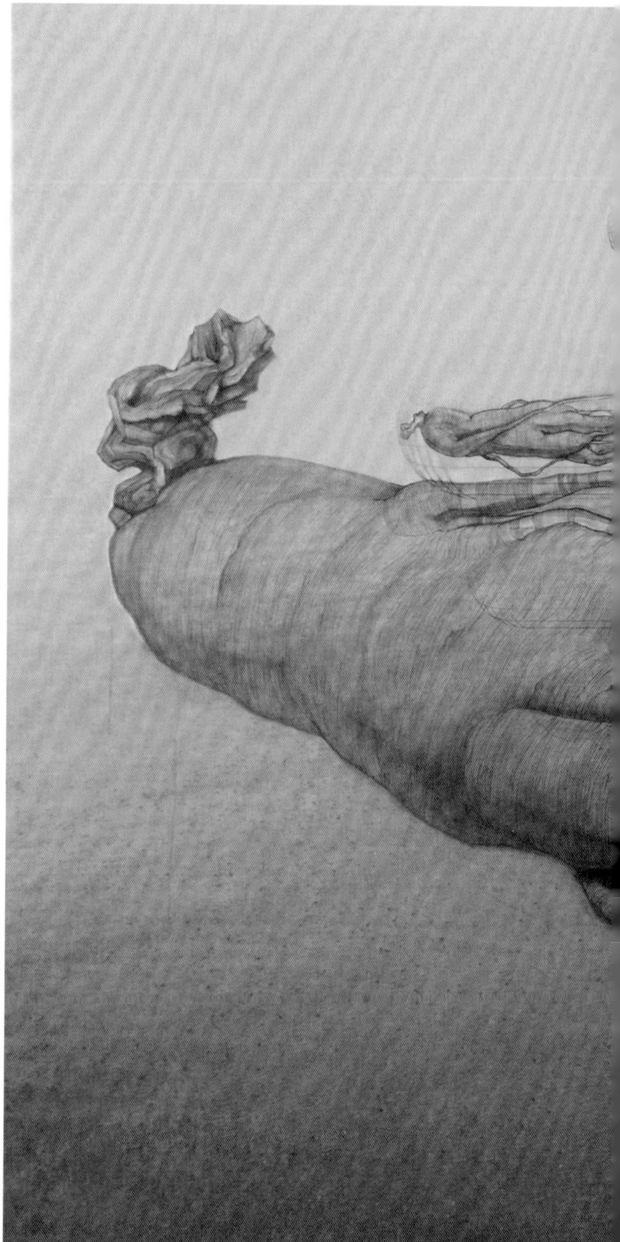

The Order of Body #01

200×140 cm
Oil Painting
2009

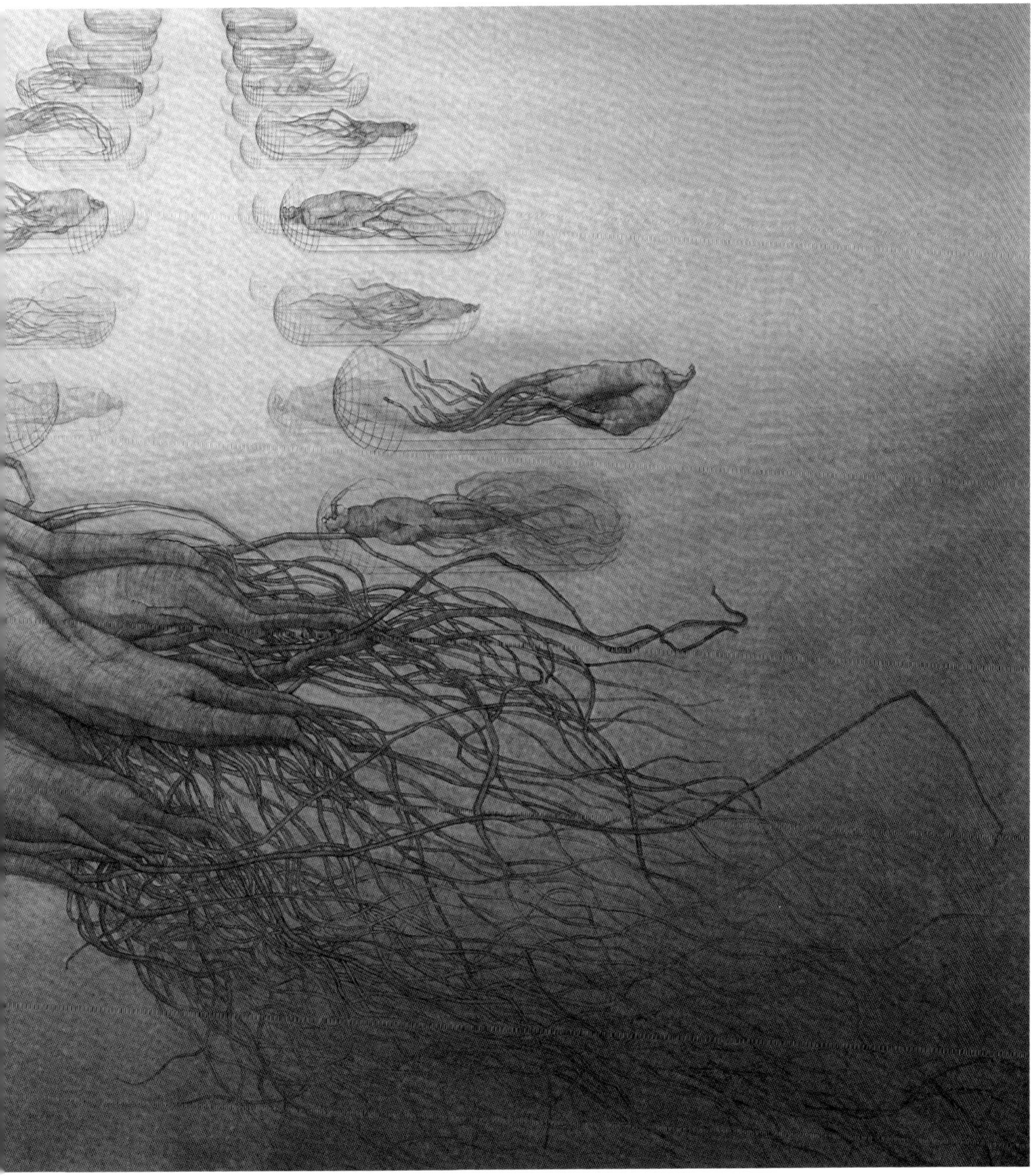

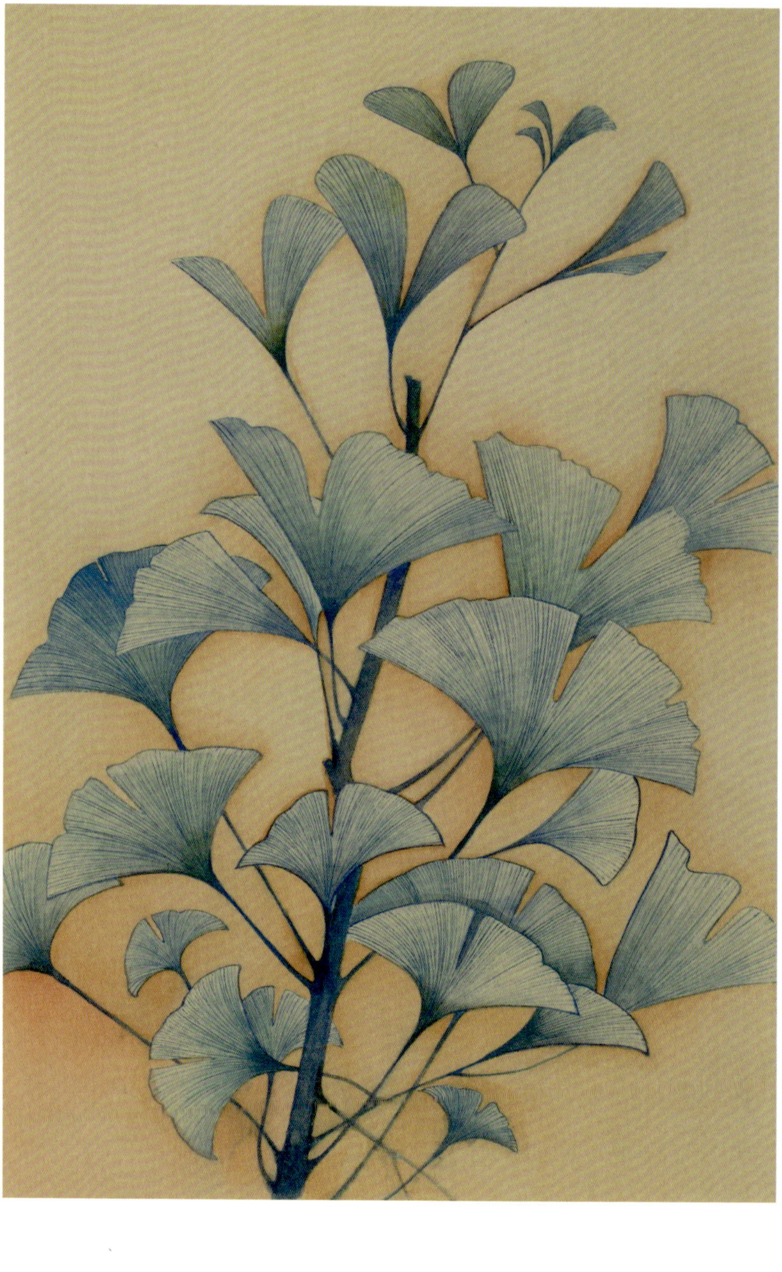

The Order of Body #4

22×32 cm
Silk Mineral Pigment
2020

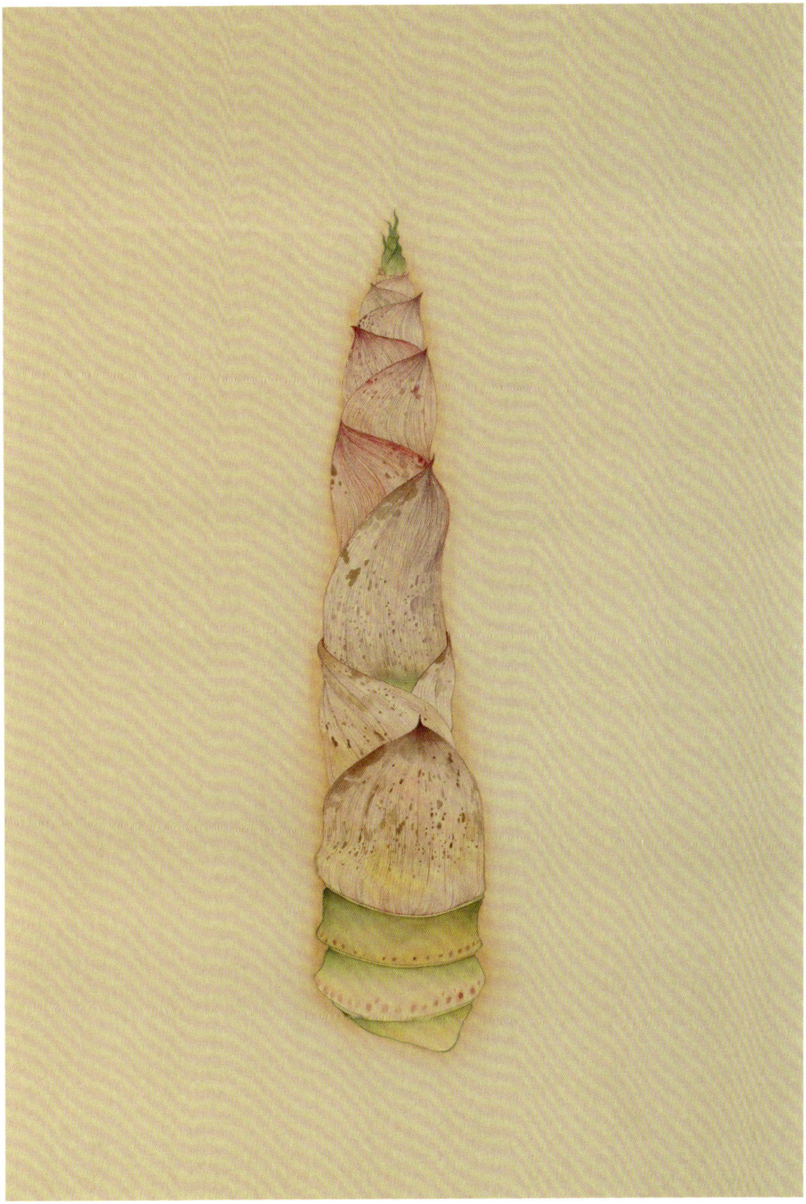

Bamboo Shoot

50×70 cm
Silk Mineral Pigment
2021

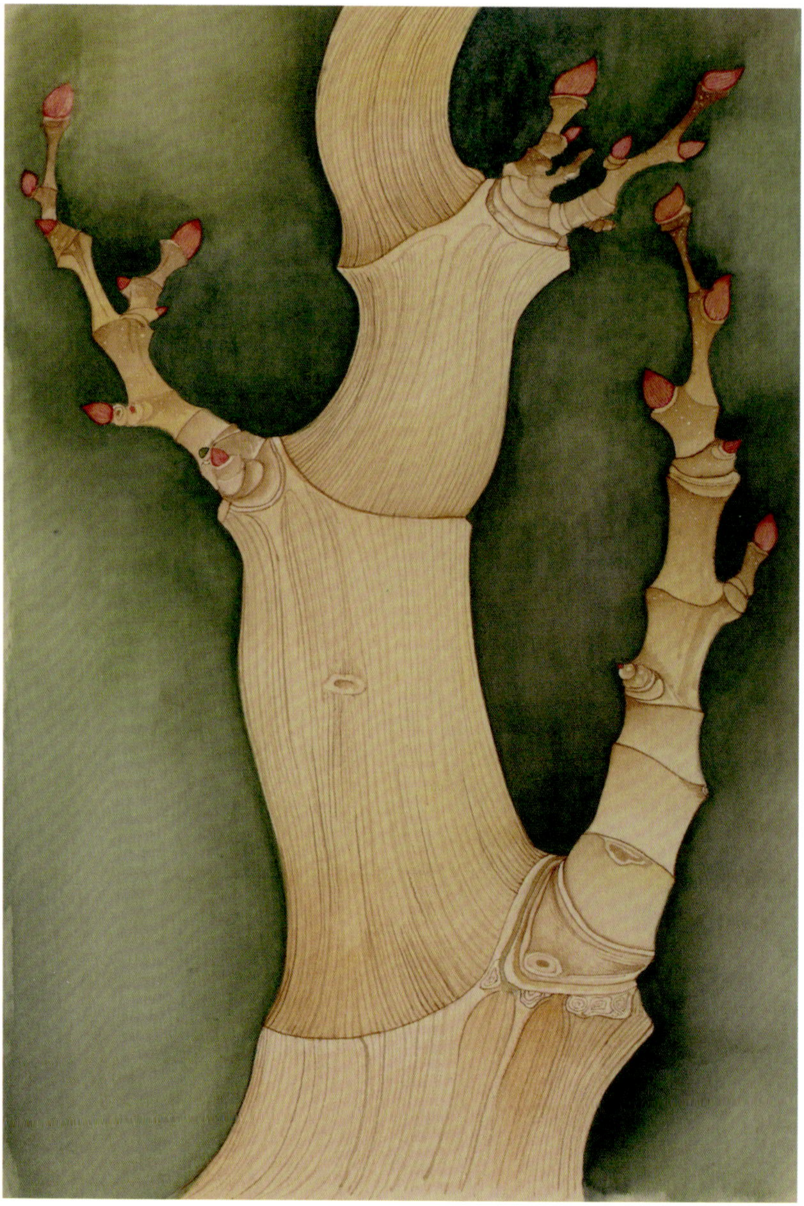

The Order of Body #5

22×32 cm
Silk Mineral Pigment
2020

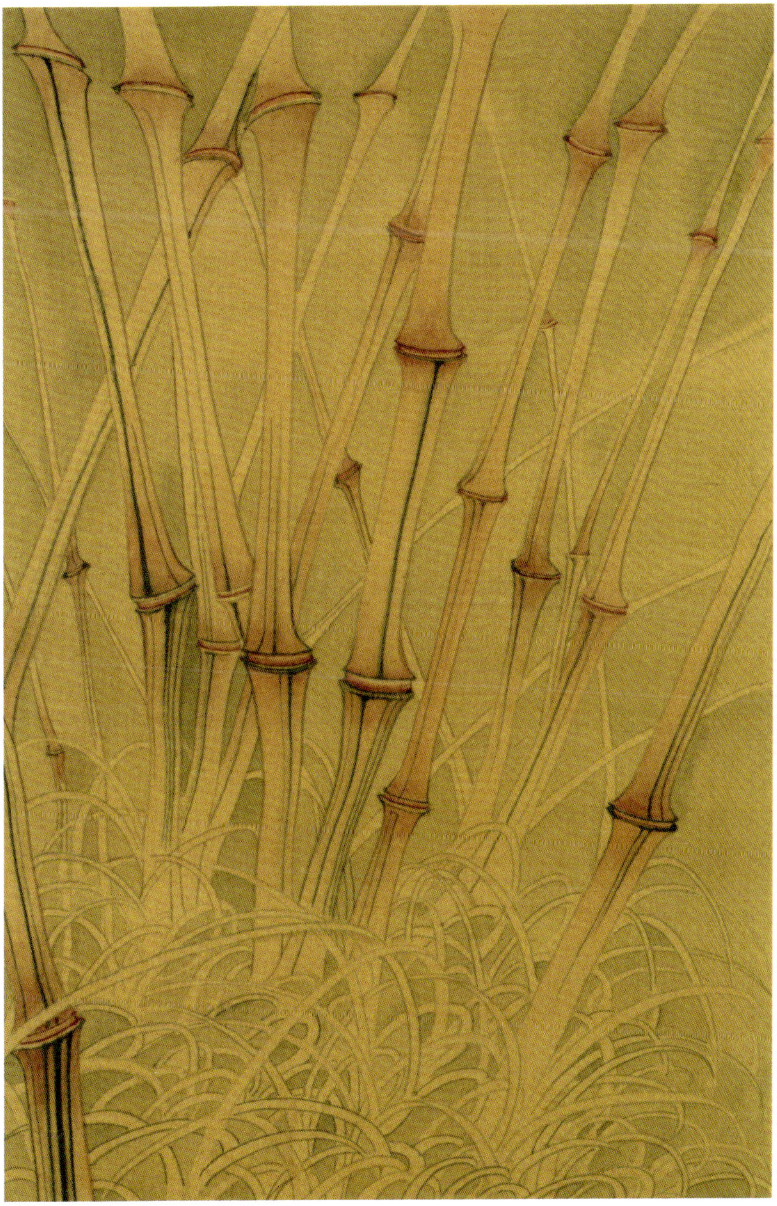

Damboo #2

22×33 cm
Silk Mineral Pigment
2017

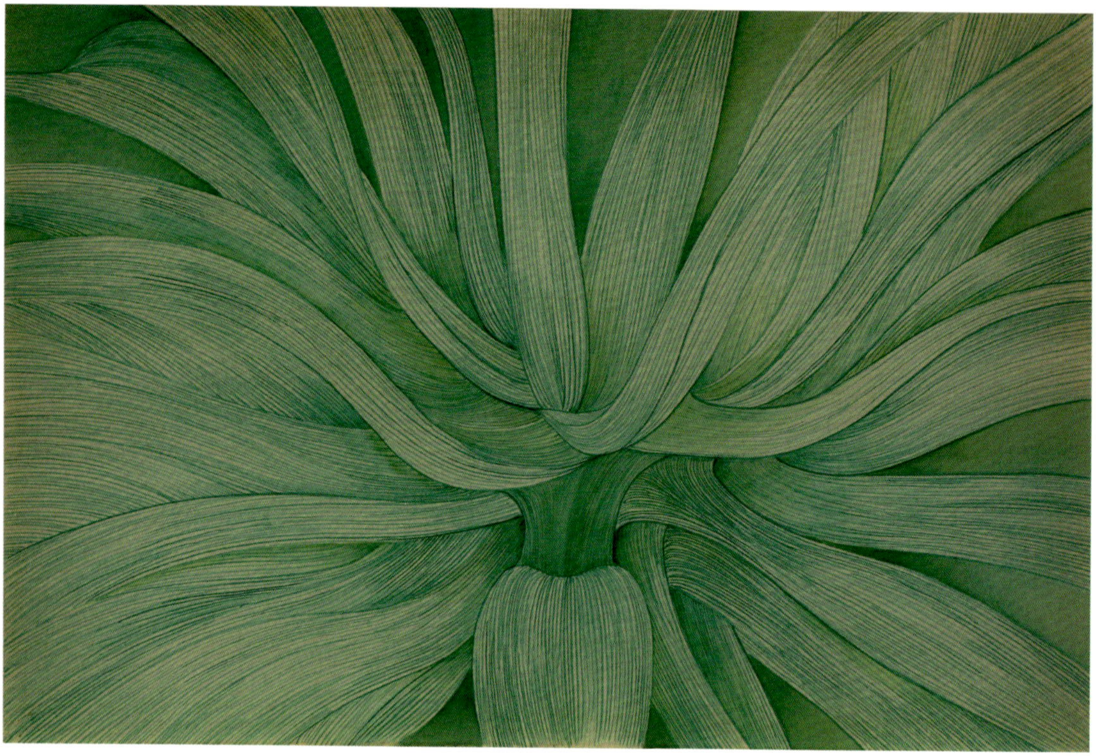

The Order of Body #7

32×22 cm
Silk Mineral Pigment
2020

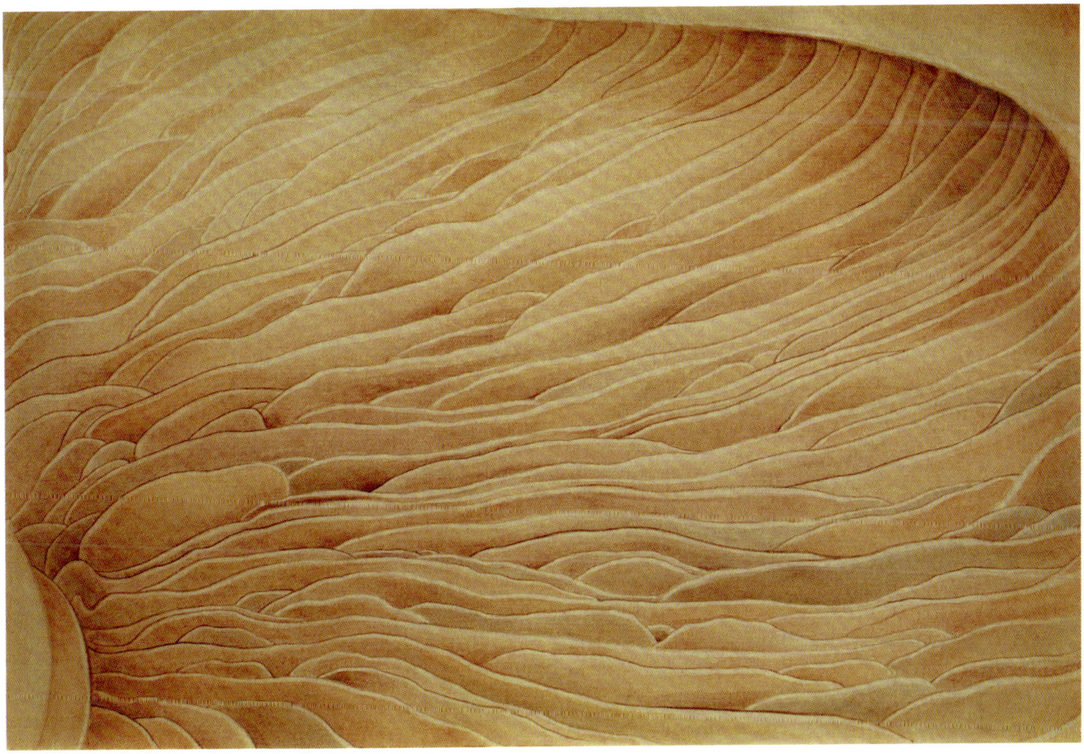

The Order of Body #2

32×22 cm
Silk Mineral Pigment
2020

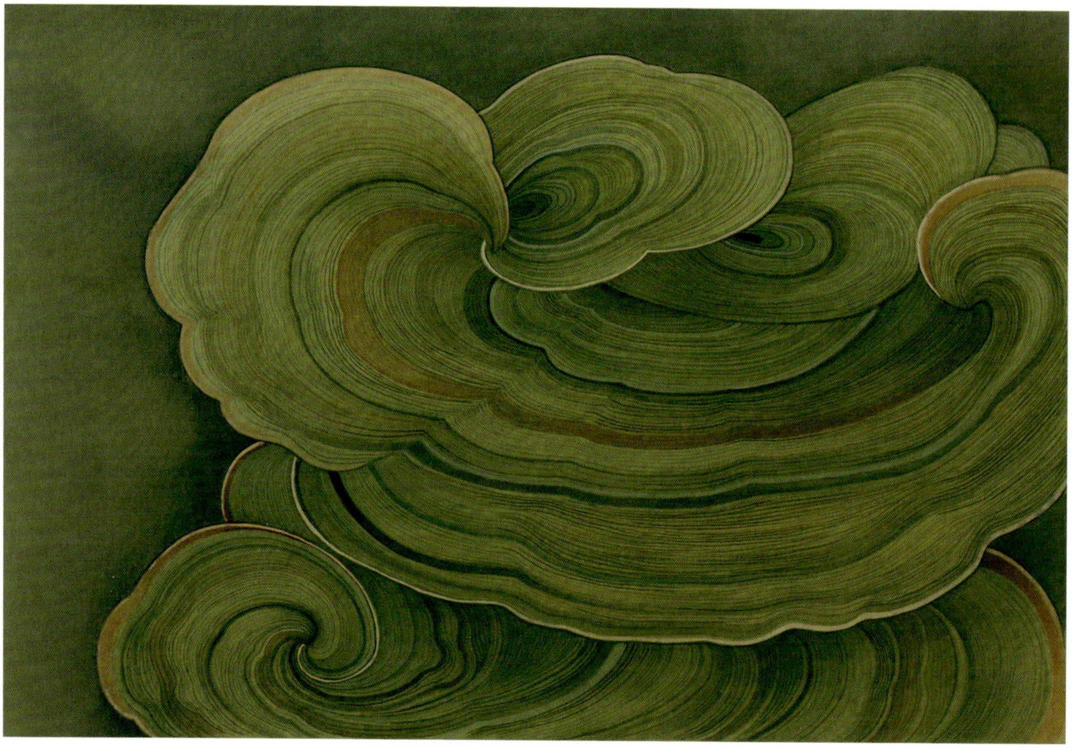

The Order of Body #6

32×22 cm
Silk Mineral Pigment
2020

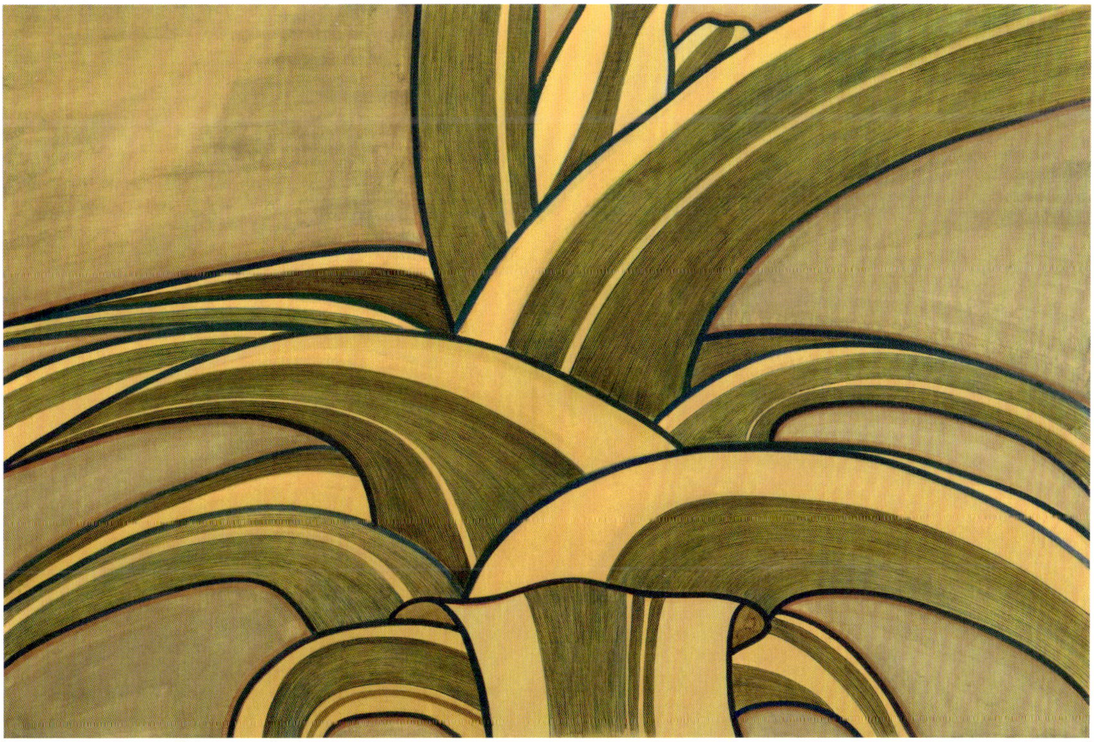

Cantury Plant

146×96 cm
Silk Mineral Pigment
2023

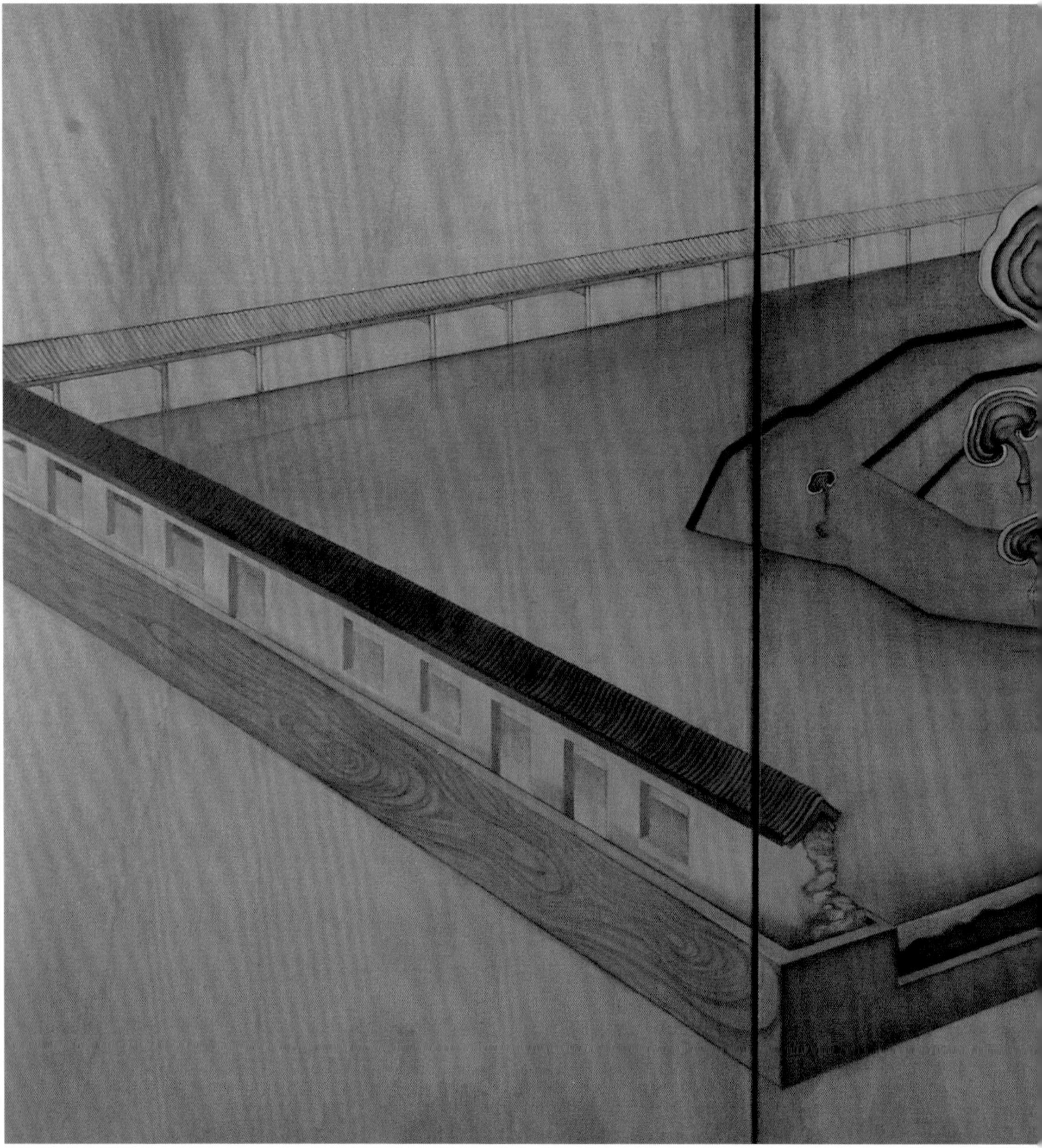

The Order of Body #02

180×100 cm
Silk Mineral Pigment
2009

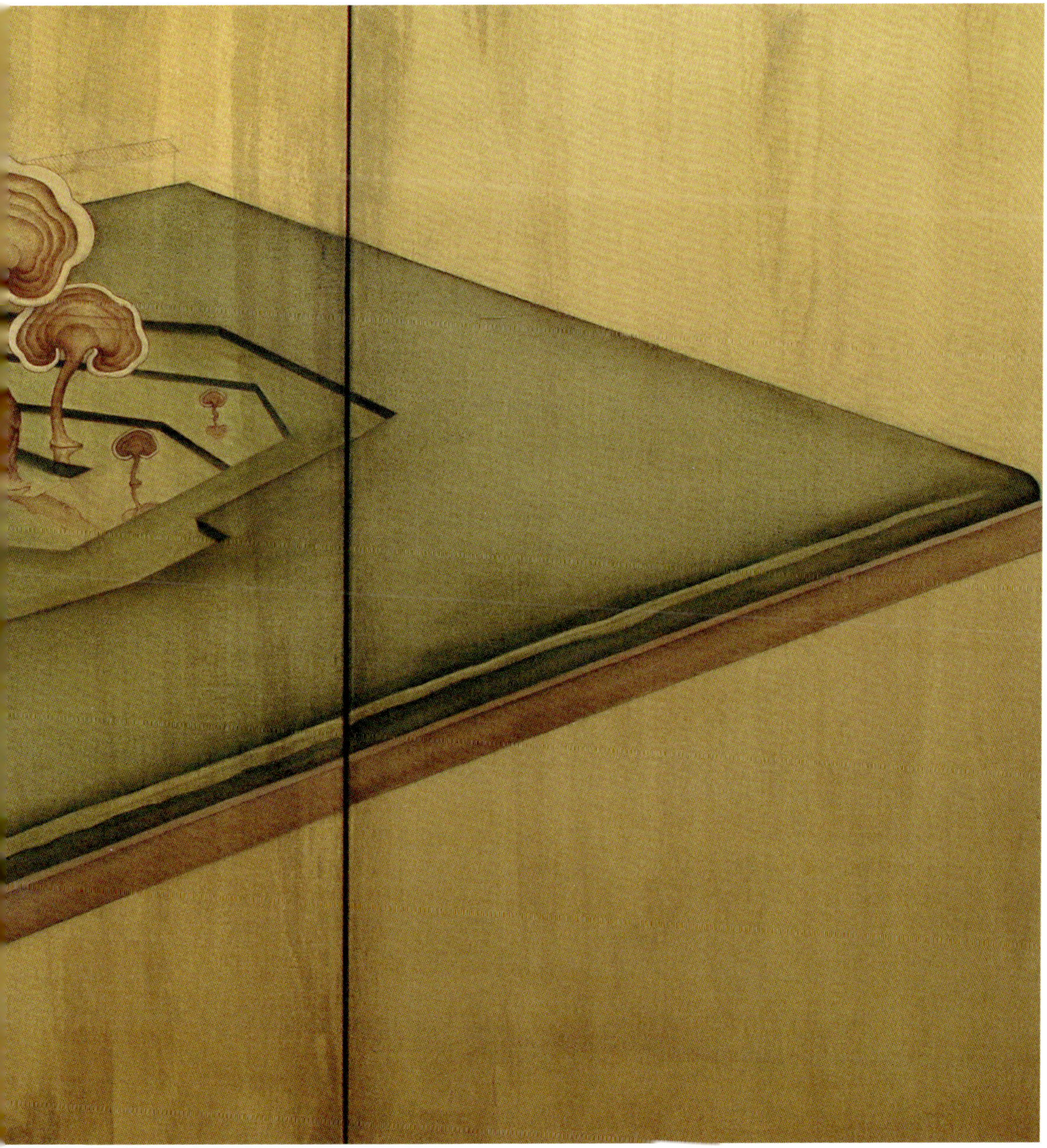

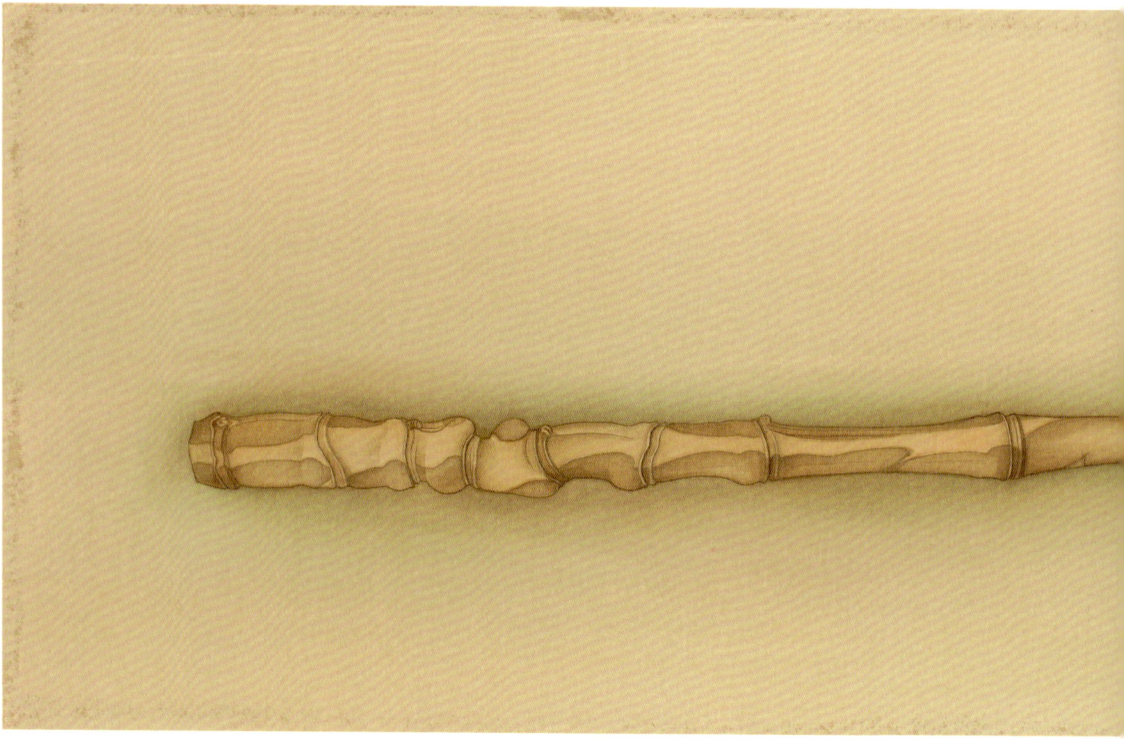

Bamboo #1

90×40 cm
Silk Mineral Pigment
2016

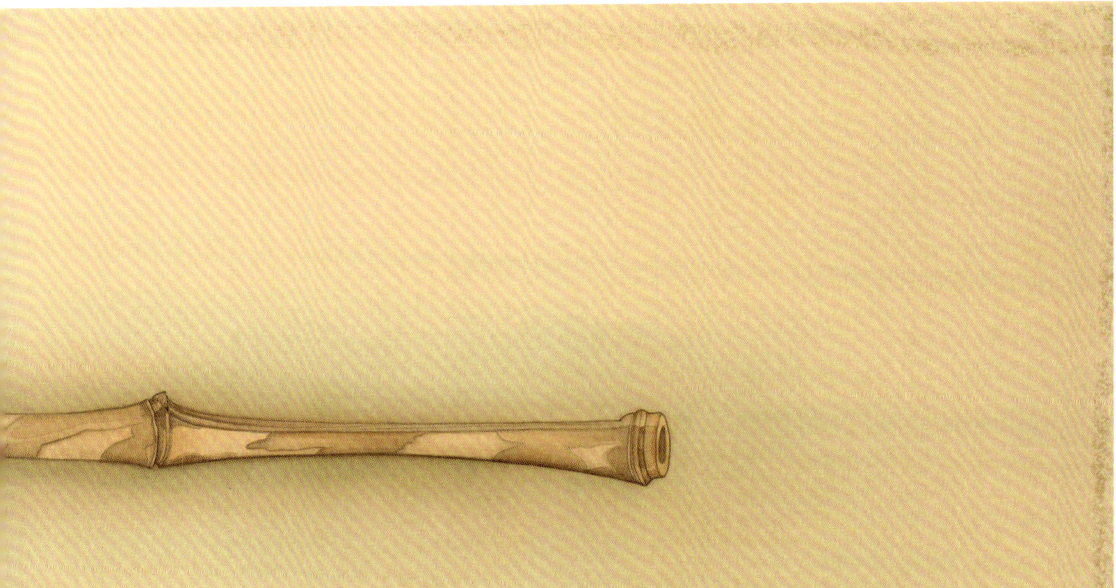

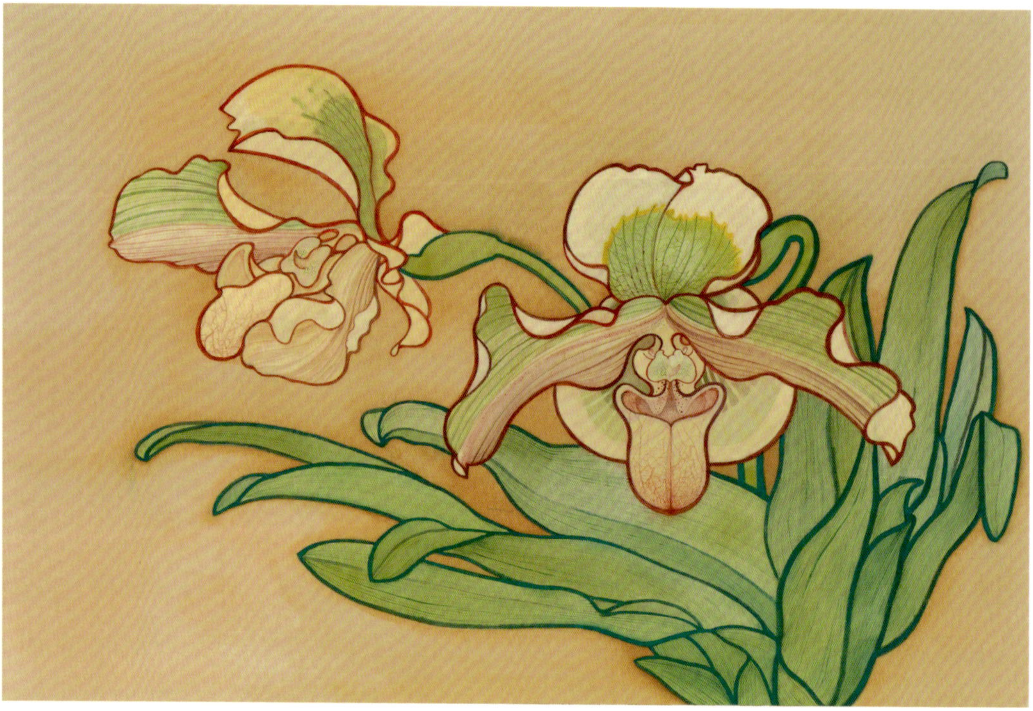

Paphiopedilum

150×100 cm
Silk Mineral Pigment
2022

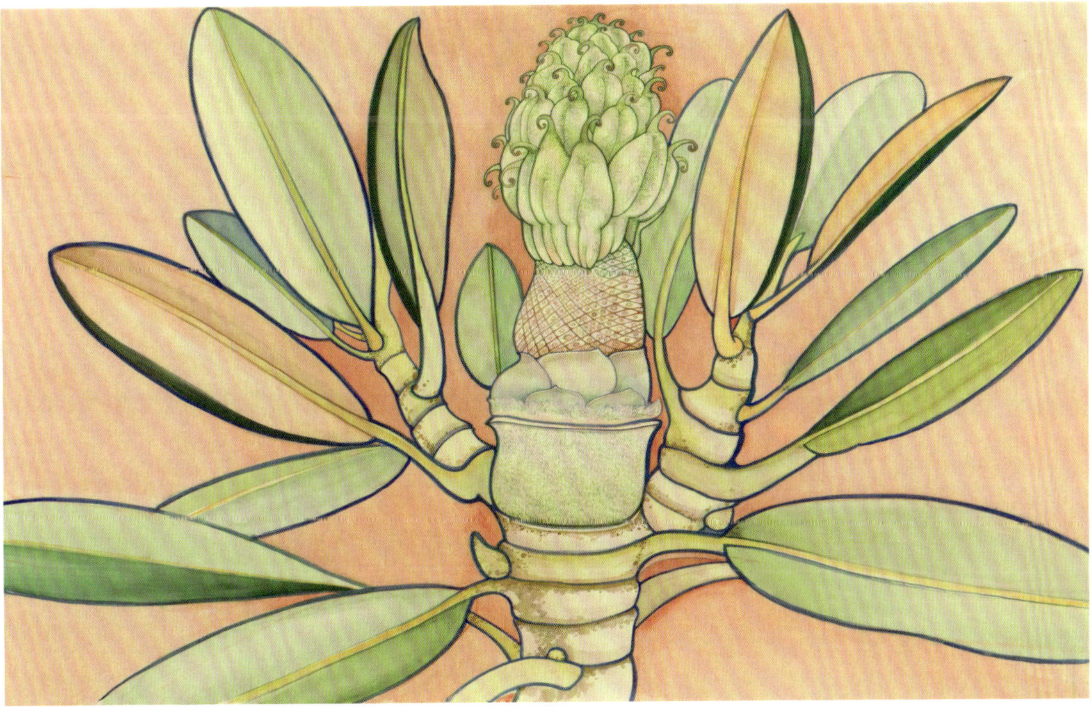

Lotus Magnolia

150×100 cm
Silk Mineral Pigment
2021

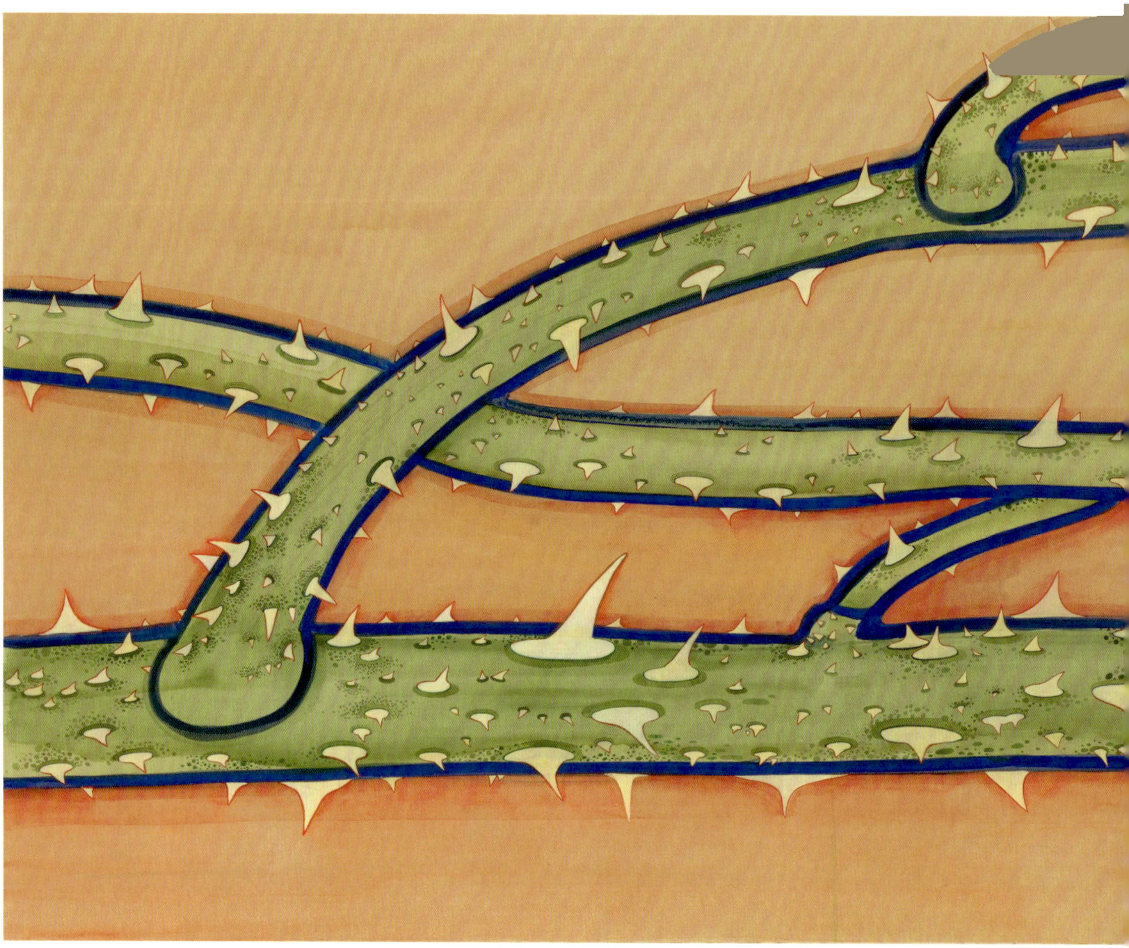

Rose

260×100 cm
Silk Mineral Pigment
2022

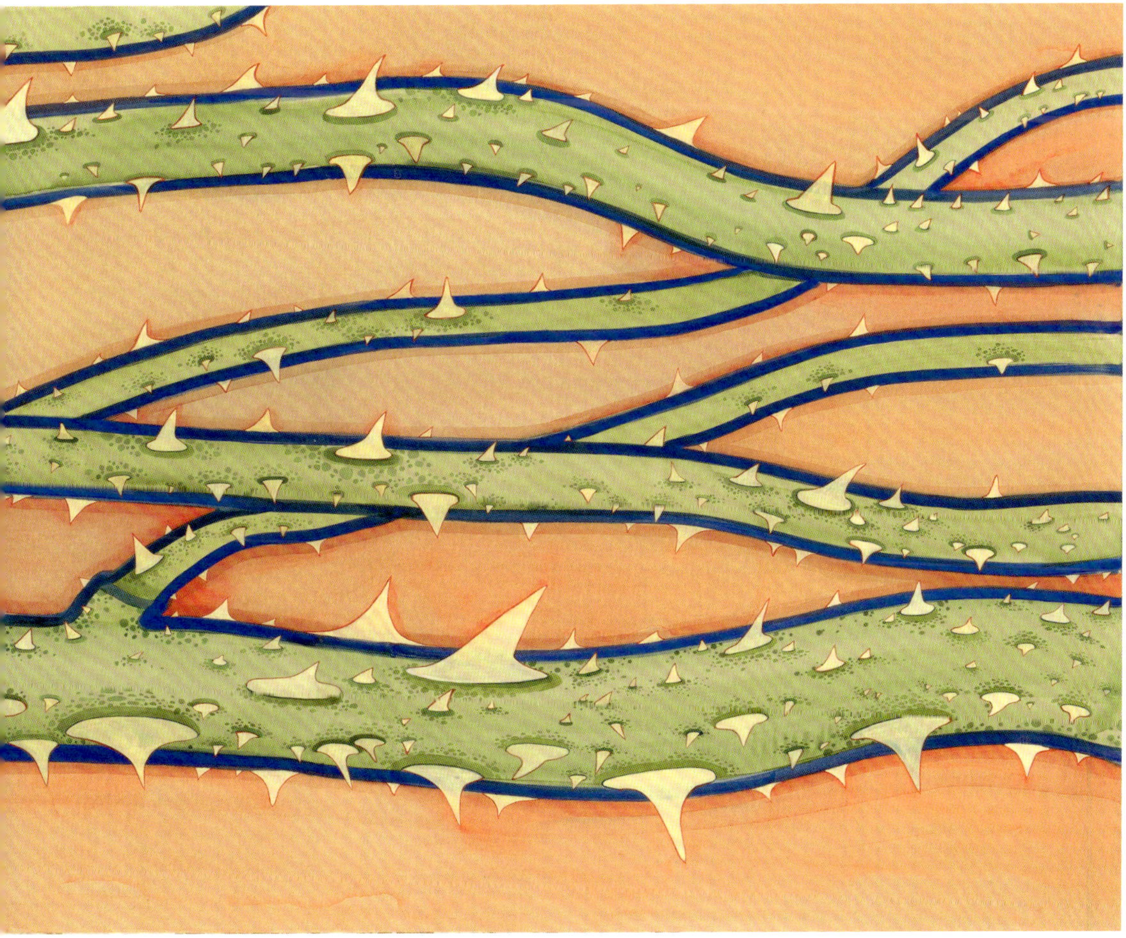

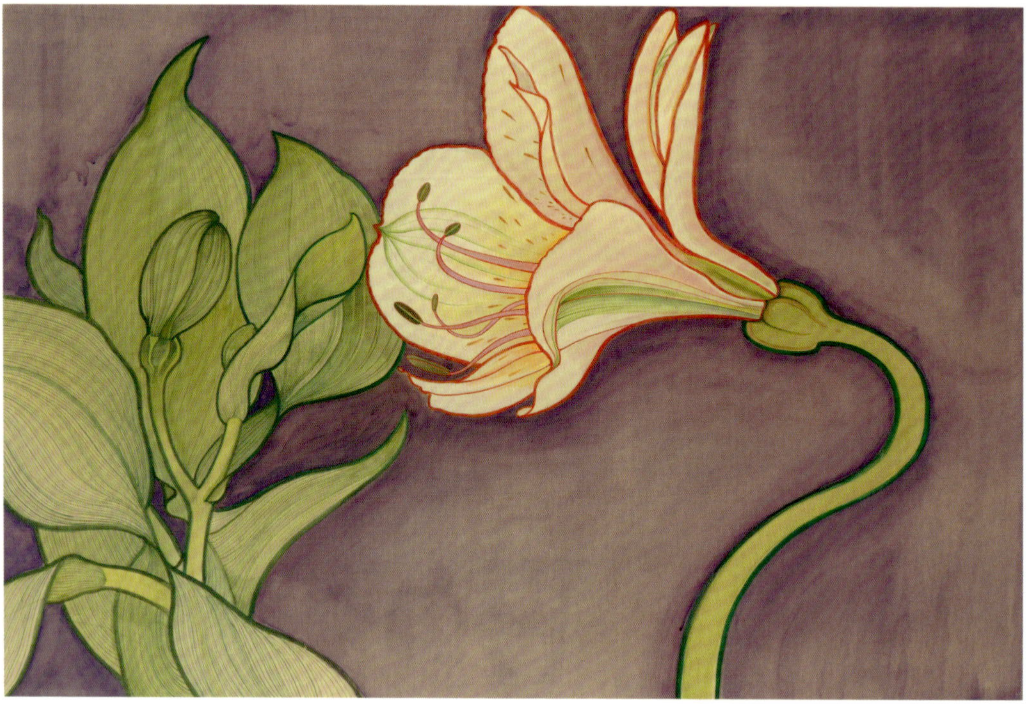

Narcissus

150×100 cm
Silk Mineral Pigment
2022

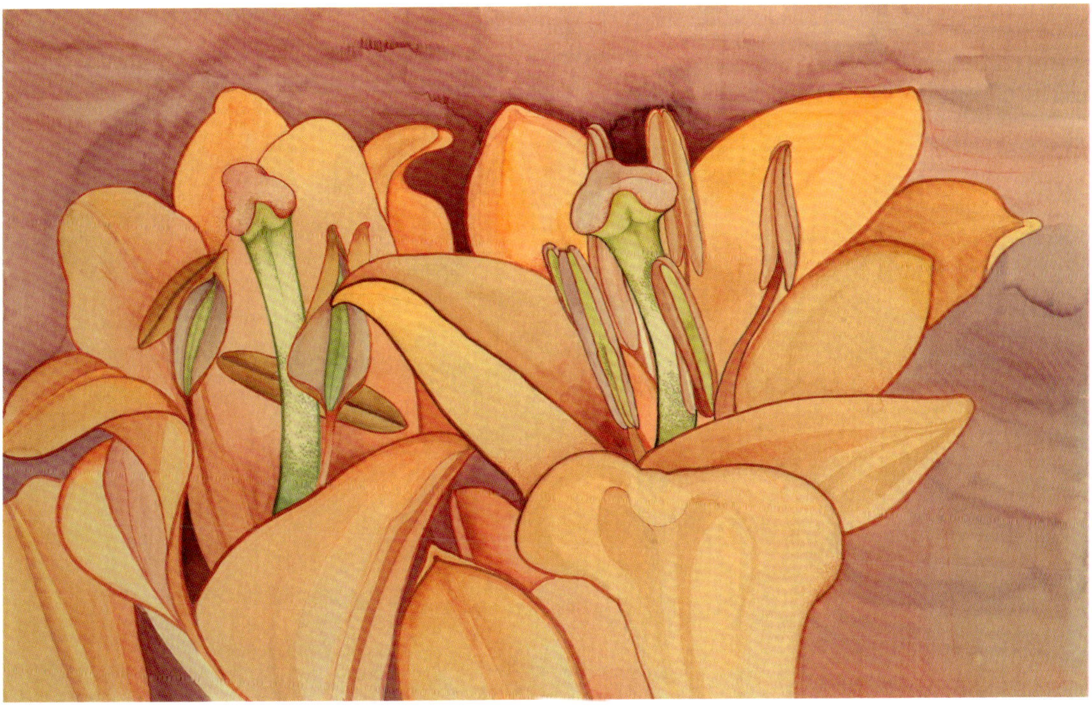

Lily

150×100 cm
Silk Mineral Pigment
2021

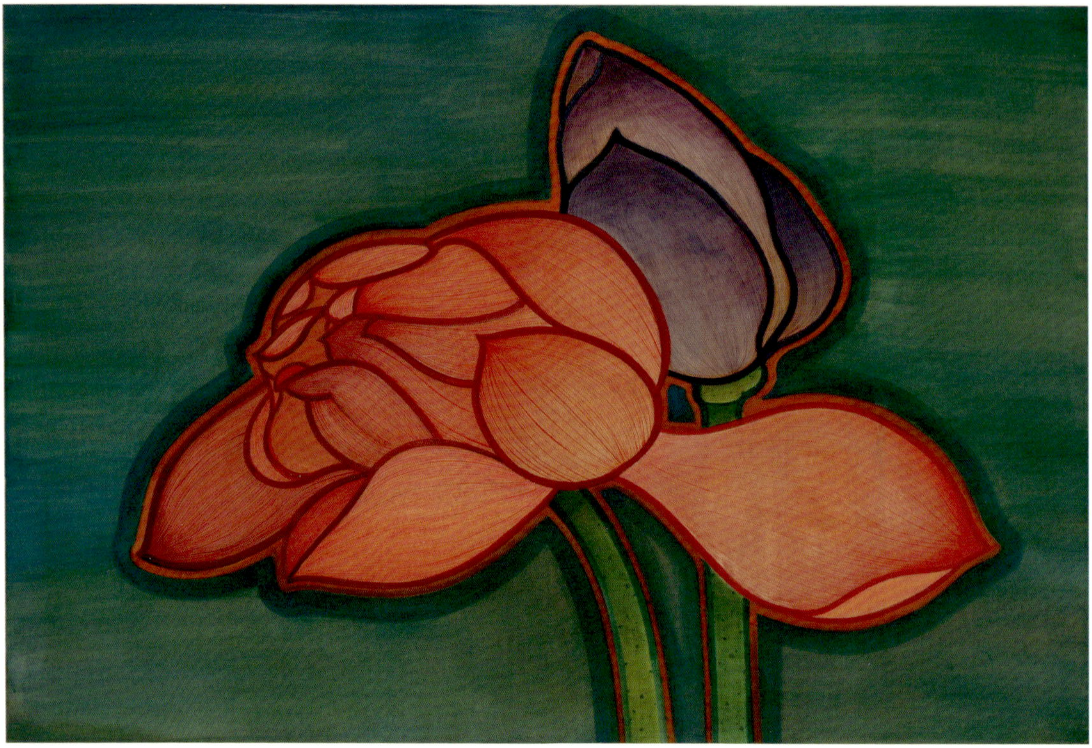

Fallen

150×100 cm
Silk Mineral Pigment
2023

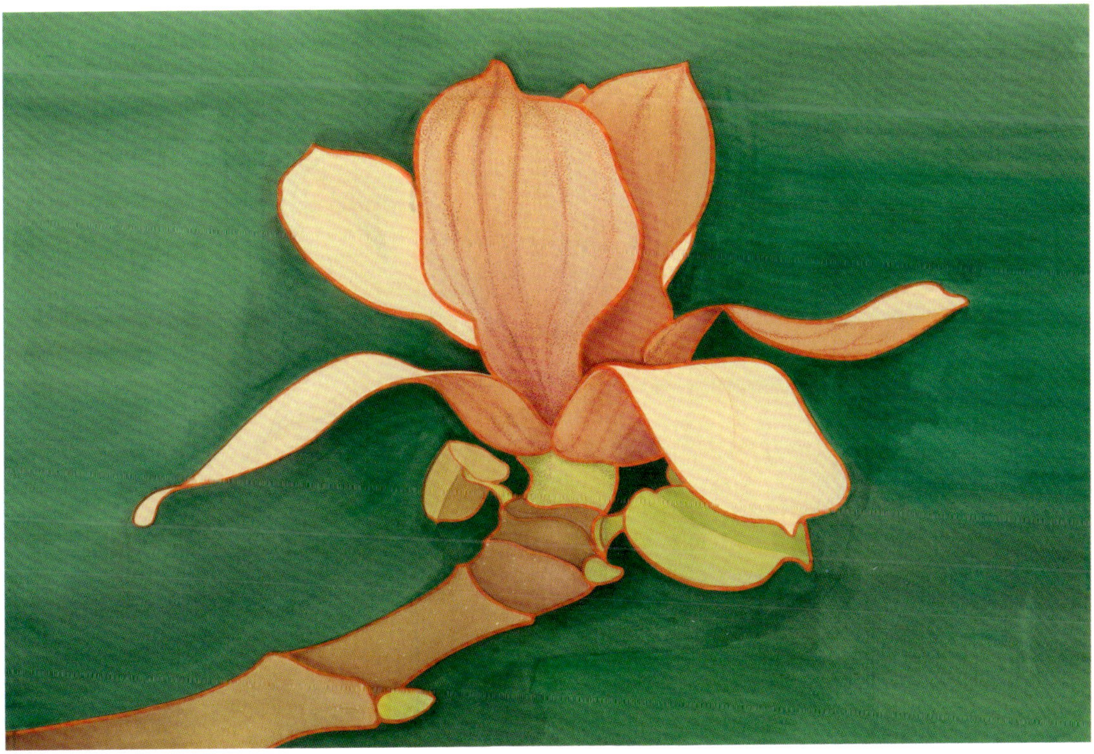

Yulan Magnolia

150 × 100 cm
Silk Mineral Pigment
2022

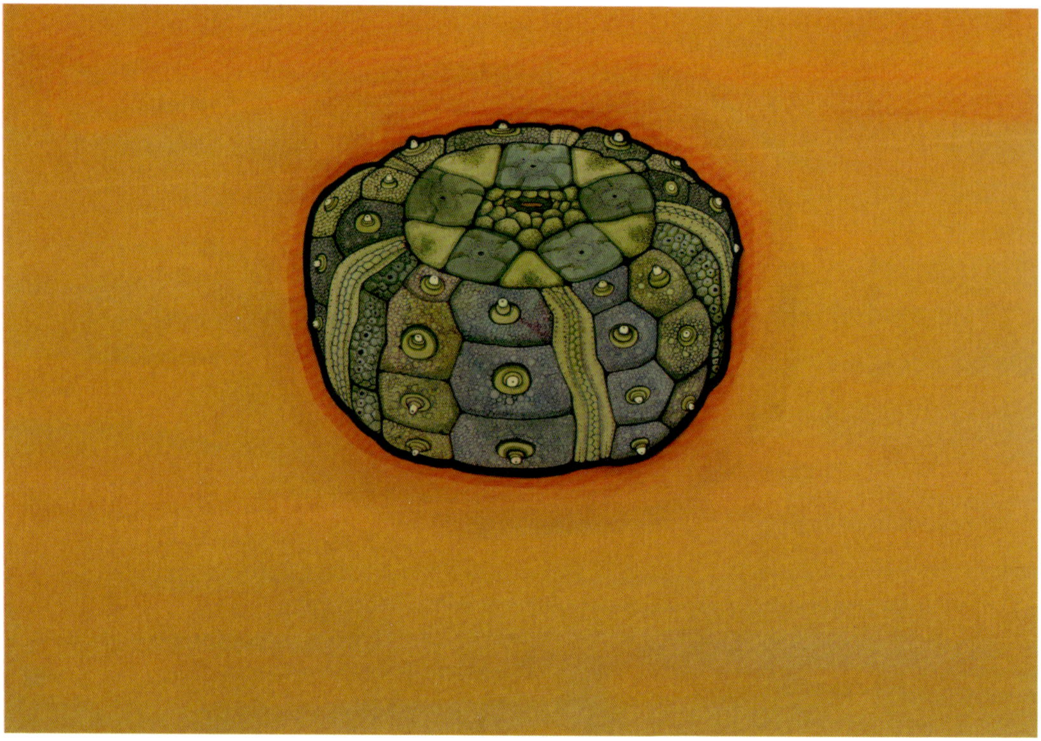

The Order of Body· Aquatic Animals #2

70×50 cm
Silk Mineral Pigment
2023

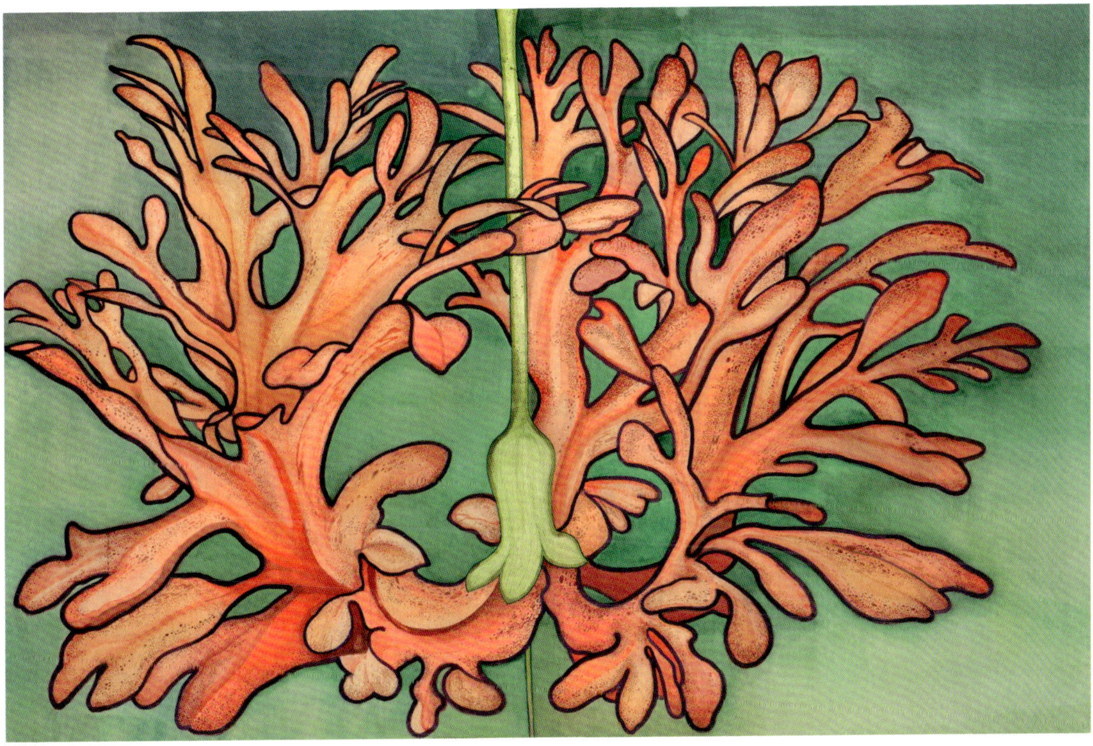

Agapetes Lacei

150×100 cm
Silk Mineral Pigment
2022

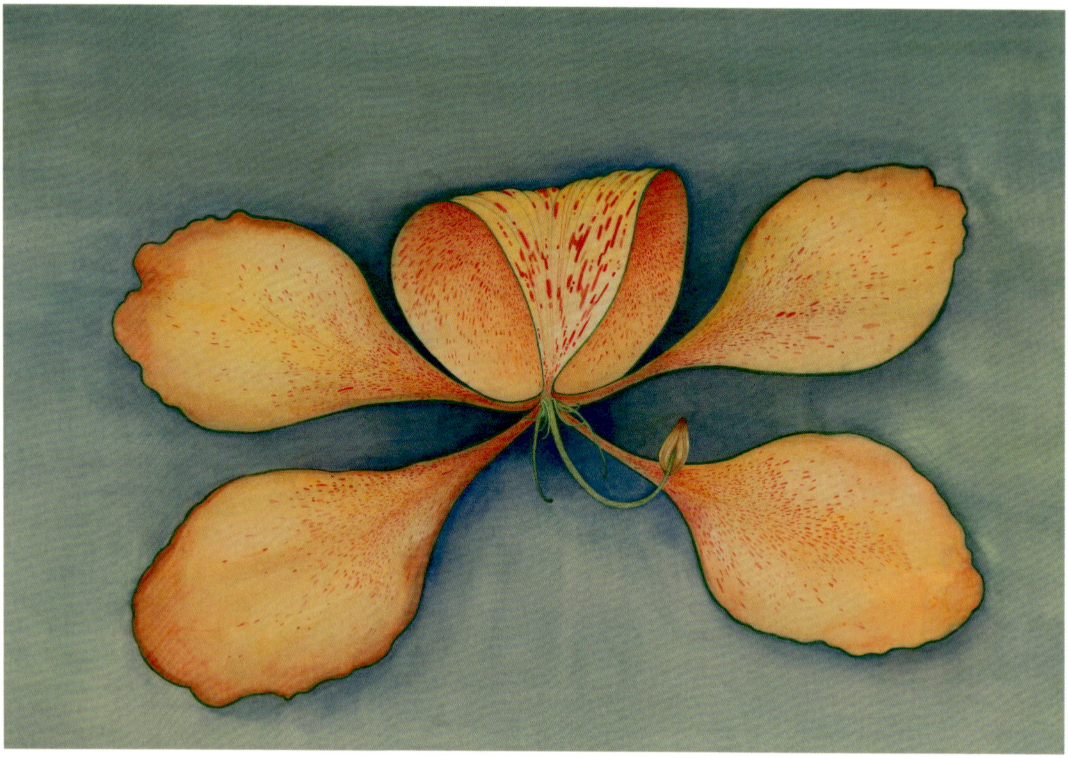

Bauhinia Variegata

70×50 cm
Silk Mineral Pigment
2021

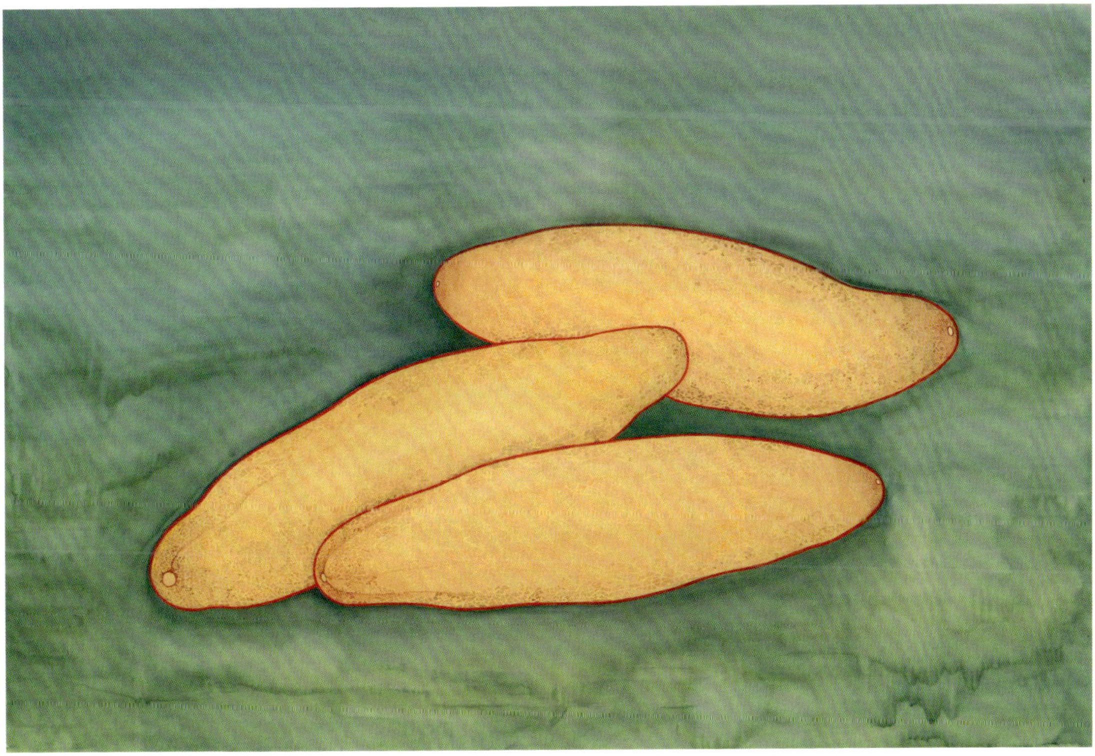

Melon

150×100 cm
Silk Mineral Pigment
2021

Lirianthe Delavayi

100×150 cm
Silk Mineral Pigment
2022

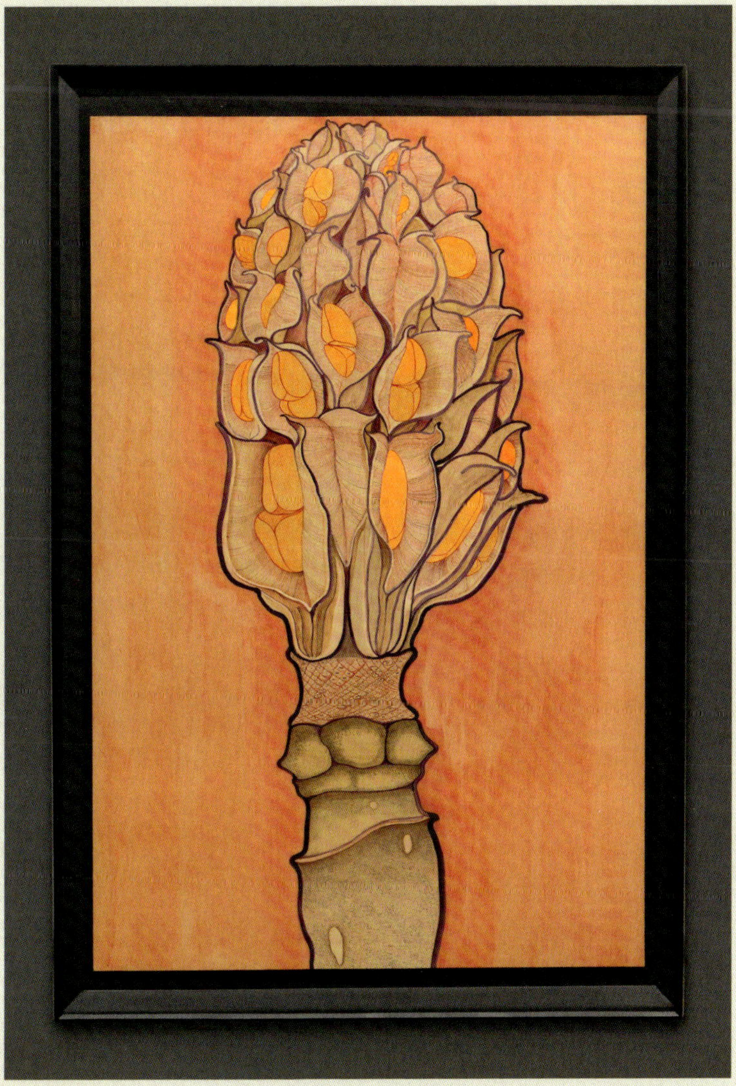

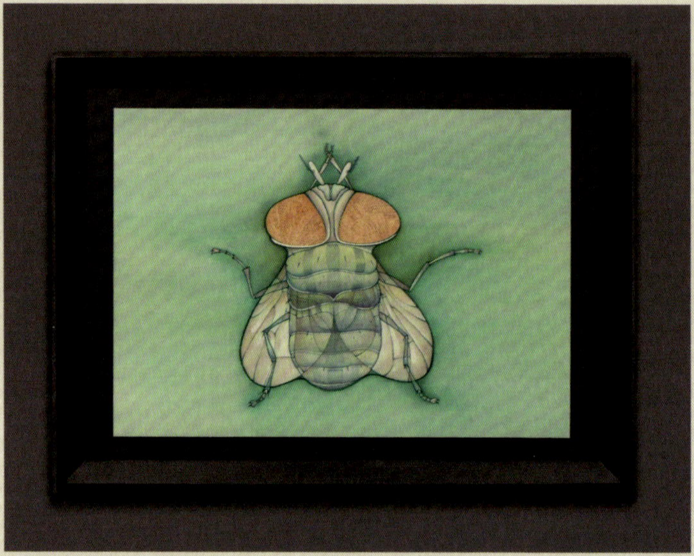

Fly

70×50 cm
Silk Mineral Pigment
2022

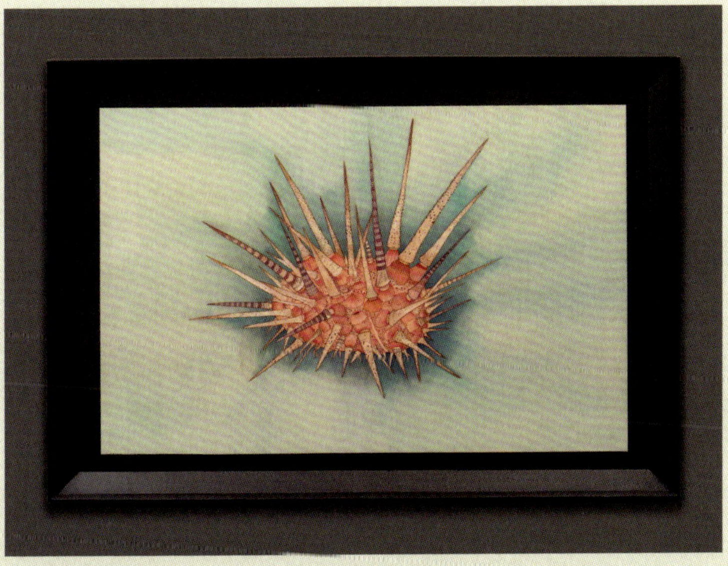

Sea Urchin

90×60 cm
Silk Mineral Pigment
2022

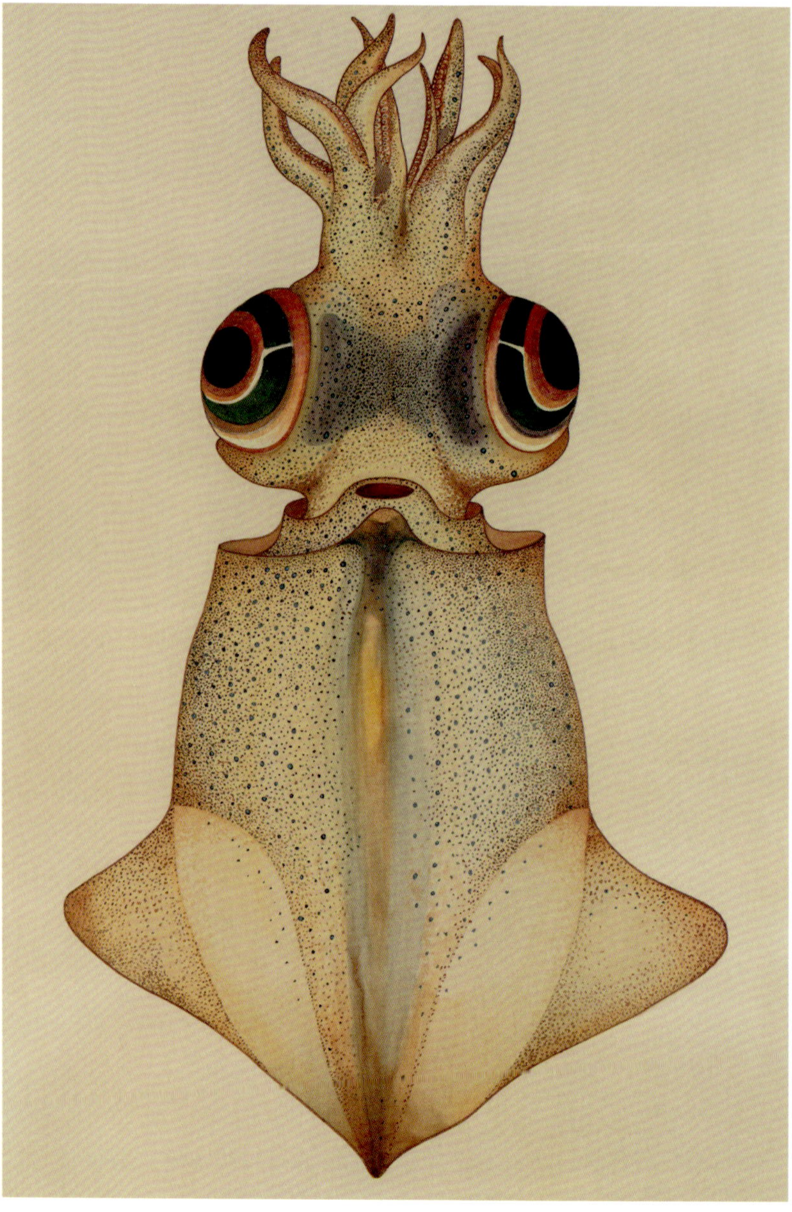

The Order of Body · Aquatic Animals #1

50×70 cm
Silk Mineral Pigment
2023

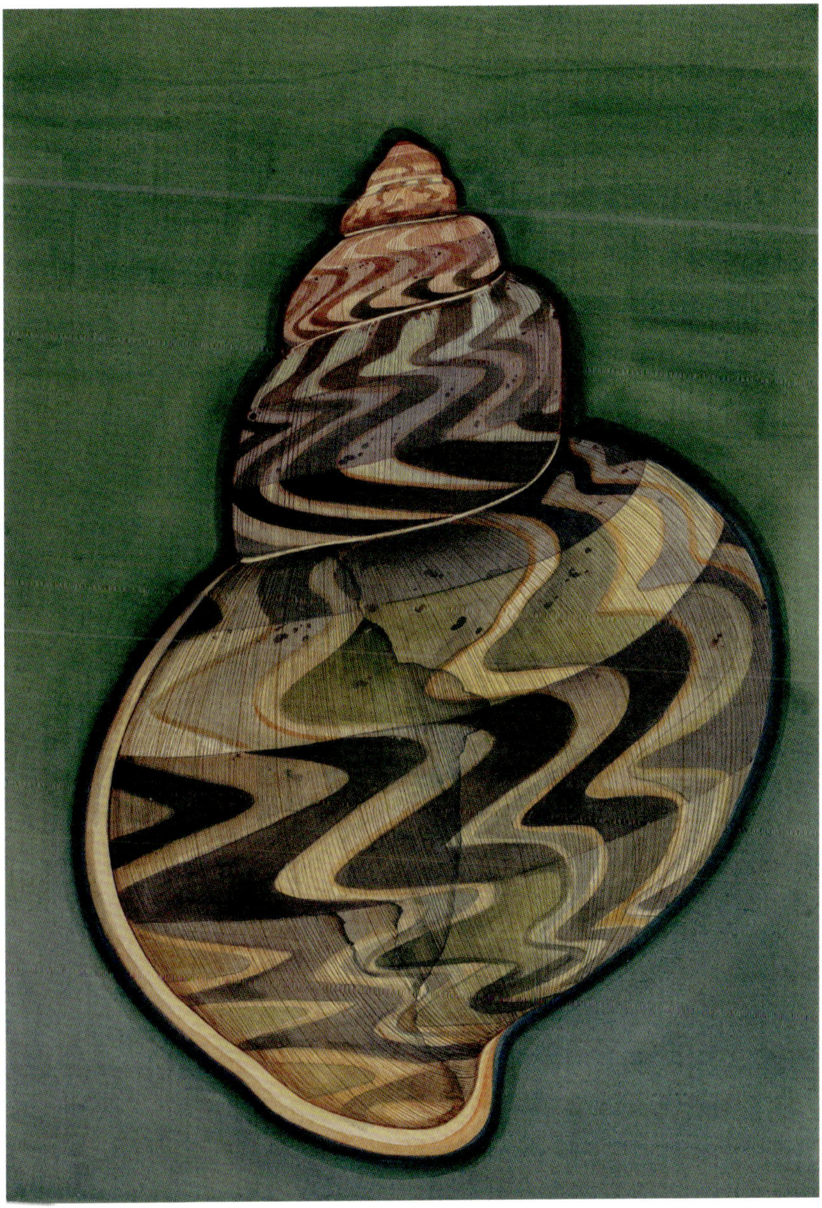

The Order of Body· Peruvian Snail

50×70 cm
Silk Mineral Pigment
2023

Ancestor

500×200 cm
Silk Mineral Pigment
2019

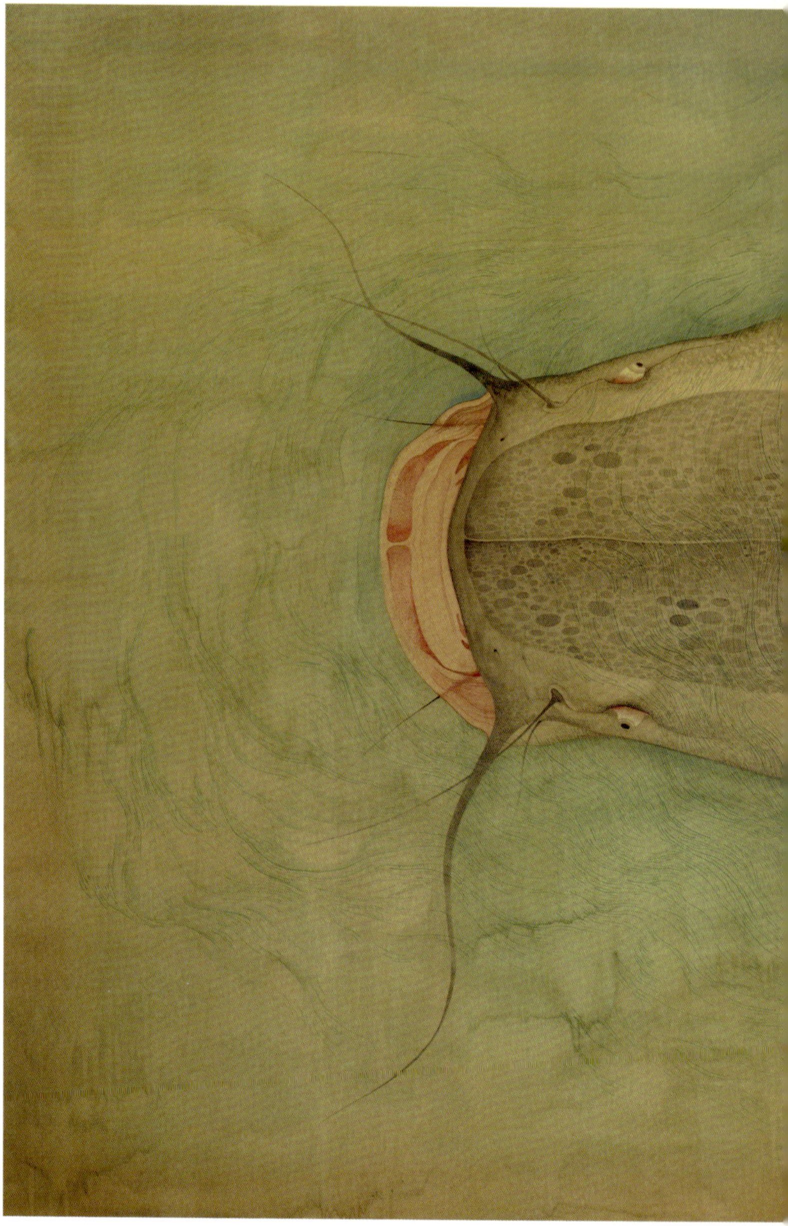

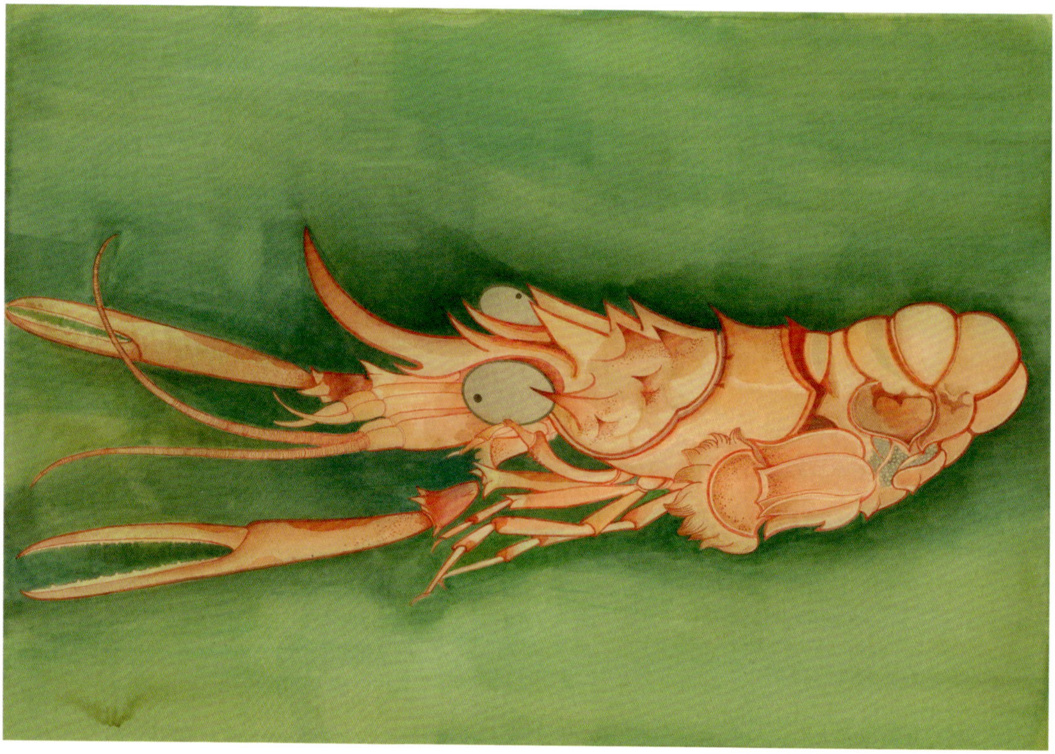

Scampi

70×50 cm
Silk Mineral Pigment
2021

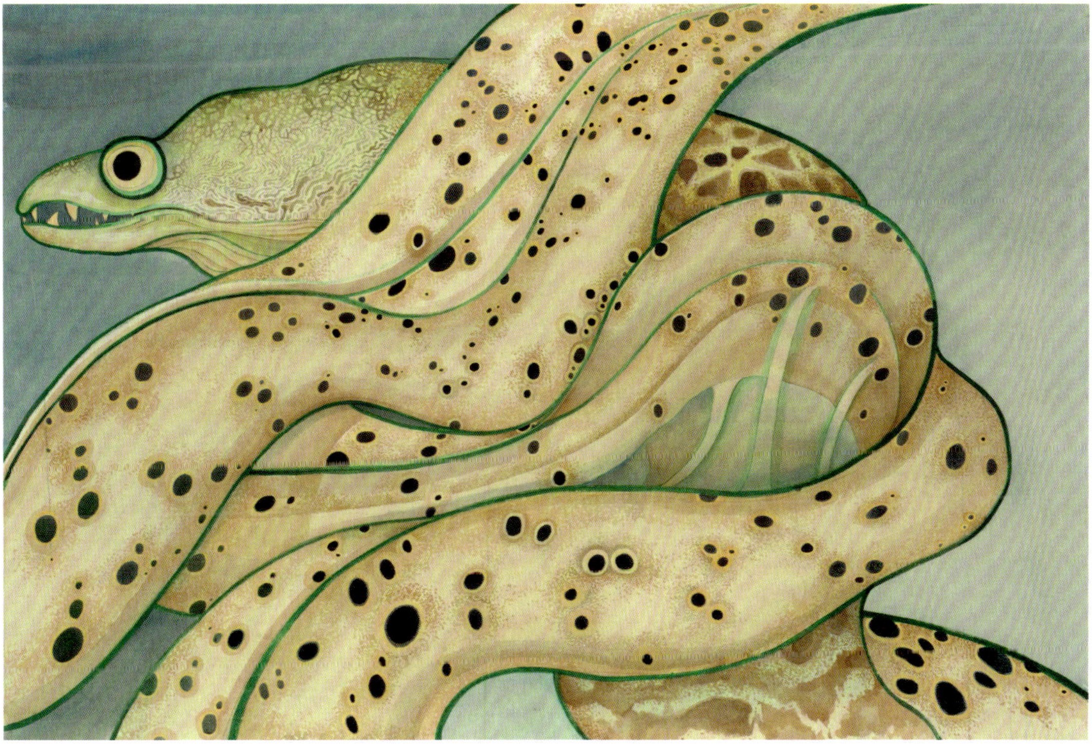

Eel

150×100 cm
Silk Mineral Pigment
2021

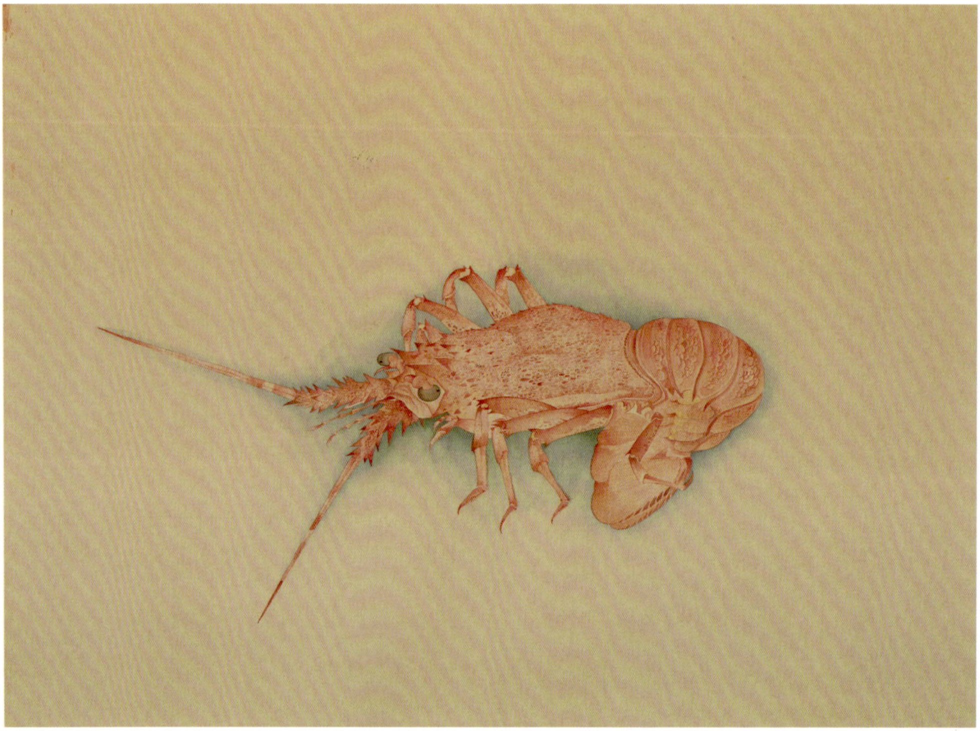

Shrimp

100×75 cm
Silk Mineral Pigment
2020

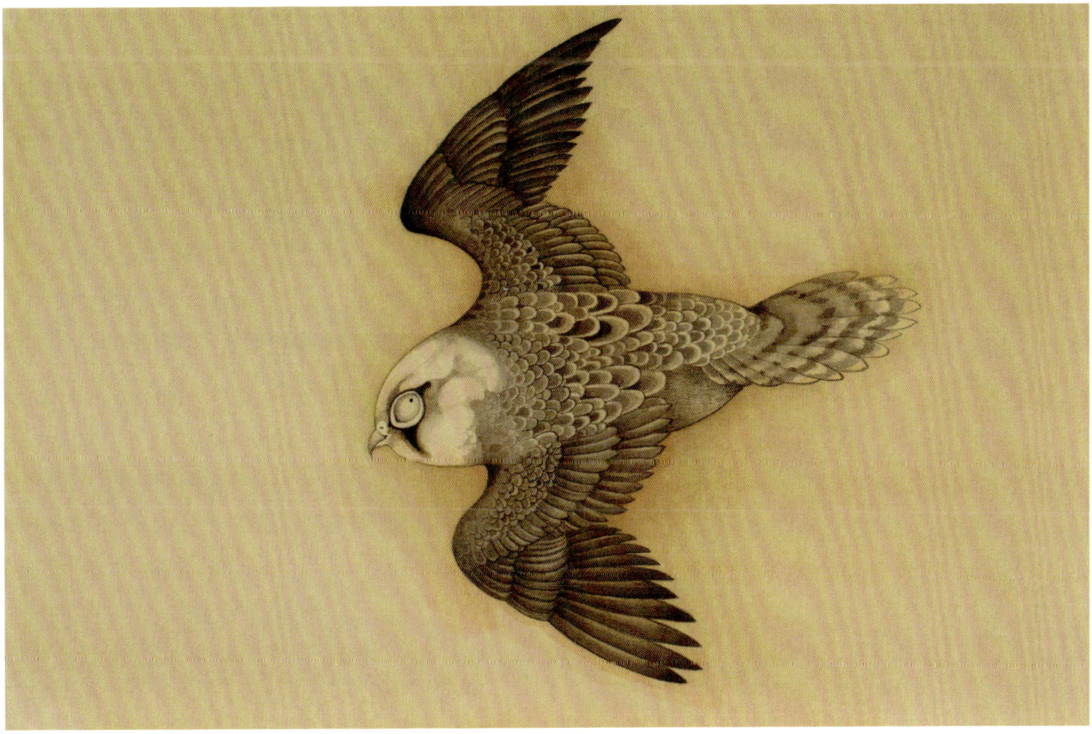

The Order of Body #3

33×22 cm
Silk Mineral Pigment
2020

Camel Bone

90×60 cm
Silk Mineral Pigment
2018

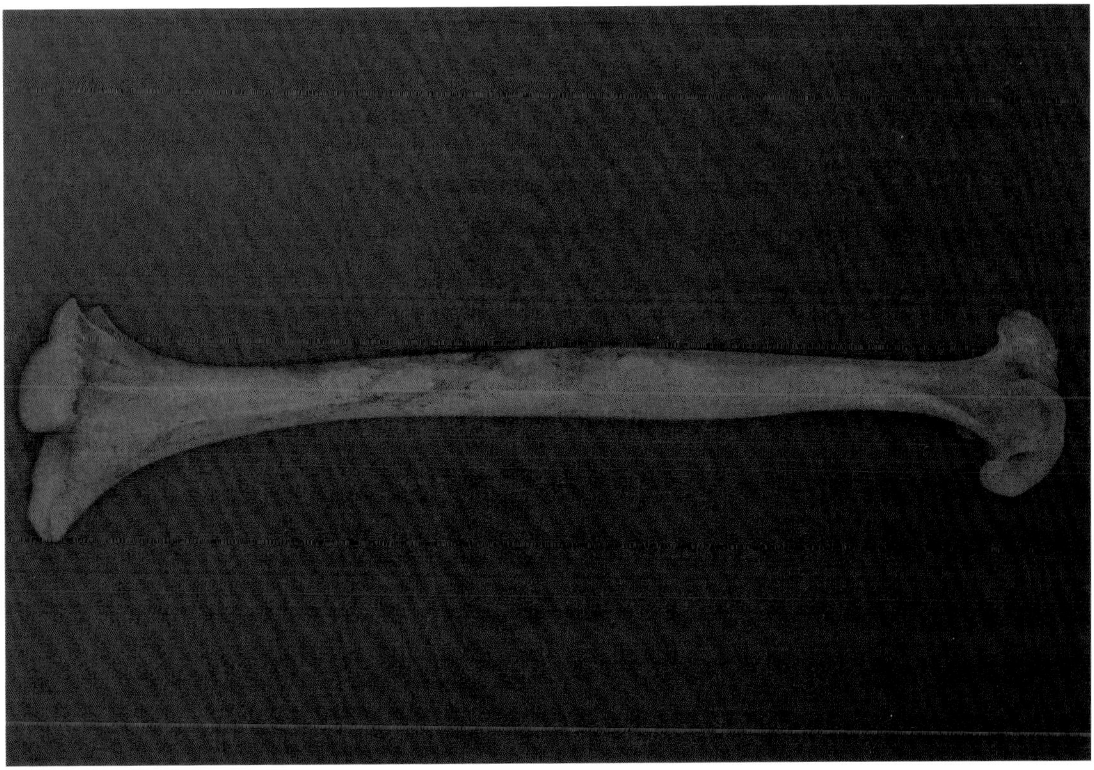

Hands

50×50 cm
Silk Mineral Pigment
2021

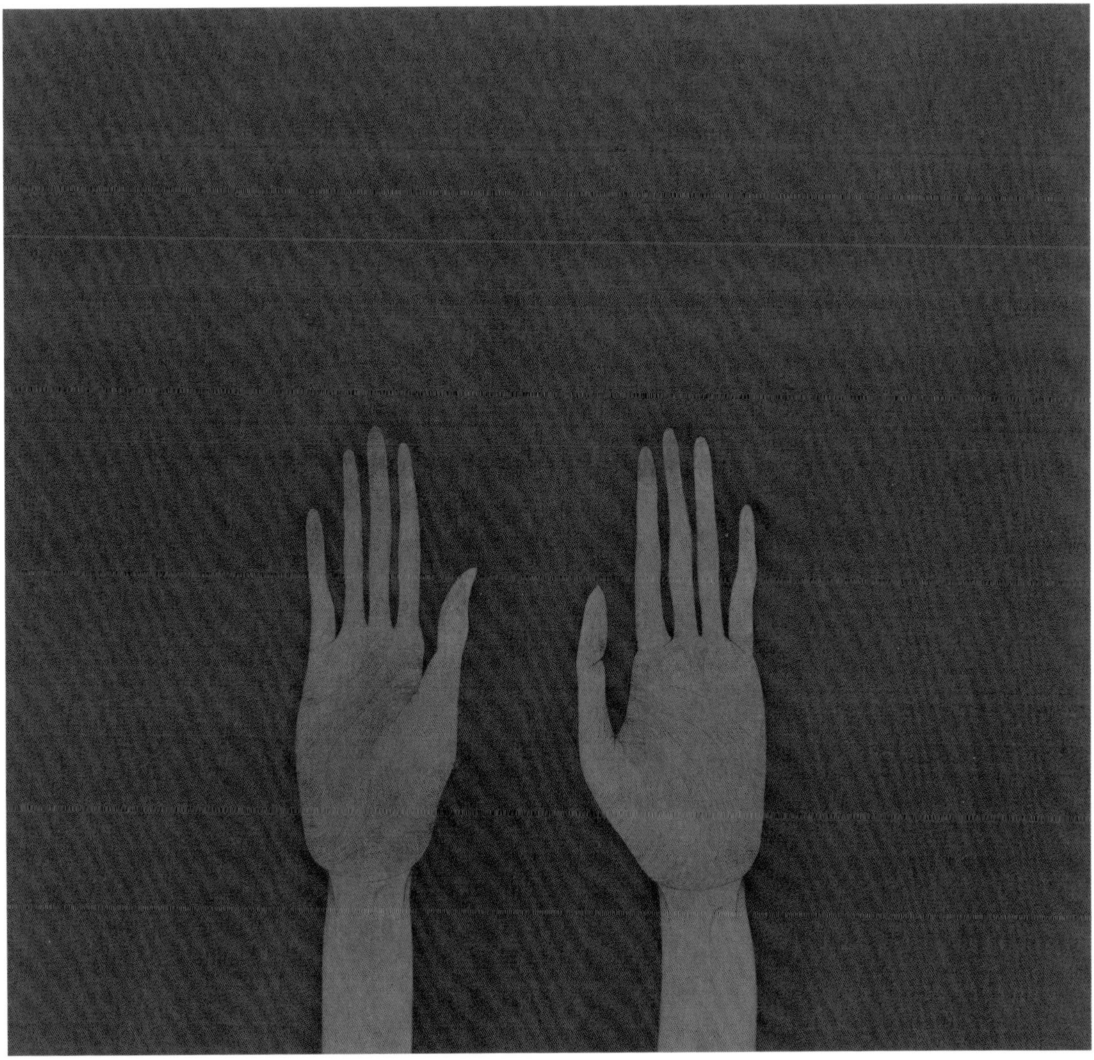

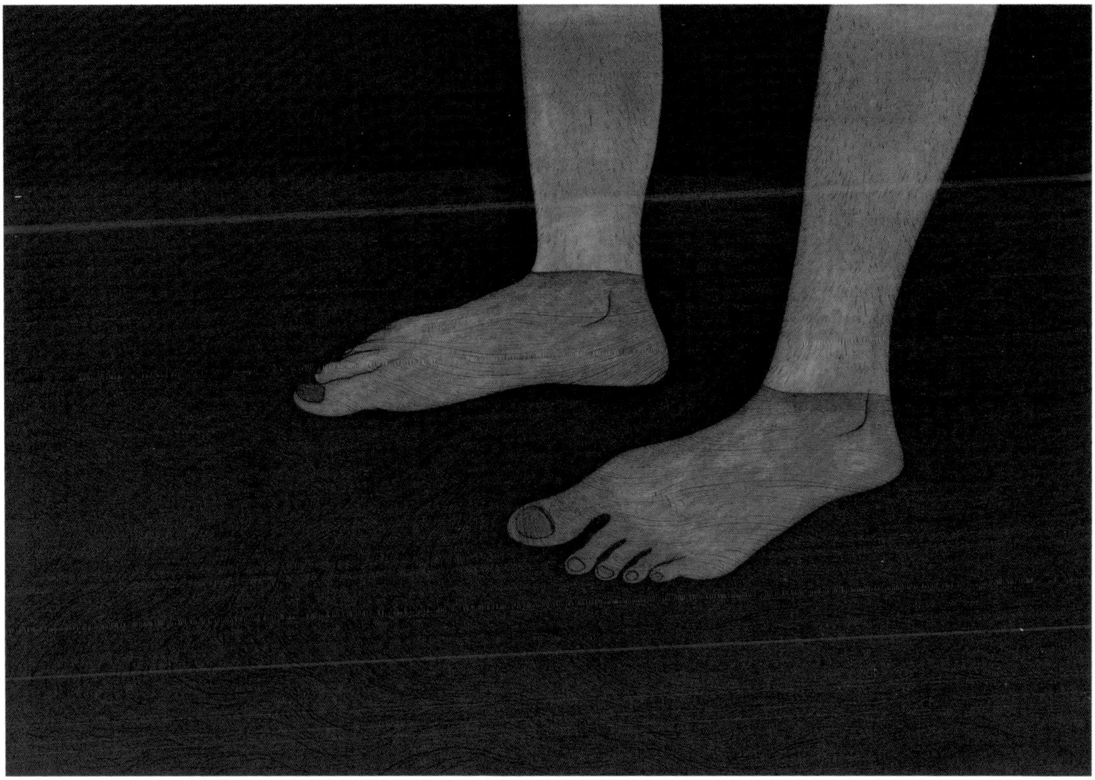

Transmit

70×50 cm
Silk Mineral Pigment
2019

Animals

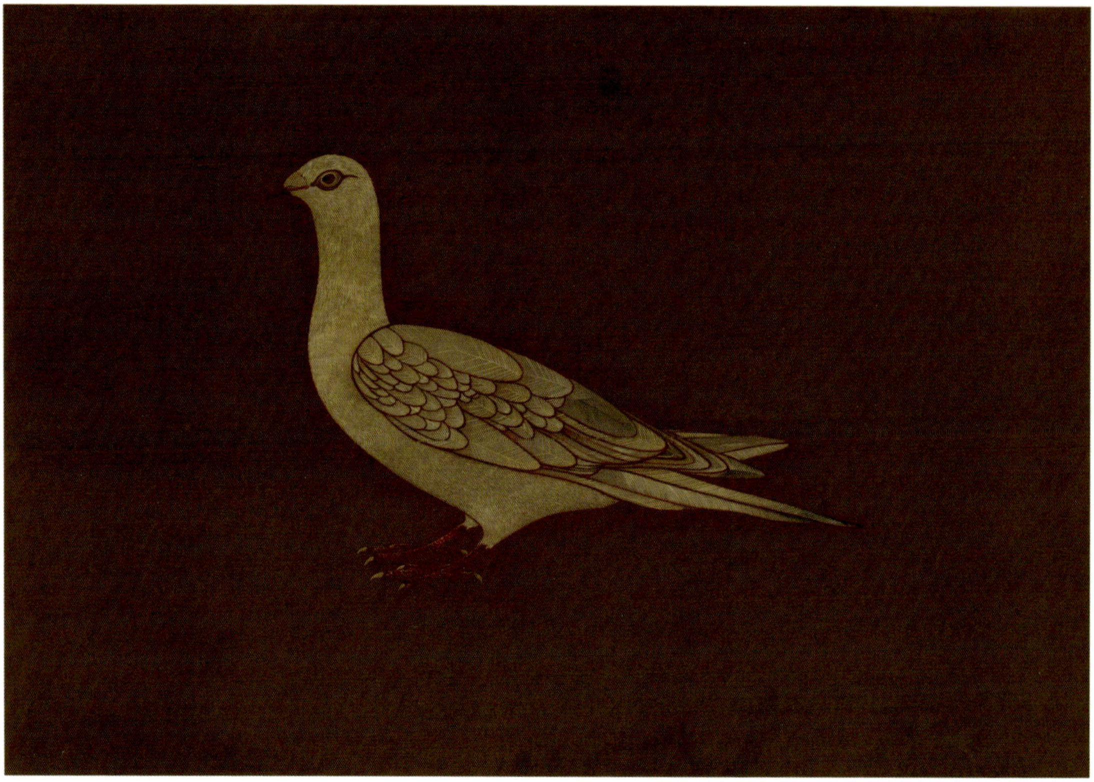

Pigeon

70×50 cm
Silk Mineral Pigment
2019

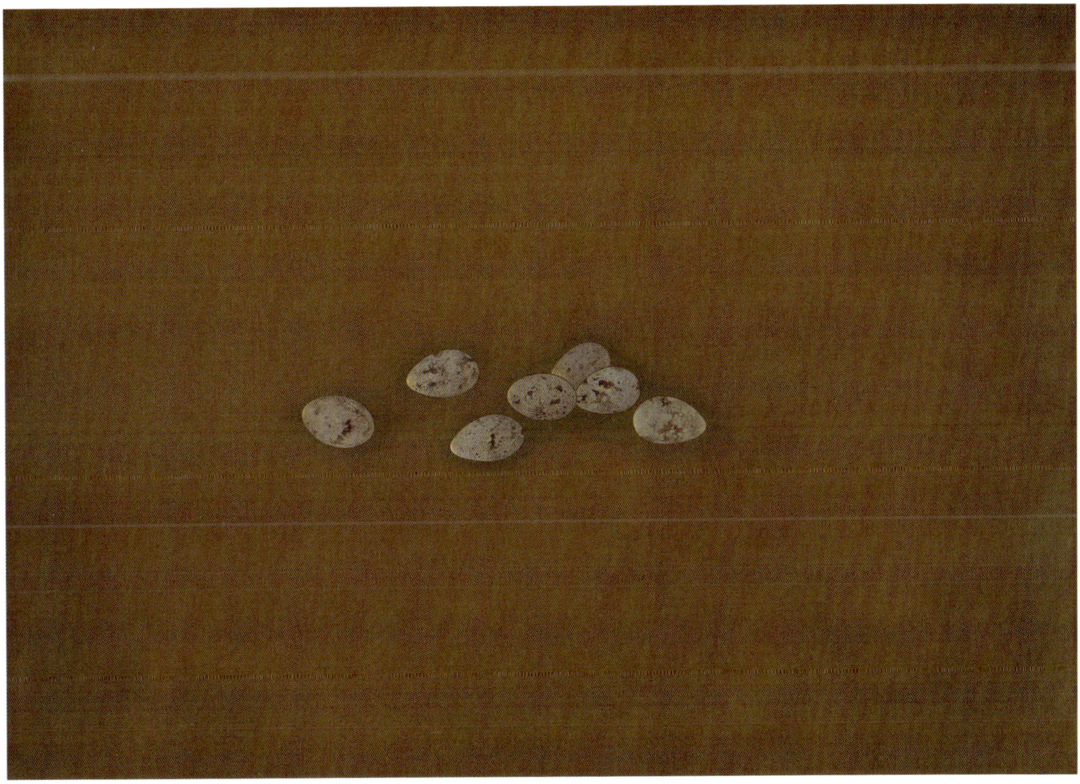

Eggs

70×50 cm
Silk Mineral Pigment
2019

White Ape

120×80 cm
Oil Painting
2012

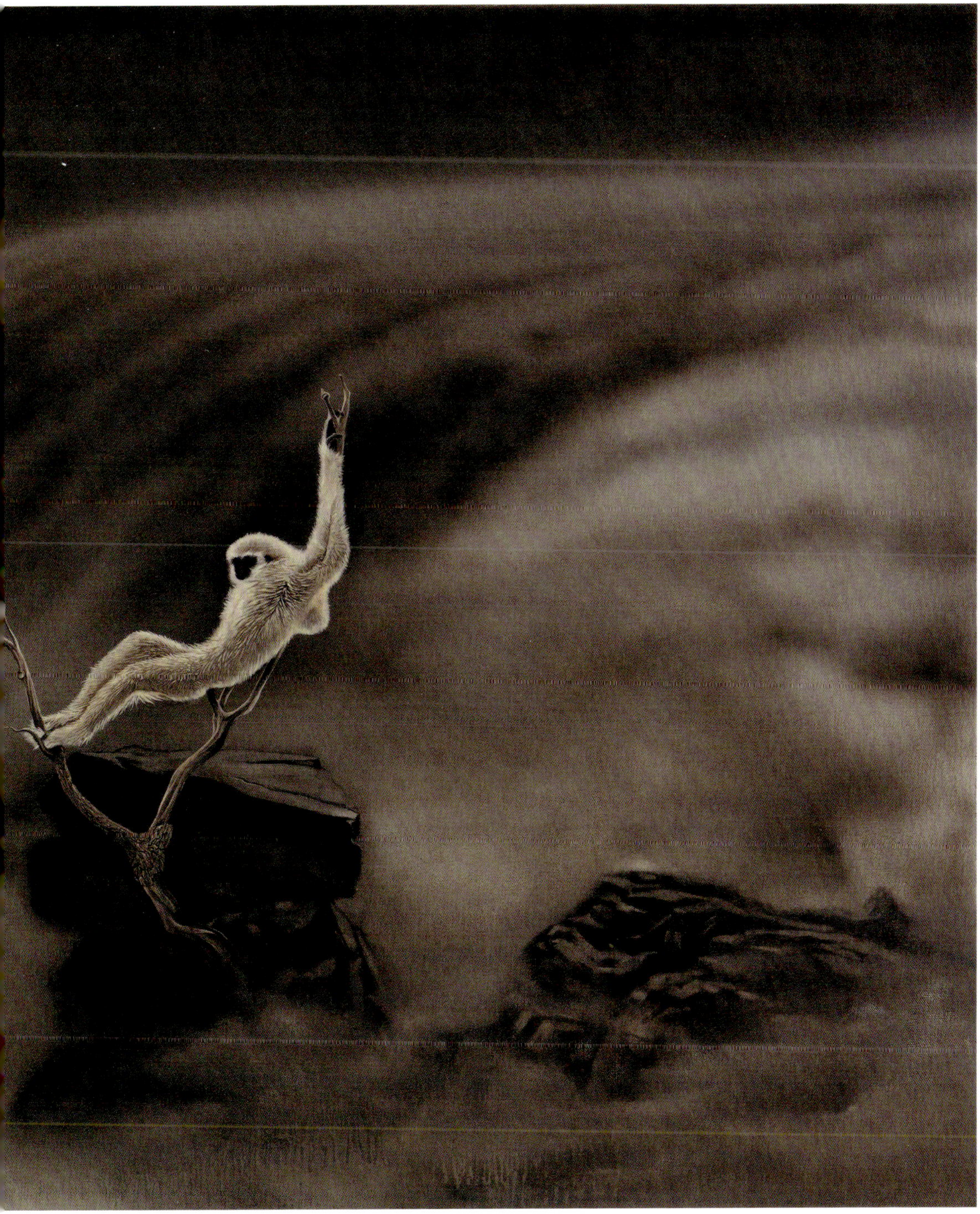

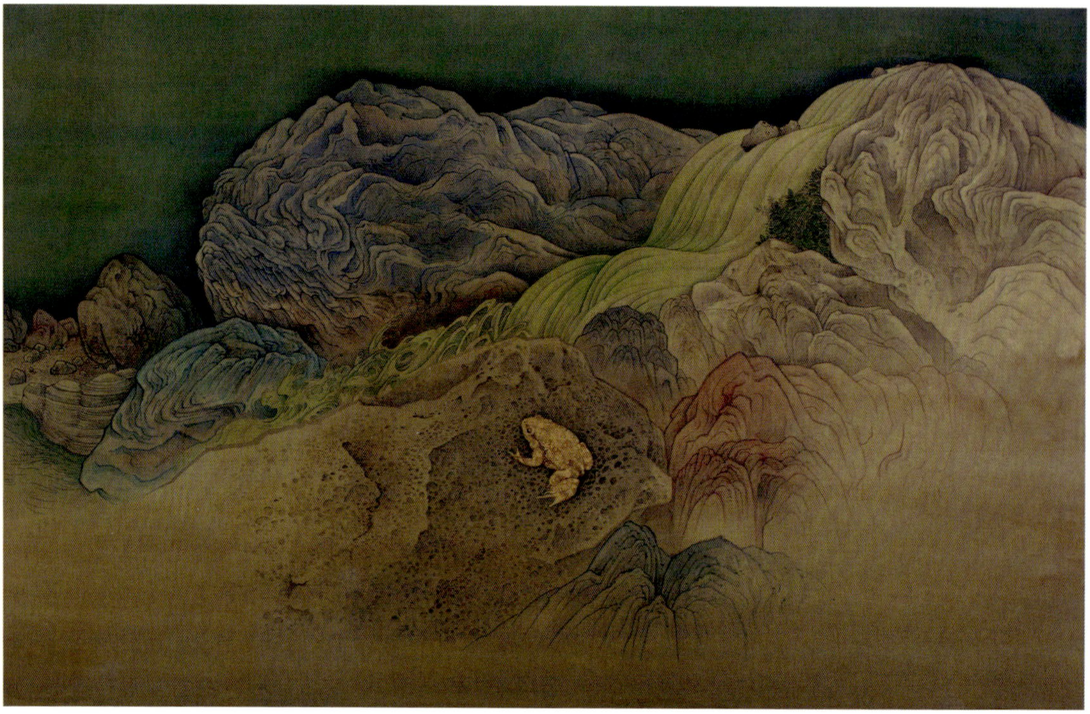

Toad

79×50 cm
Silk Mineral Pigment
2018

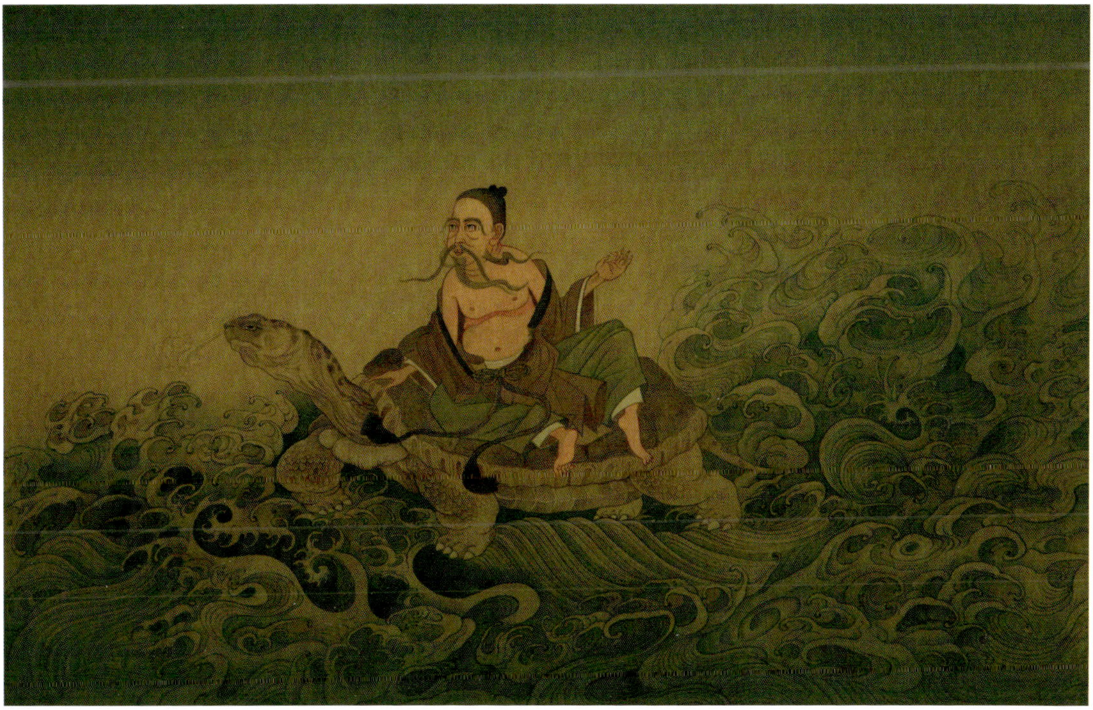

God of Rivers

55×35 cm
Silk Mineral Pigment
2016

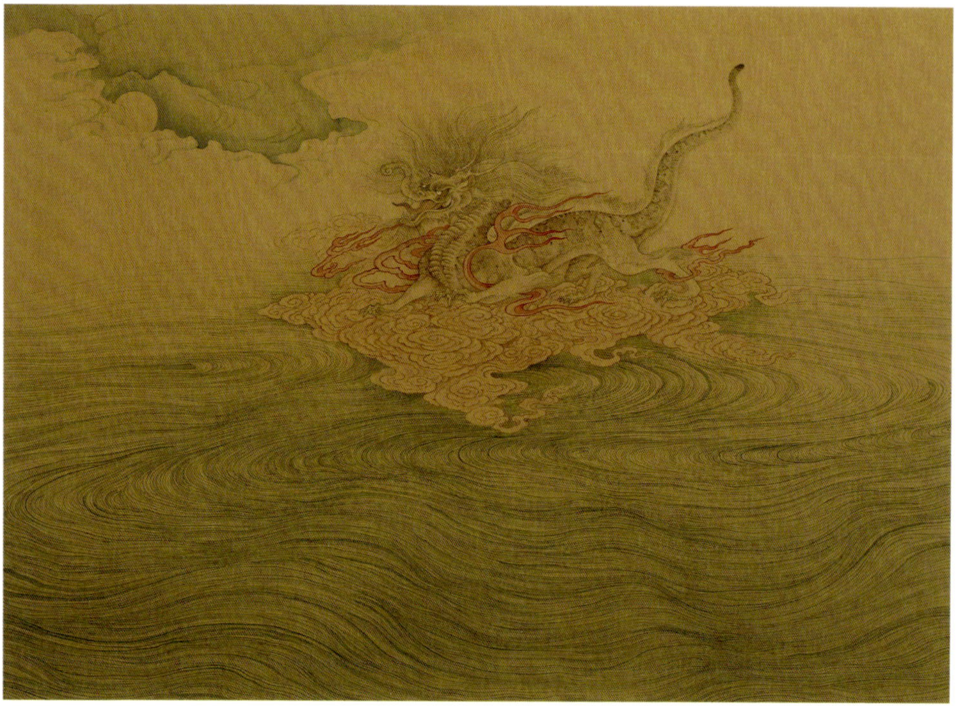

Flood Dragon

100×60 cm
Silk Mineral Pigment
2018

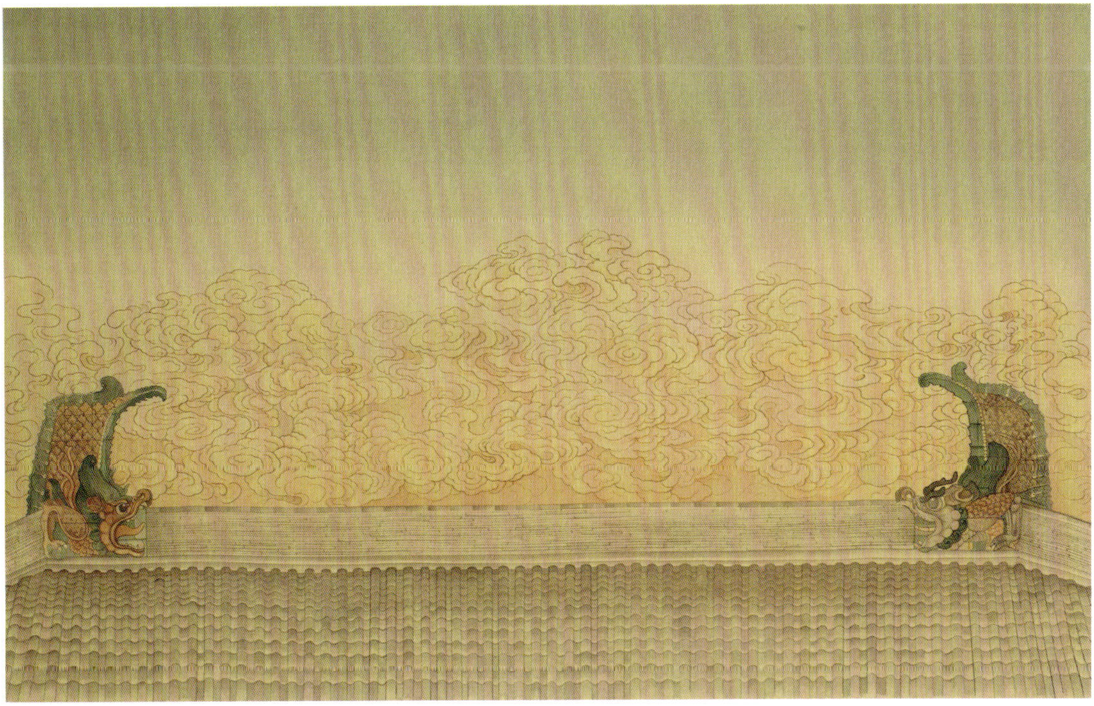

Huayan Temple

90×60 cm
Silk Mineral Pigment
2018

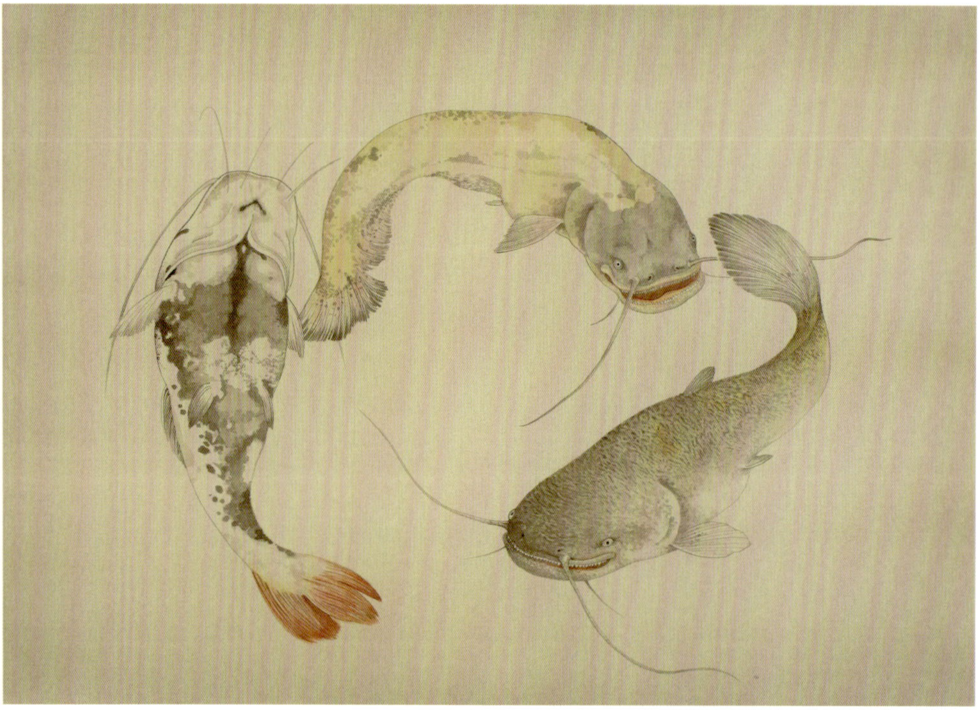

Catfish

70×50 cm
Silk Mineral Pigment
2018

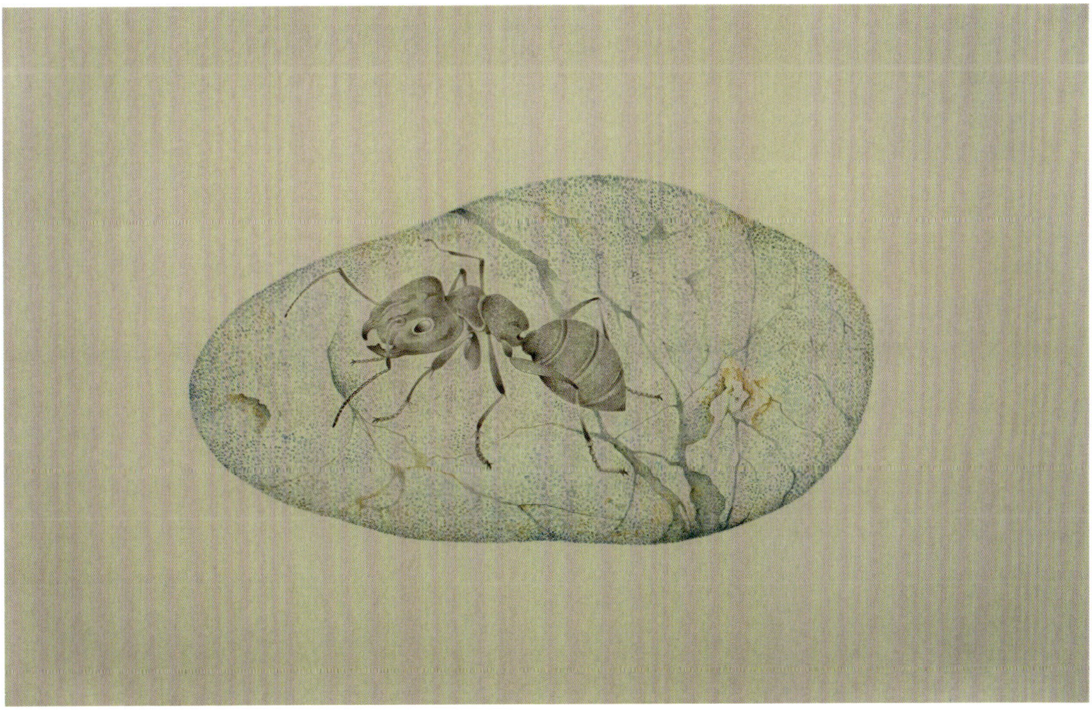

Ant

50×30 cm
Silk Mineral Pigment
2018

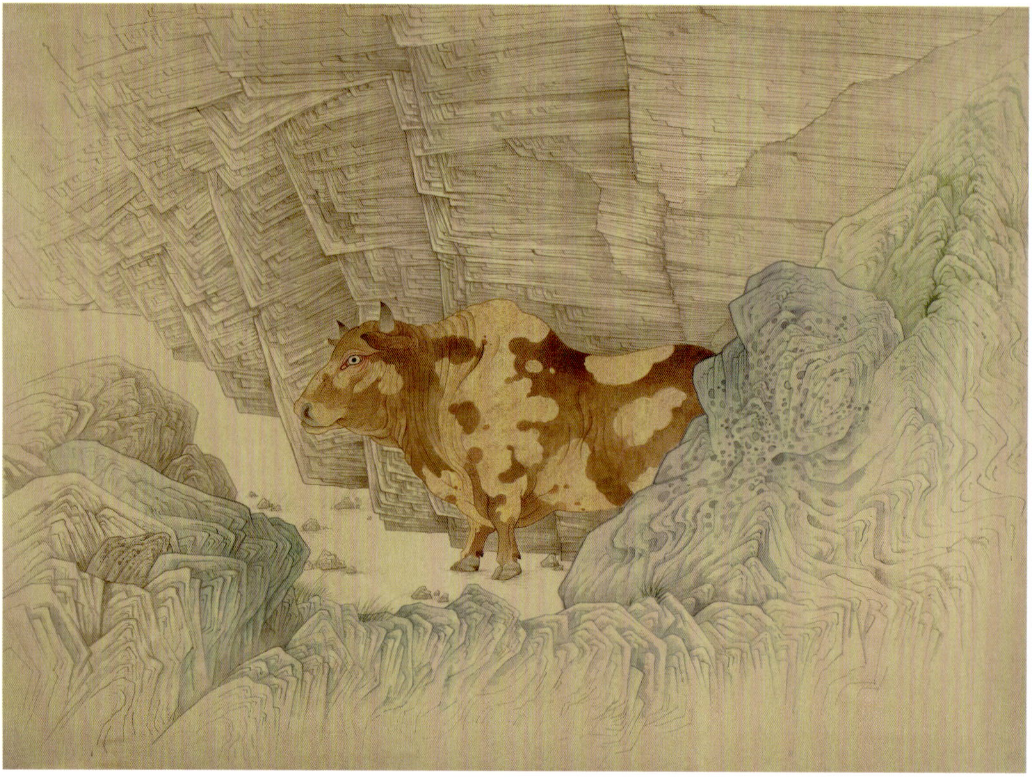

Cow

70×50 cm
Silk Mineral Pigment
2018

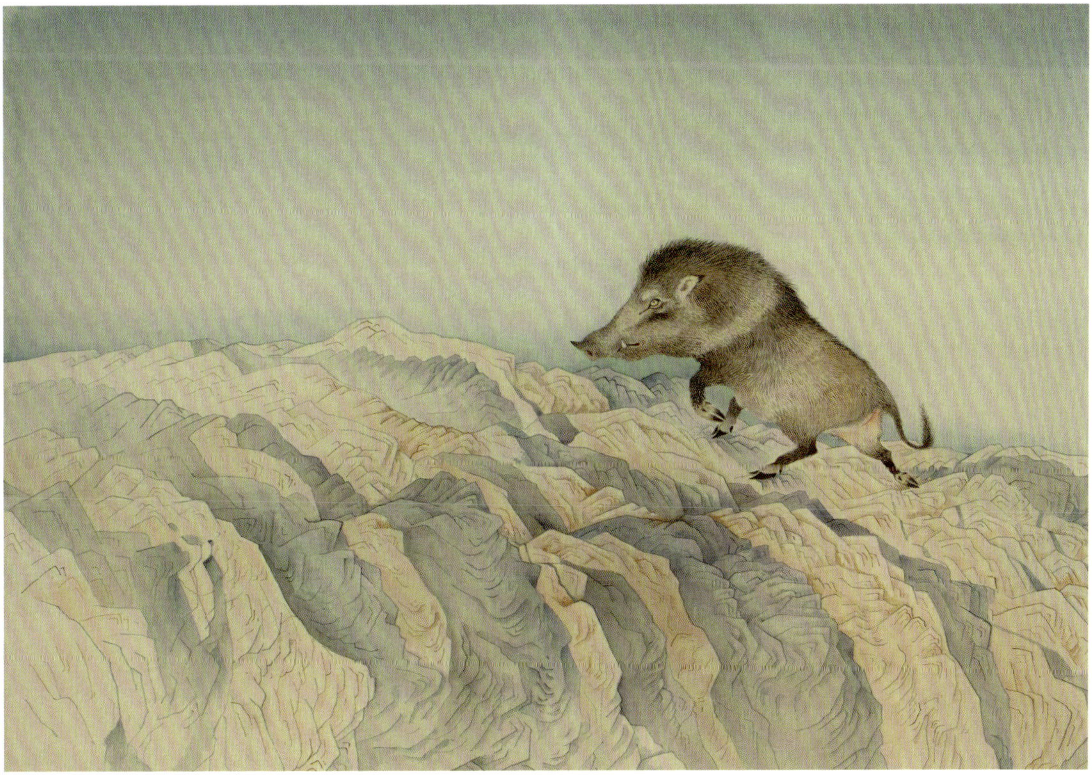

Boar

70×50 cm
Silk Mineral Pigment
2018

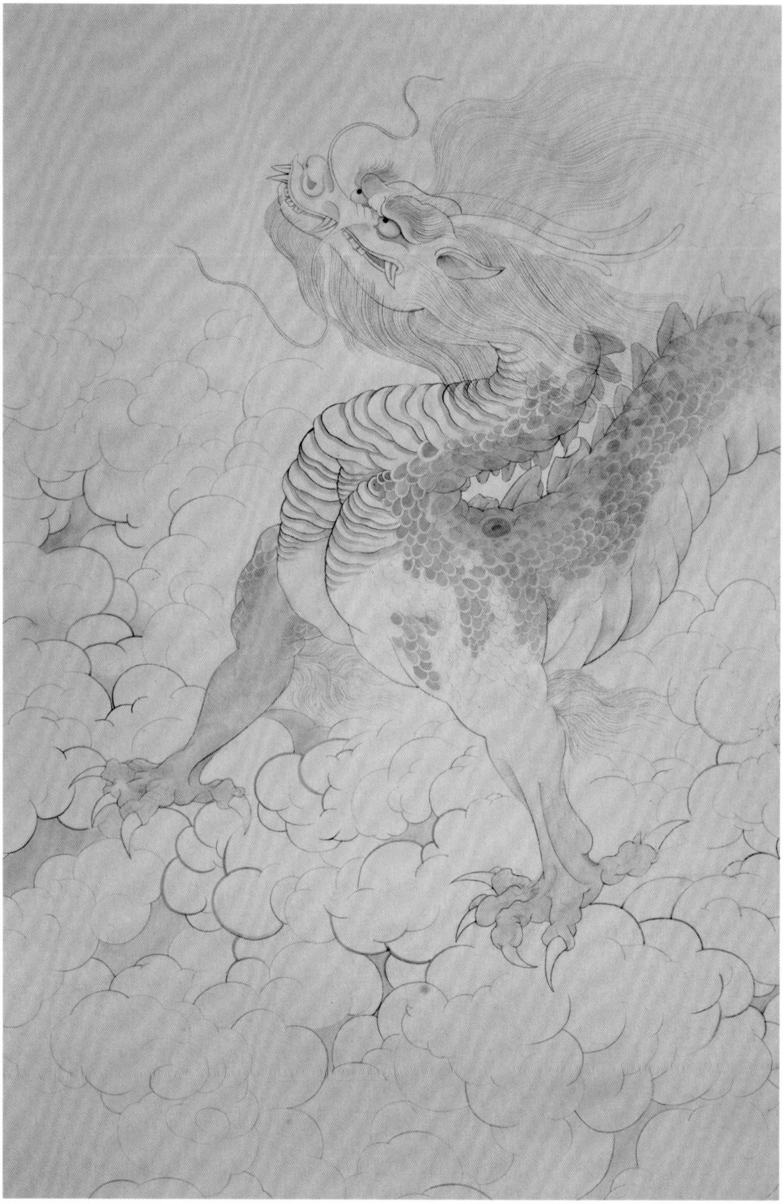

In the Clouds

200×300 cm
Mural
2015

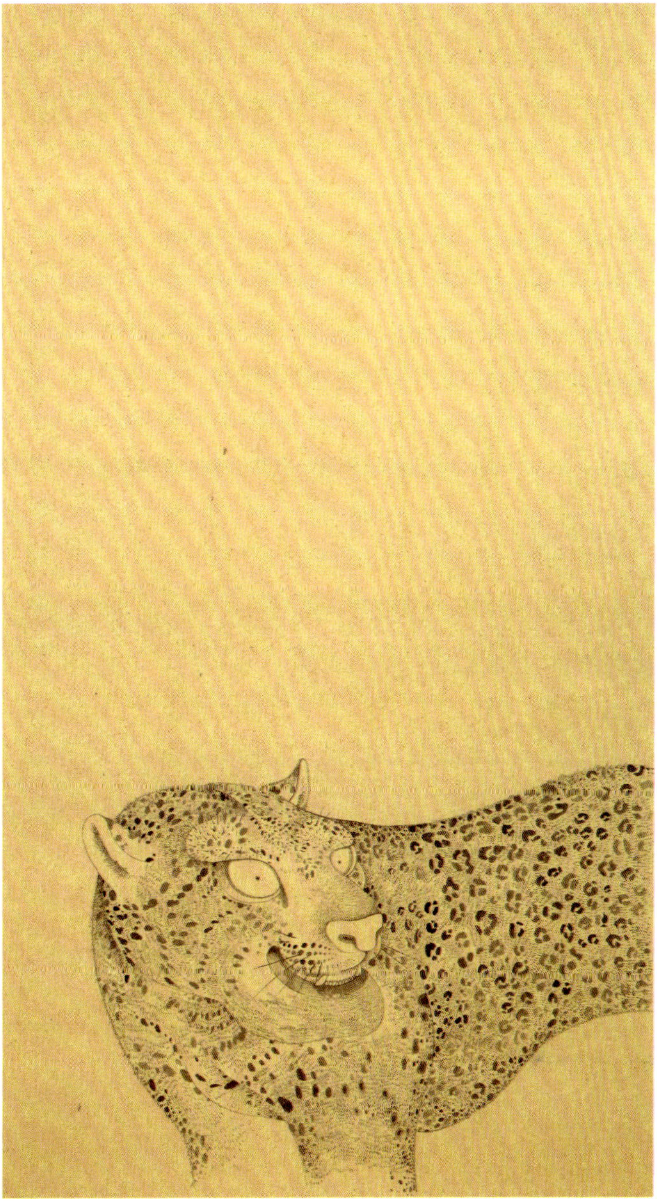

Leopard

42×72 cm
Mineral Pigment on Paper
2019

Curious Tiger

22×66 cm
Silk Mineral Pigment
2018

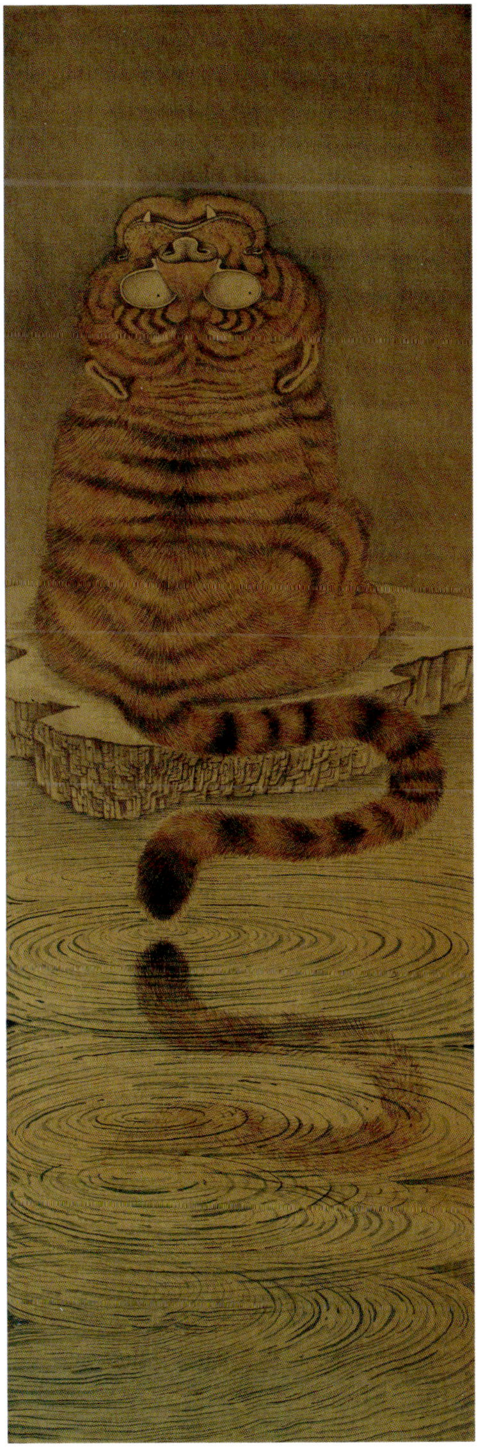

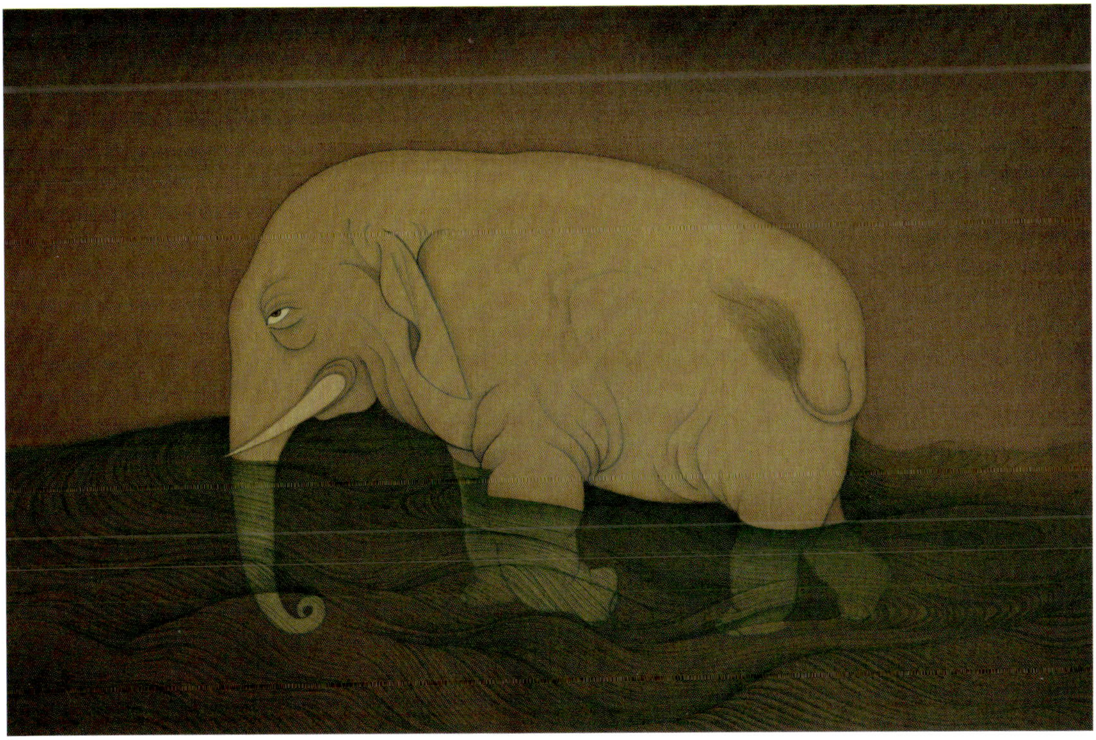

Elephant

55×35 cm
Silk Mineral Pigment
2016

Portaiture

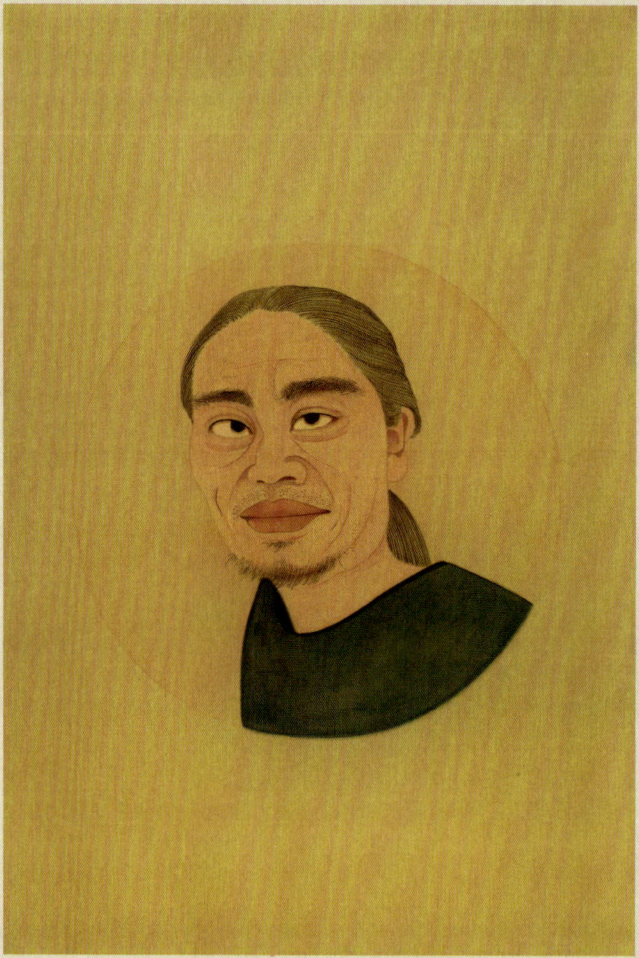

Portaiture #1

22×33 cm
Silk Mineral Pigment
2019

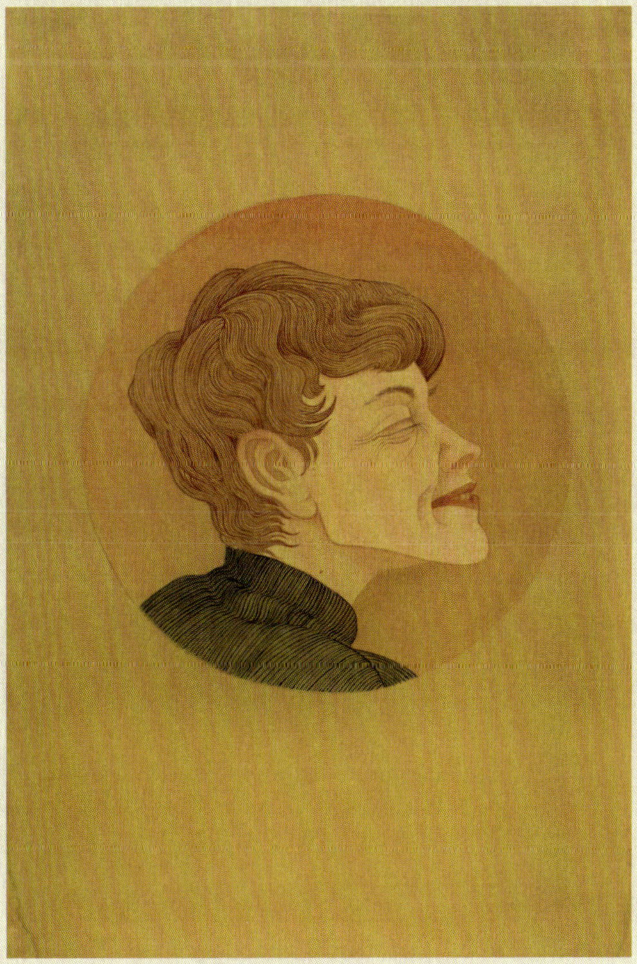

Portaiture #2

22×33 cm
Silk Mineral Pigment
2019

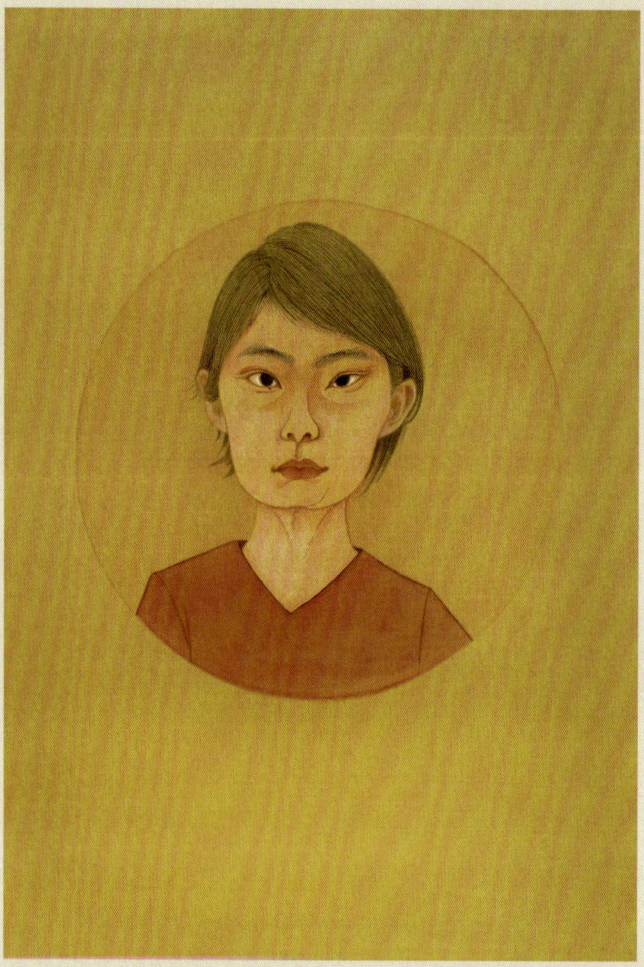

Portaiture #3

22×33 cm
Silk Mineral Pigment
2019

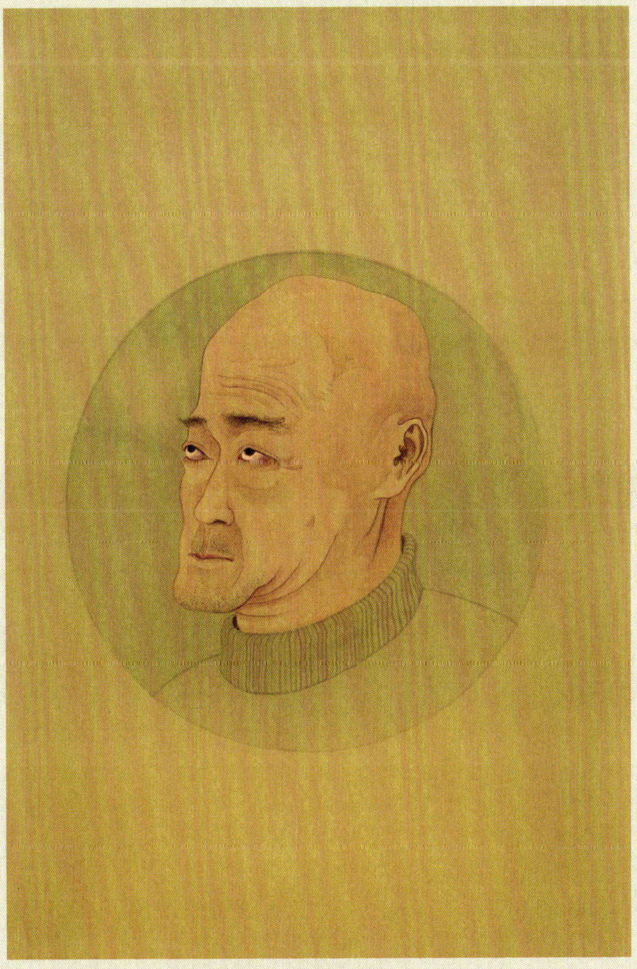

Portaiture #4

22×33 cm
Silk Mineral Pigment
2019

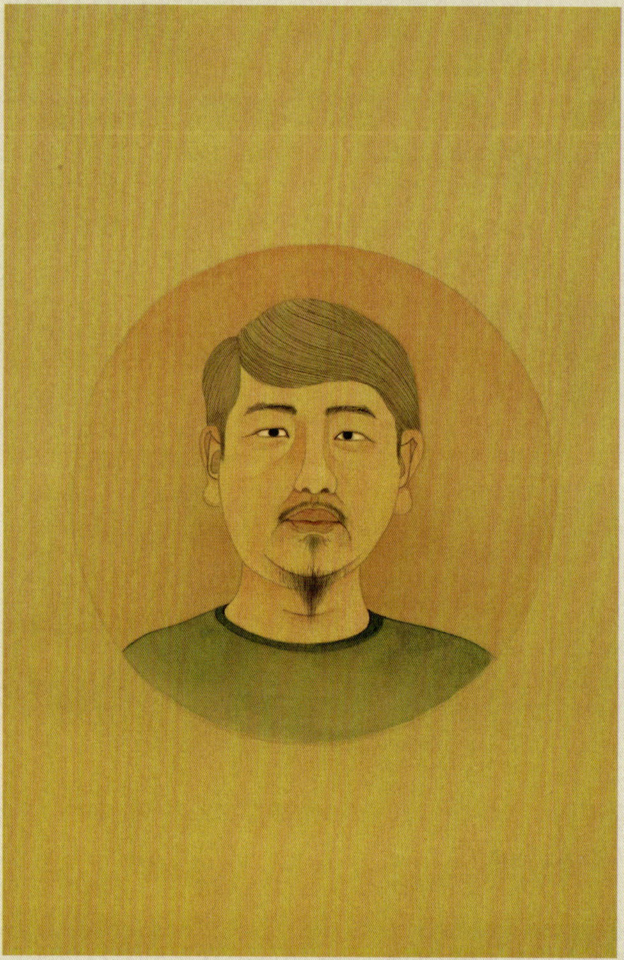

Portaiture #5

22×33 cm
Silk Mineral Pigment
2019

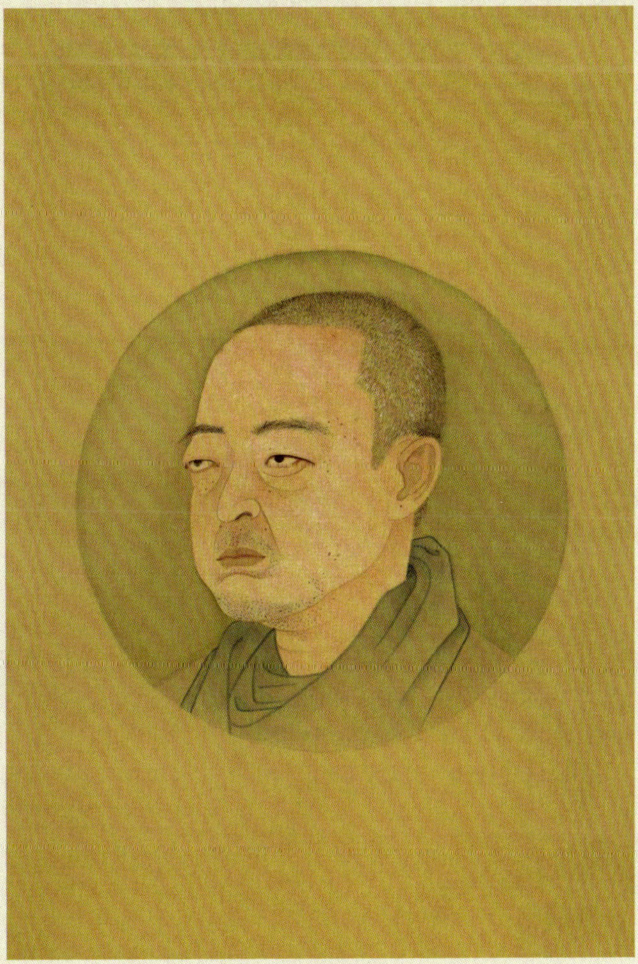

Portaiture #6

22×33 cm
Silk Mineral Pigment
2019

APPENDIX

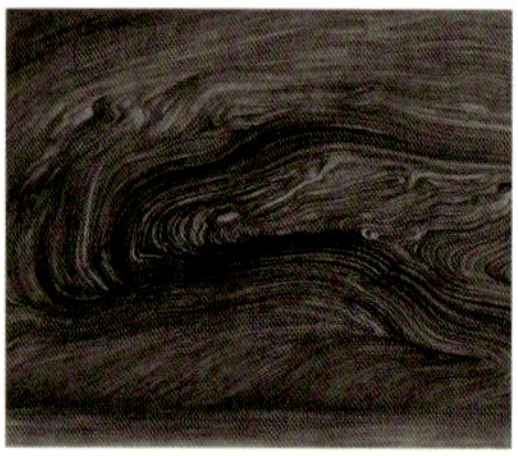
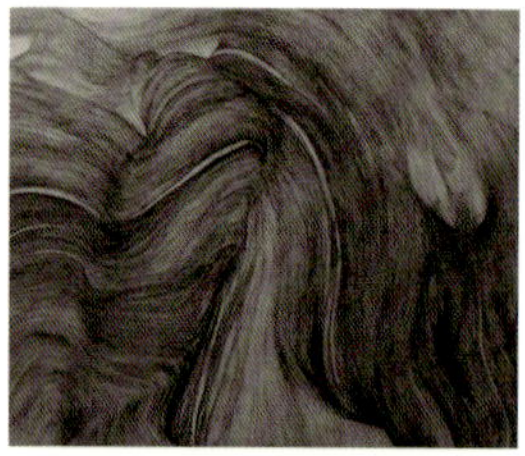

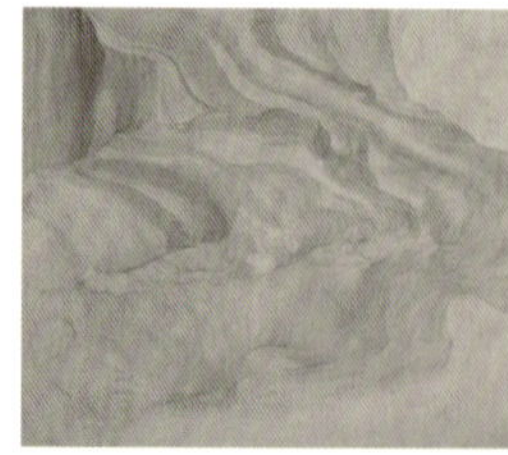
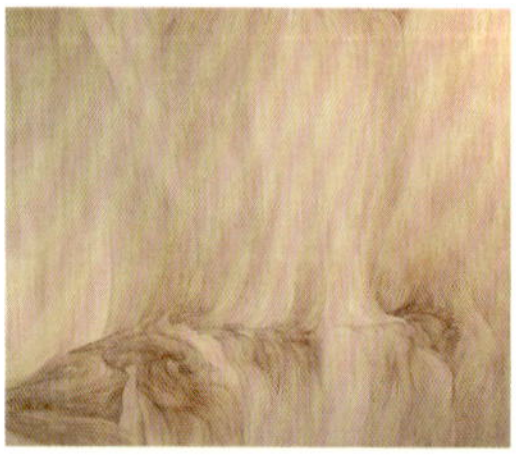
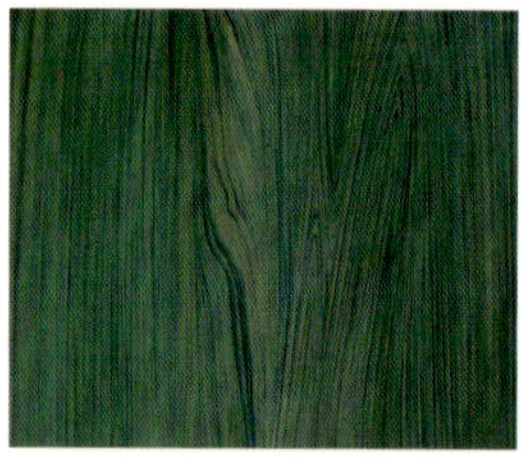

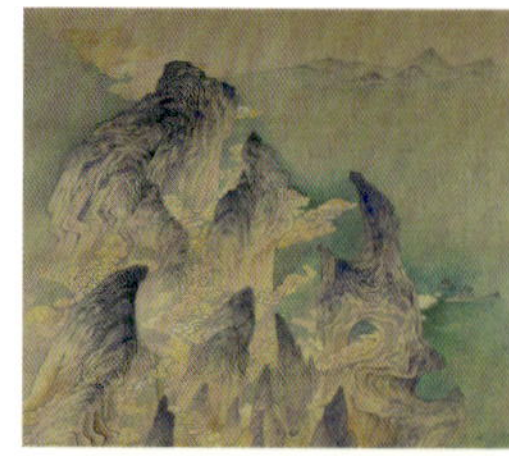
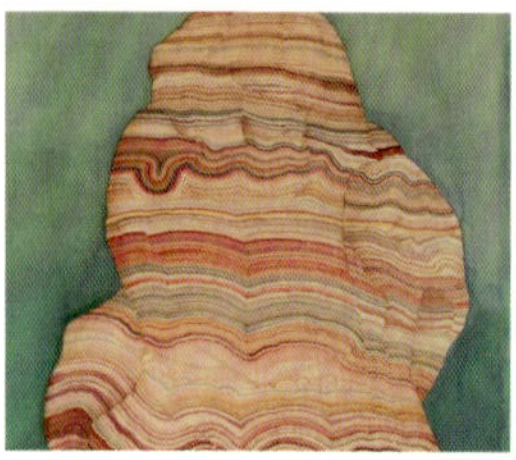
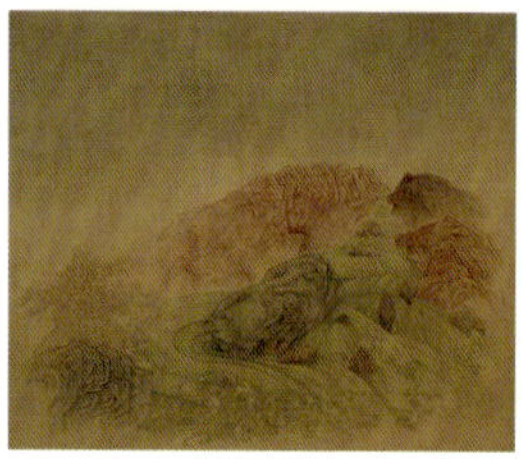
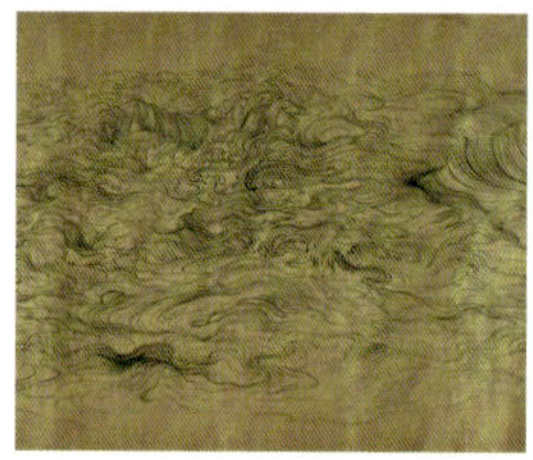

p. 054 1. Vacuous Silence #1
p. 055 2. Vacuous Silence #2
p. 057 3. Vacuous Silence #3
p. 056 4. Vacuous Silence #4
p. 052 5. Vacuous Silence #5
p. 060 6. Vacuous Silence #6
p. 058 7. Vacuous Silence #7
p. 126 8. Cavern Silk
p. 116 9. Cloud #4
p. 064 10. Contemplate #25screen
p. 144 11. Contemplate #2
p. 134 12. Contemplate #6

1	2	3	4
5	6	7	8
9	10	11	12

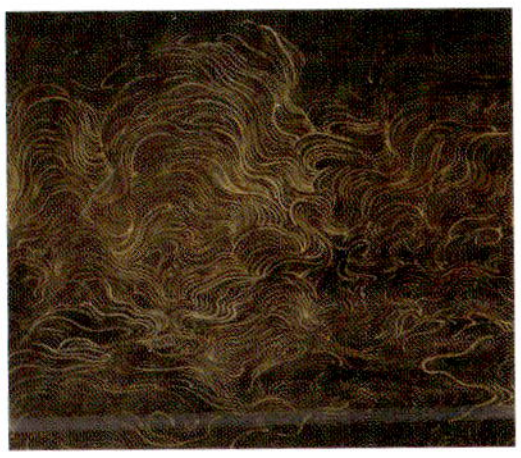
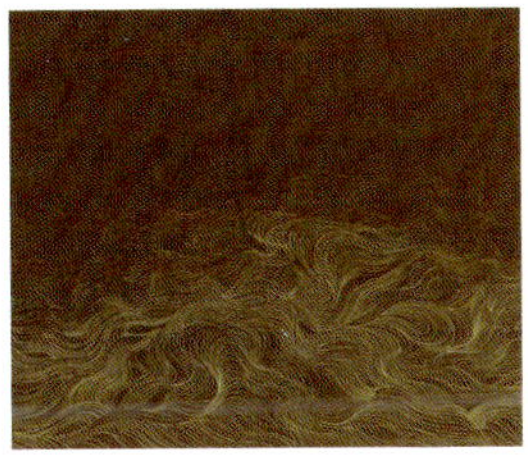
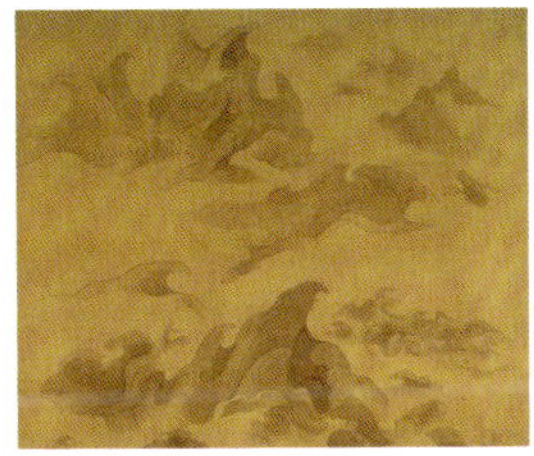

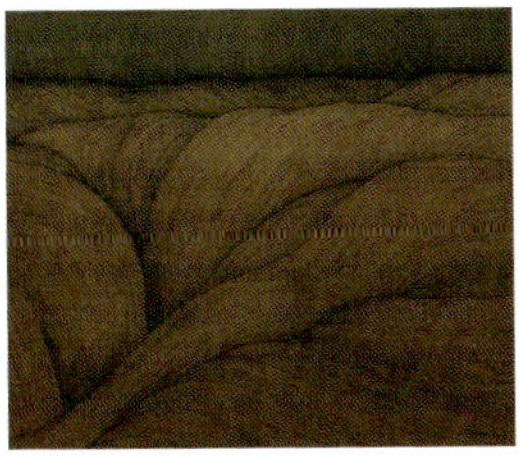
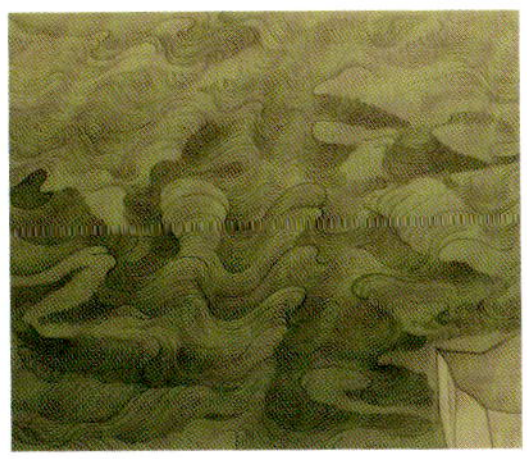

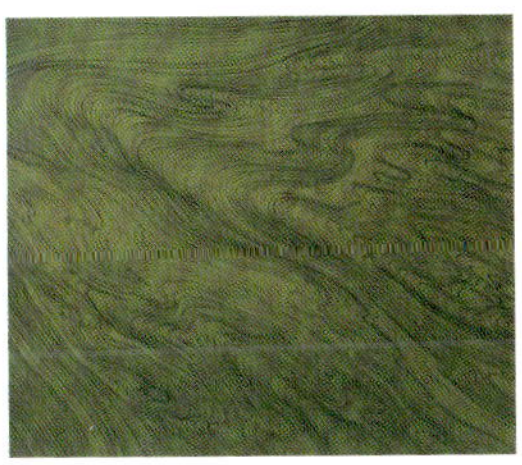
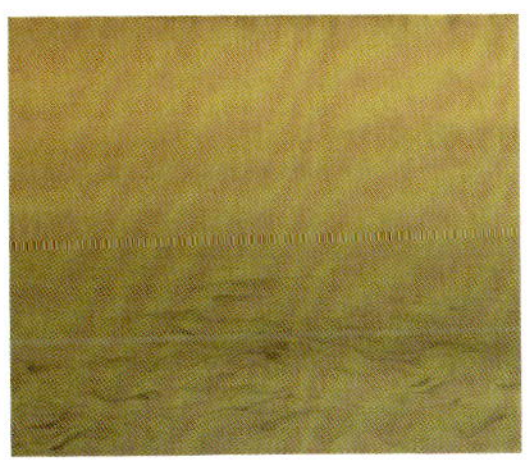
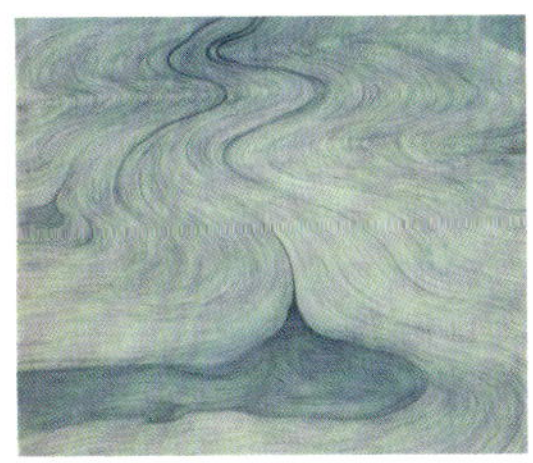
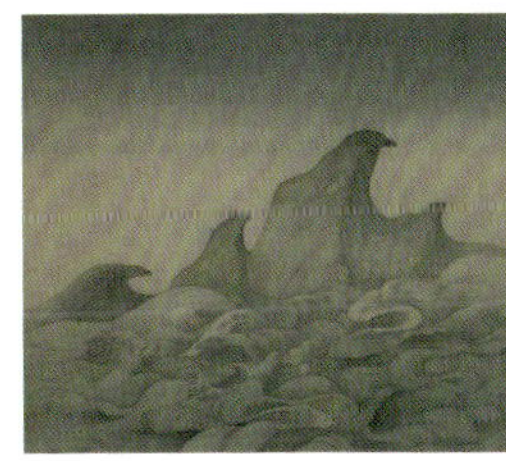

13	14	15	16
17	18	19	20
21	22	23	24

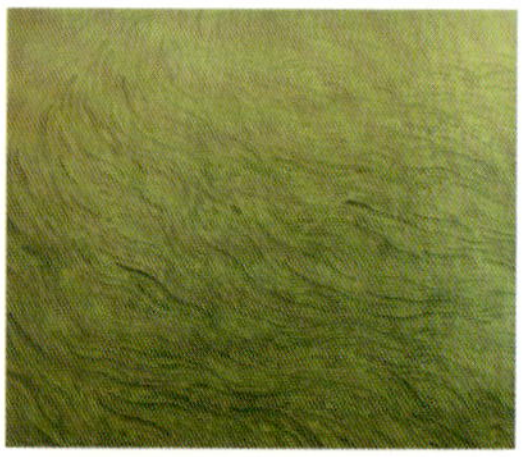
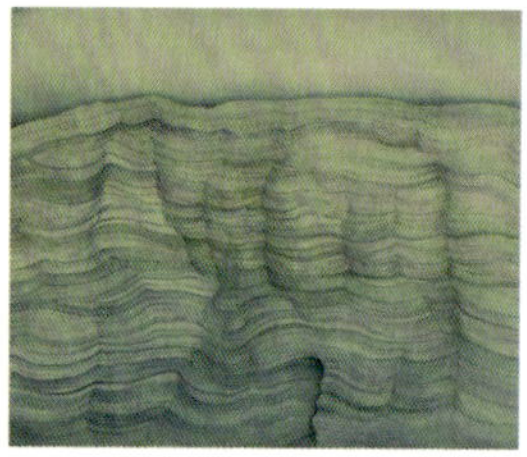
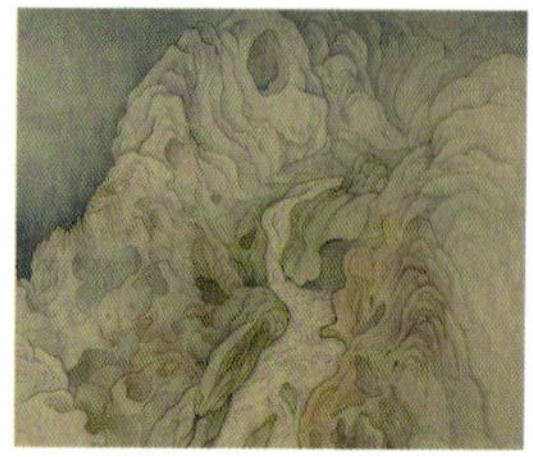

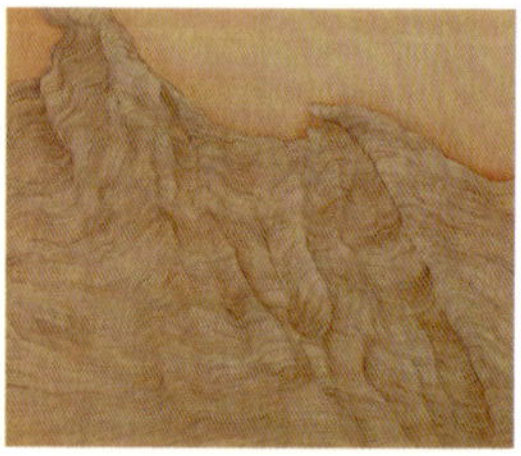
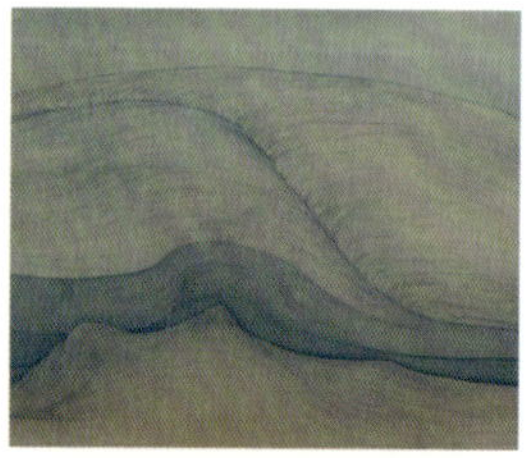

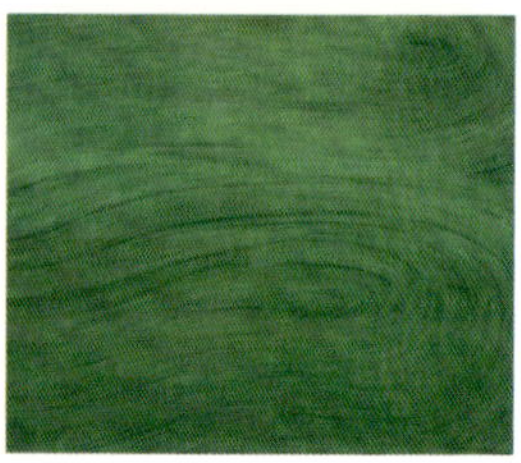
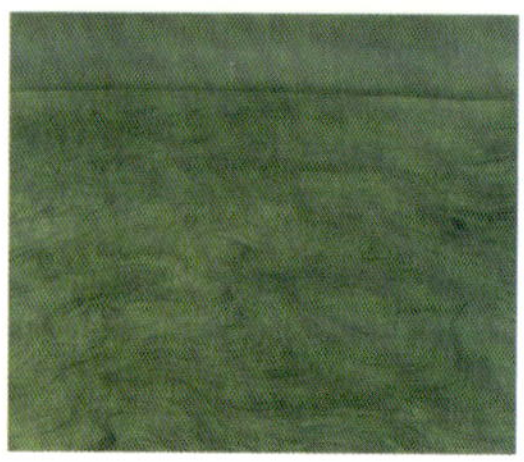
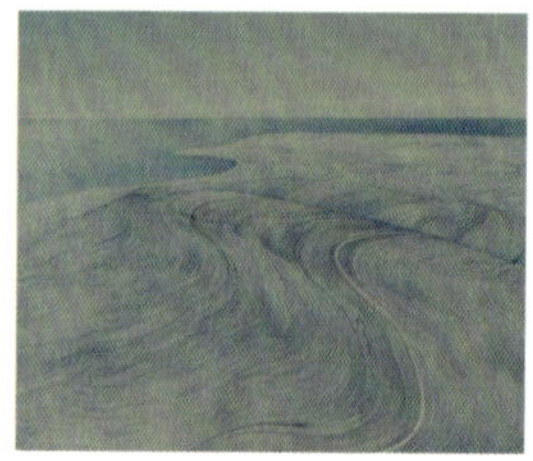
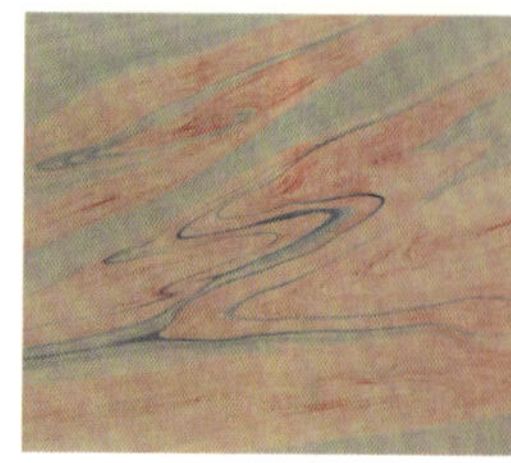

25	26	27	28
29	30	31	32
33	34	35	36

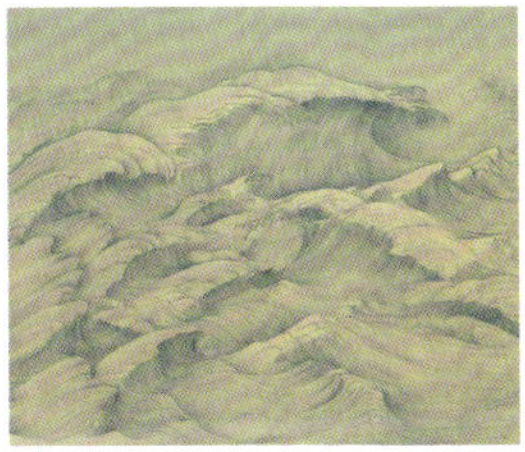
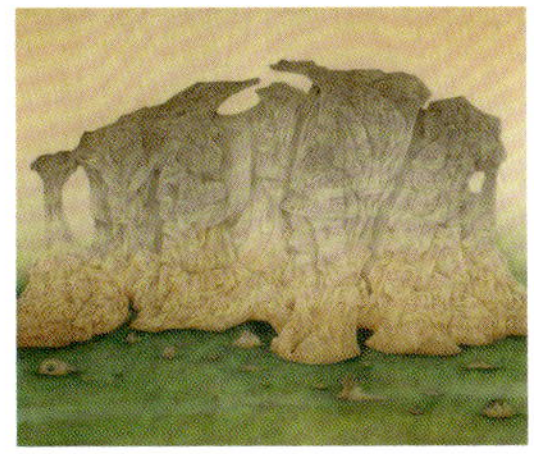
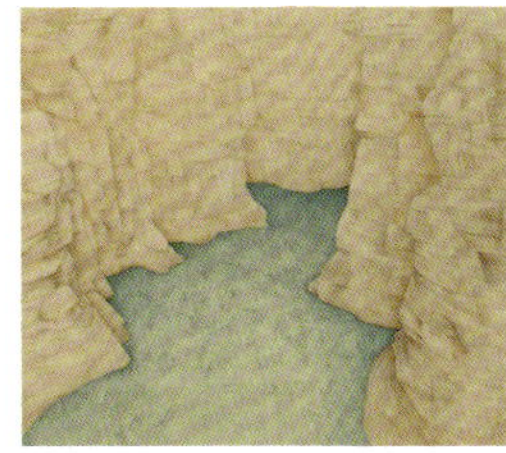
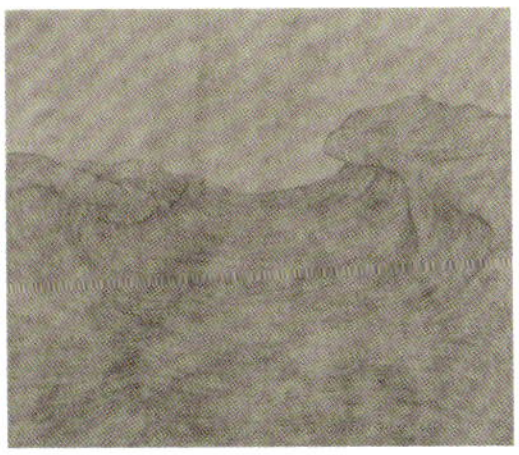
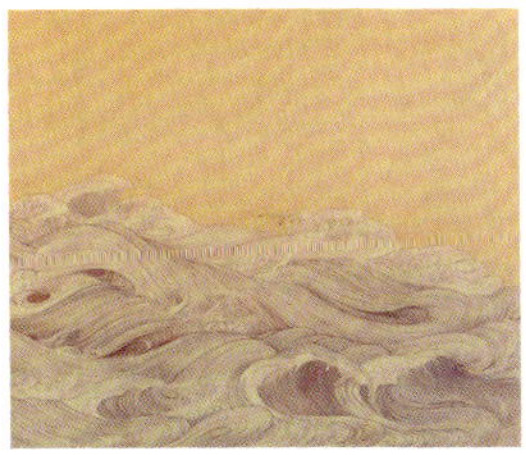
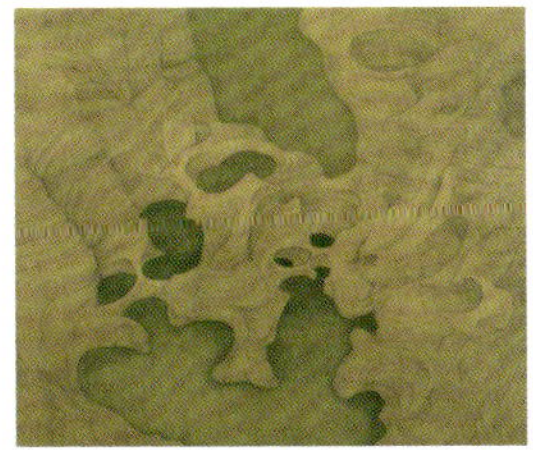
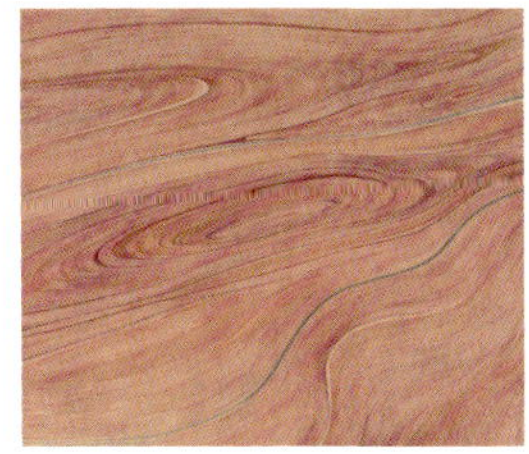
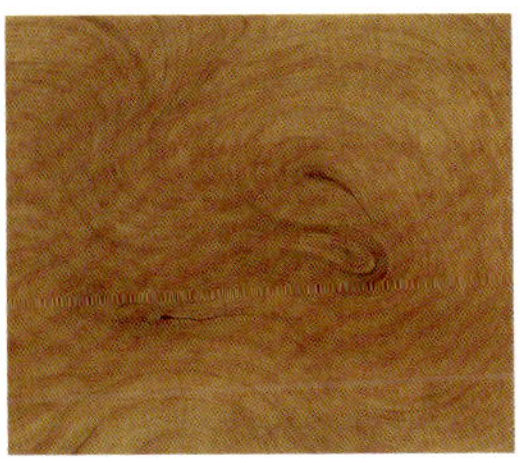
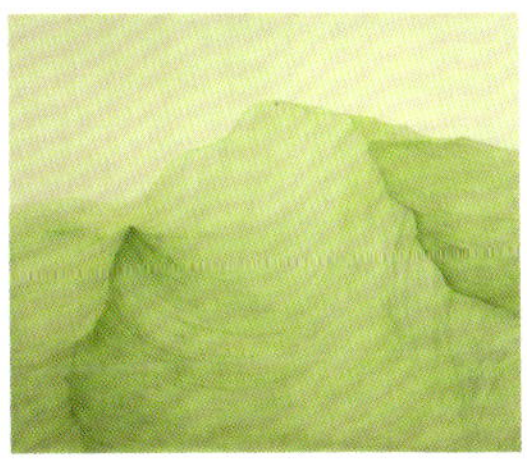
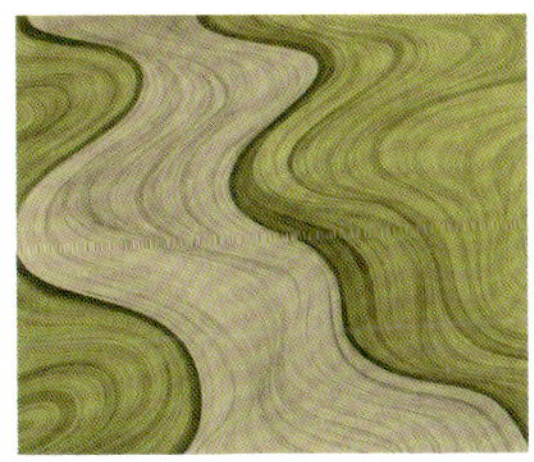
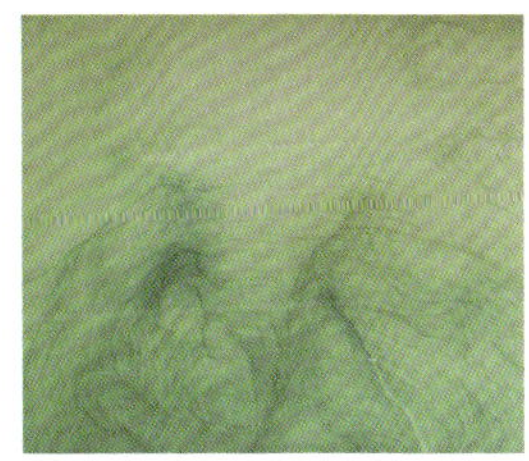

37	38	39	40
41	42	43	44
45	46	47	48

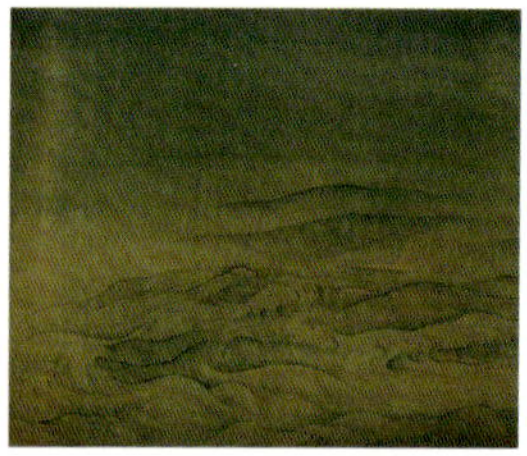
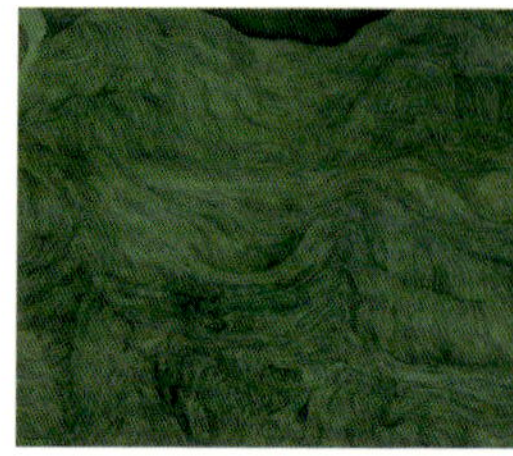
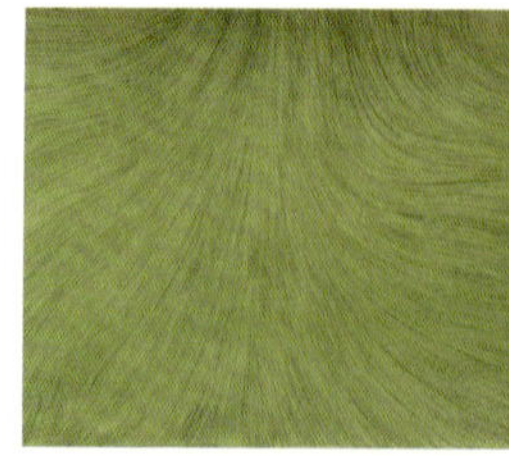
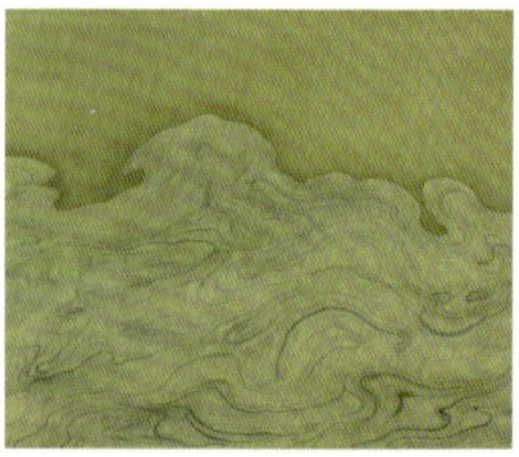
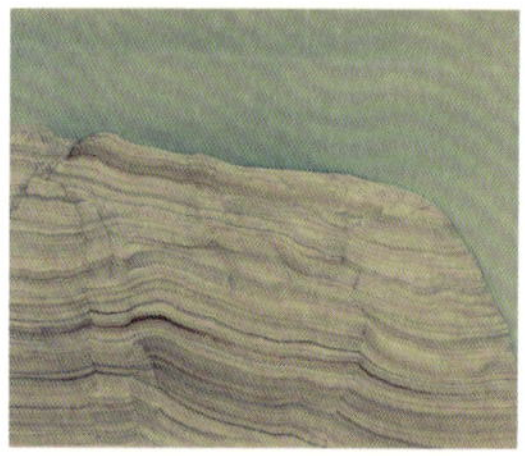
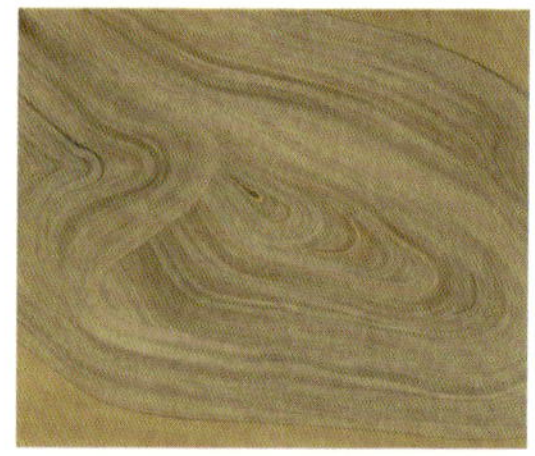

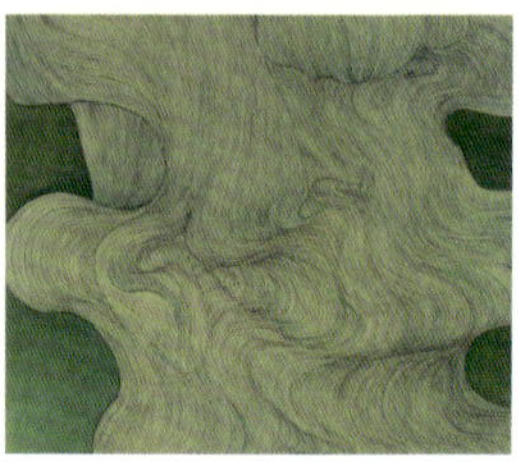
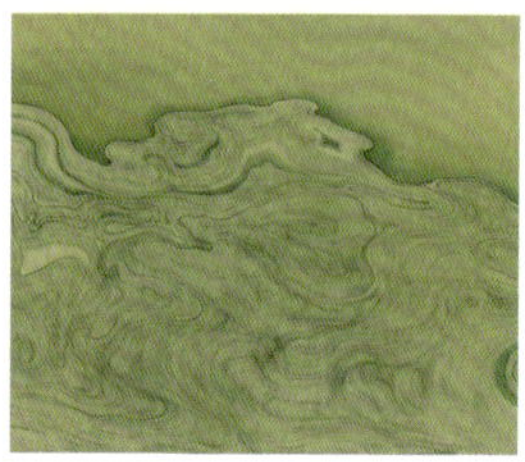
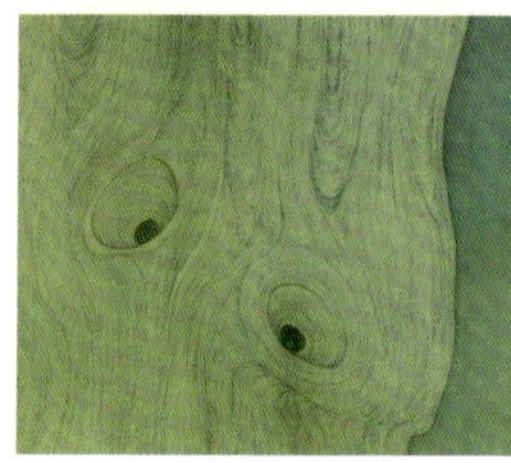
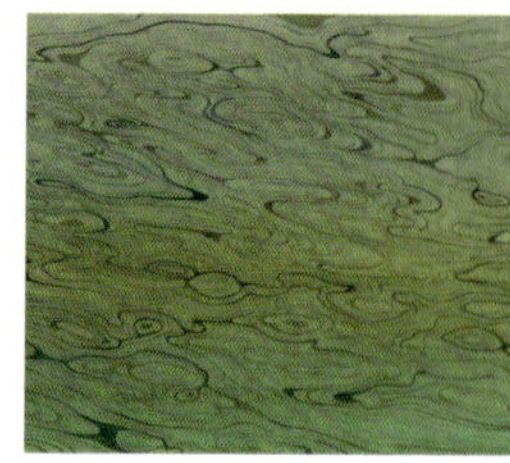

p. 070 49. Contemplate #51
p. 071 50. Contemplate #52
p. 069 51. Contemplate #53
p. 095 52. Contemplate #60
p. 100 53. Contemplate #61
p. 098 54. Contemplate #62
p. 078 55. Contemplate #63
p. 146 56. Contemplate #65
p. 125 57. Contemplate #69
p. 132 58. Contemplate #70 & 71
p. 124 59. Contemplate #72
p. 077 60. Contemplate #73

49	50	51	52
53	54	55	56
57	58	59	60

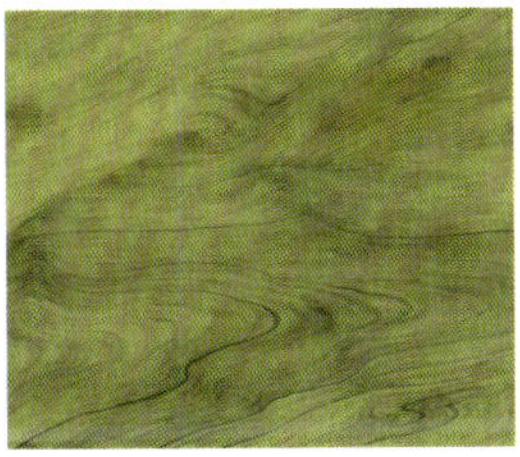
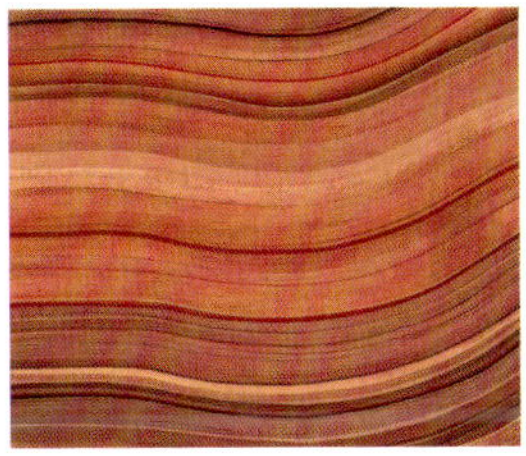
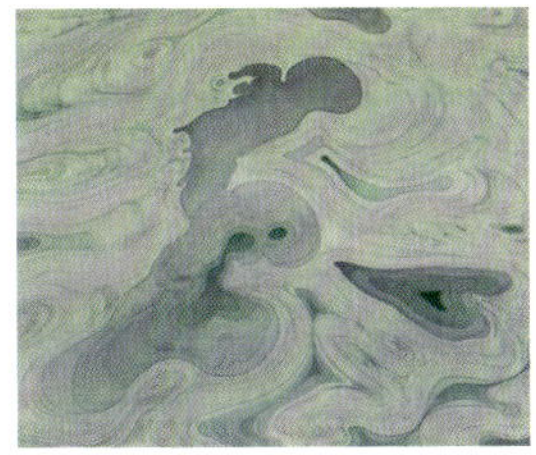
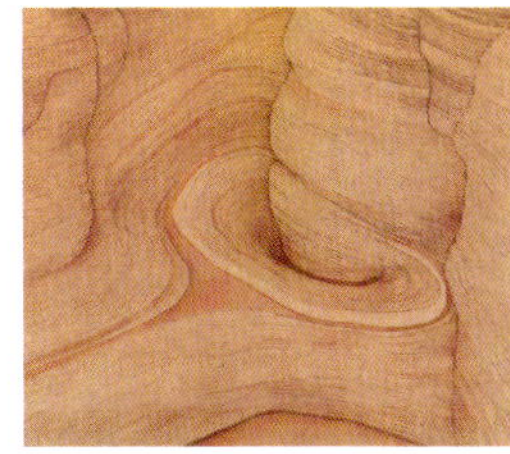

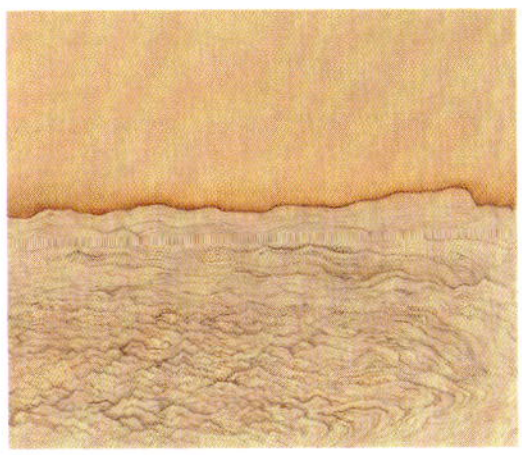
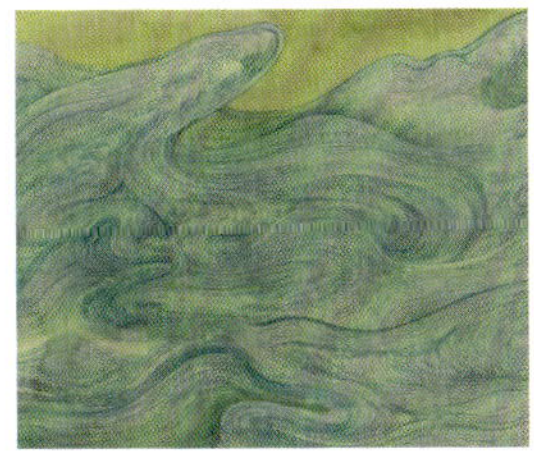
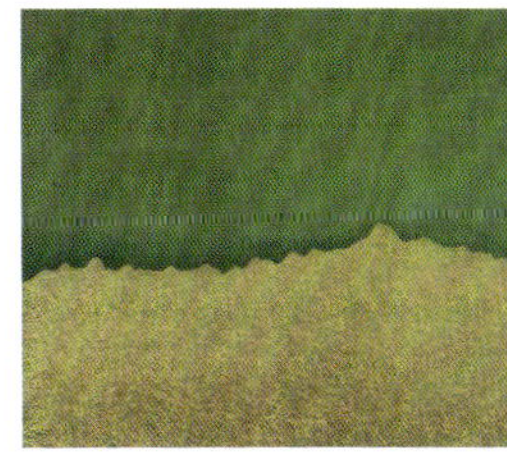
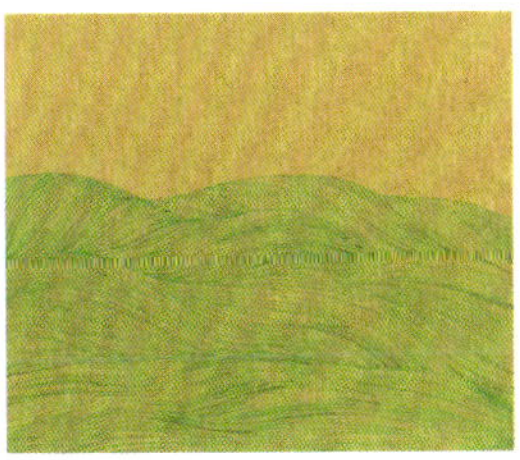
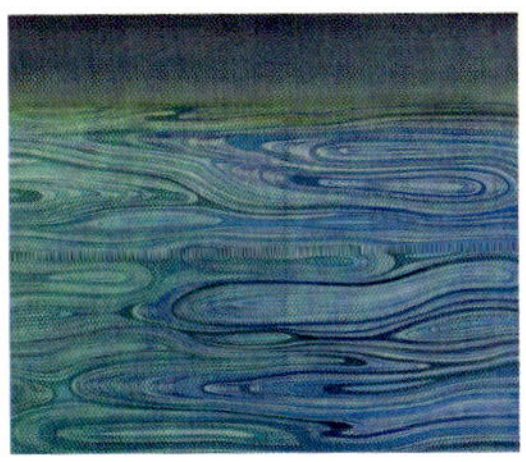
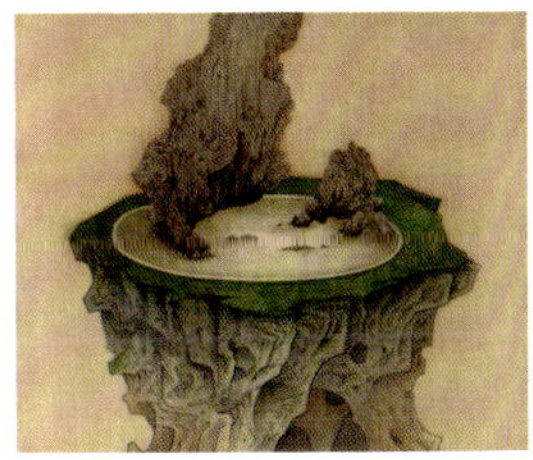
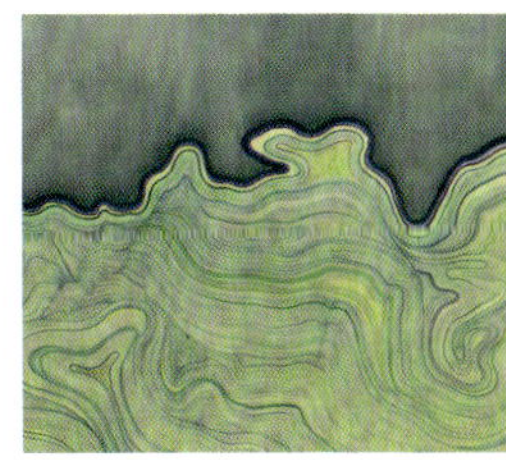

p. 075 61. Contemplate #74
p. 083 62. Contemplate #75
p. 099 63. Contemplate #76
p. 068 64. Contemplate #77
p. 090 65. Contemplate #78
p. 094 66. Contemplate #79
p. 088 67. Contemplate #88
p. 118 68. Contemplate-Mine #3
p. 129 69. Contemplate-Mine #4
p. 101 70. Contemplate-Mine #86
p. 123 71. Garden
p. 120 72. Hadean

61	62	63	64
65	66	67	68
69	70	71	72

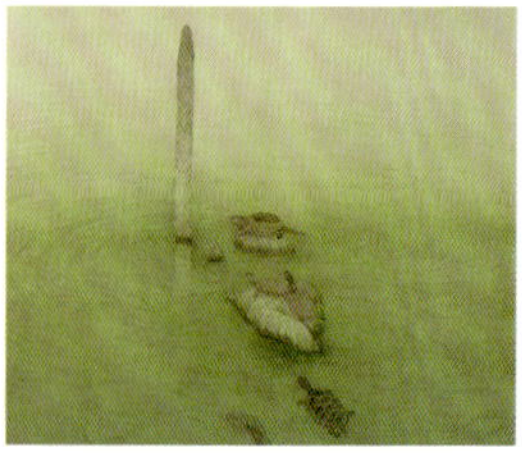
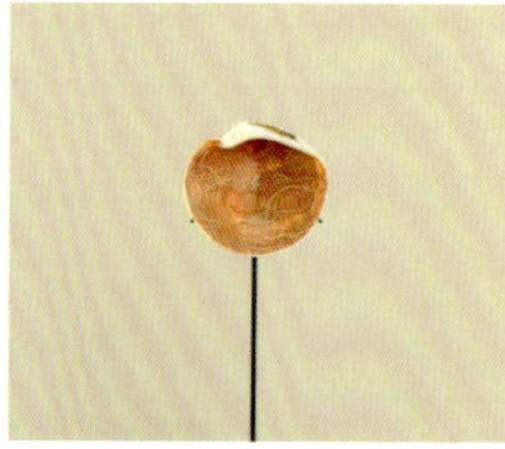
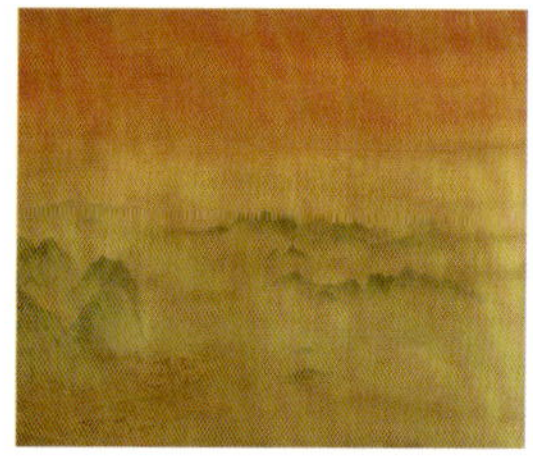
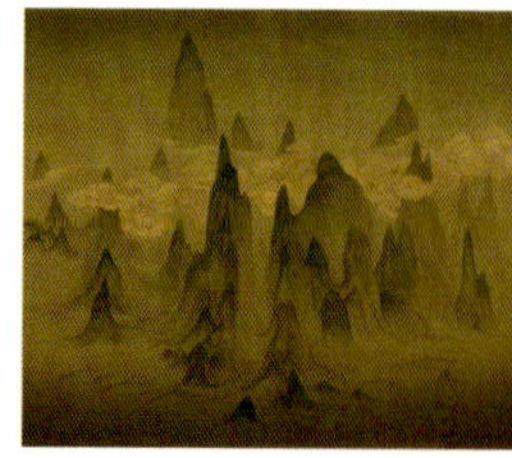
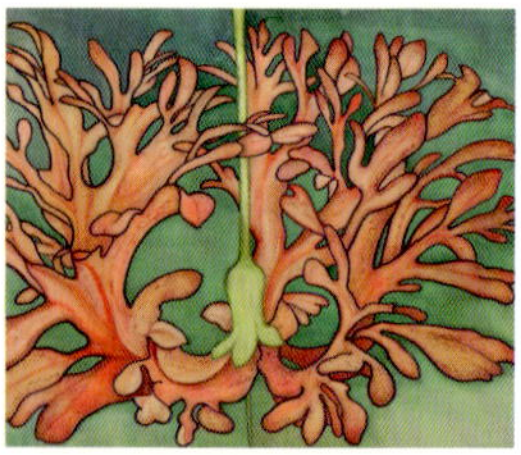
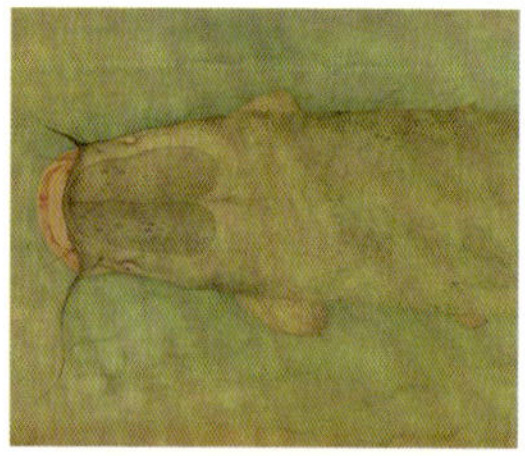
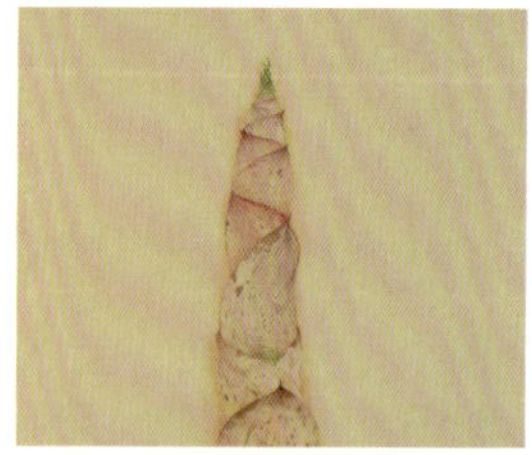
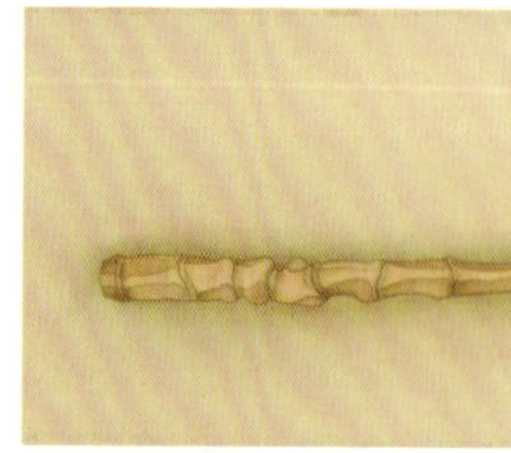
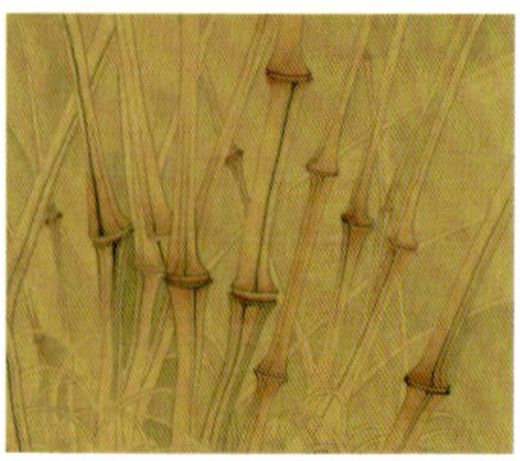
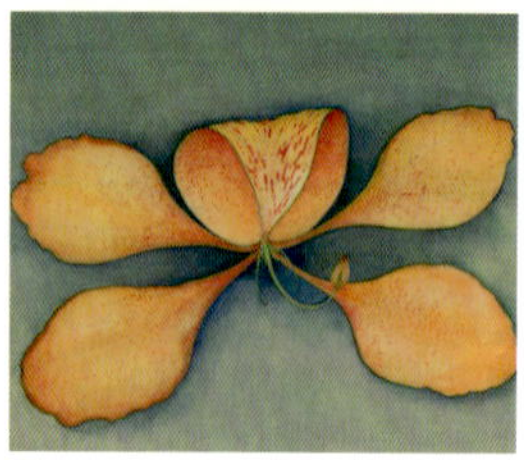
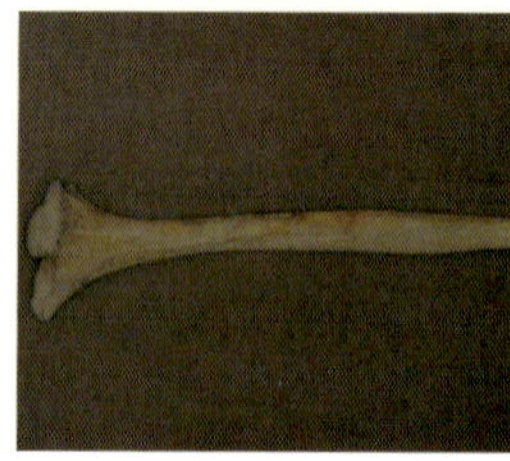
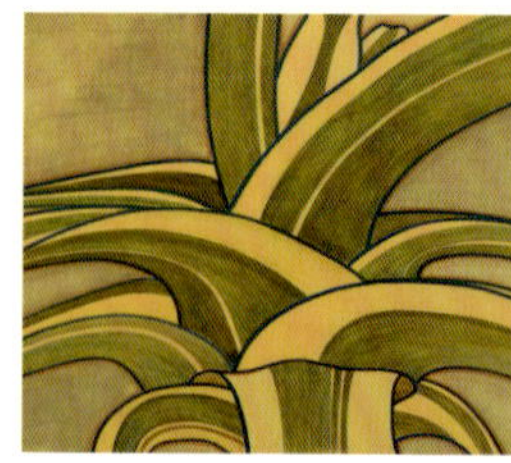

73	74	75	76
77	78	79	80
81	82	83	84

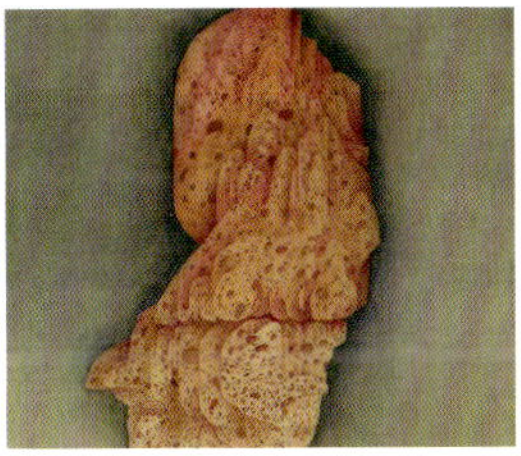
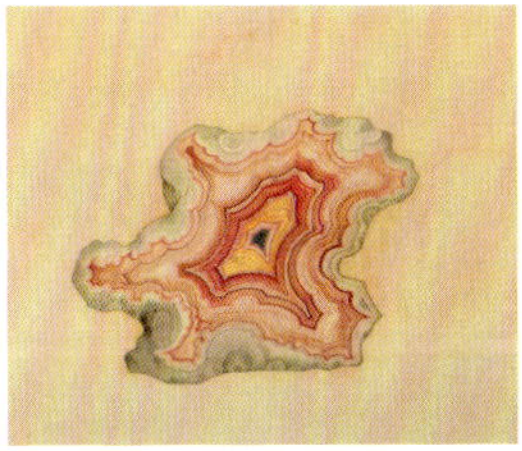
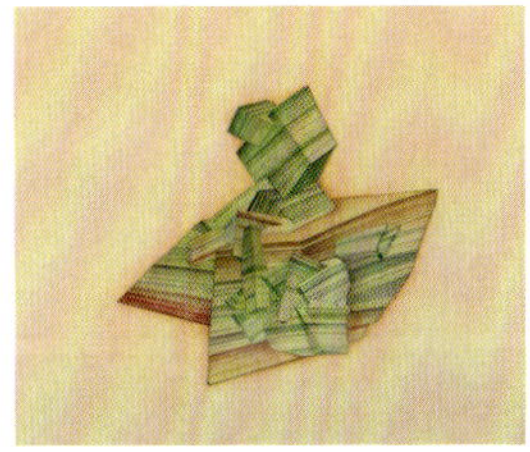
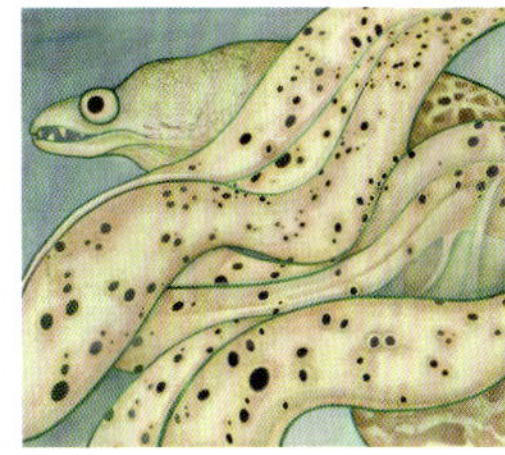
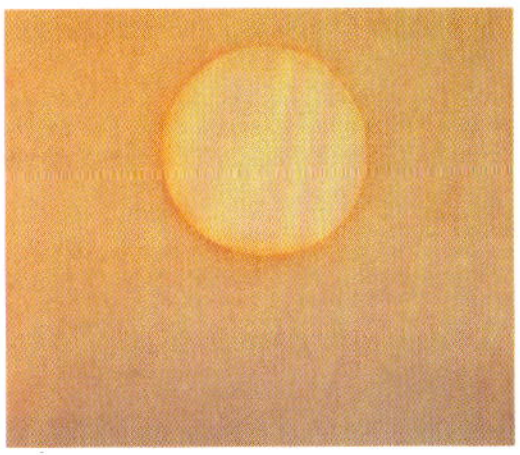
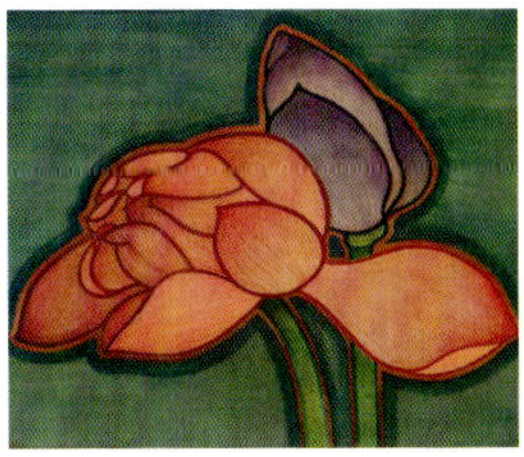
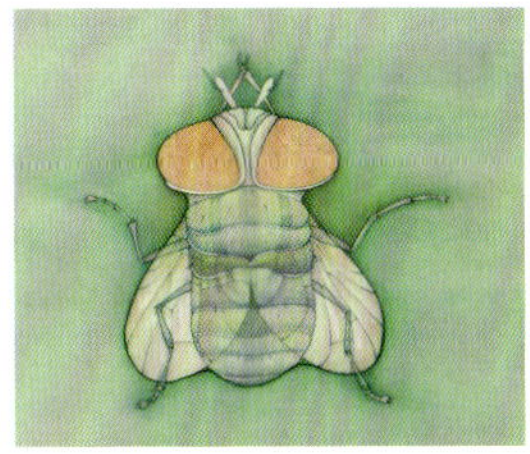
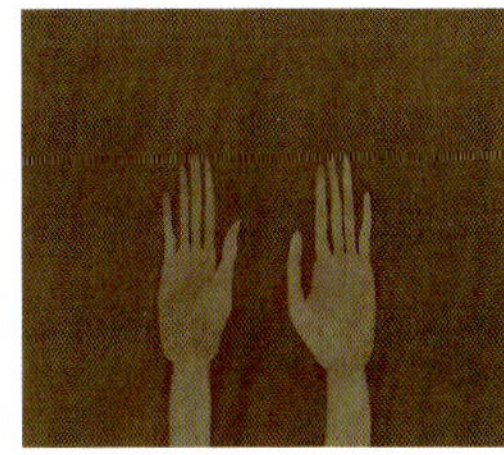
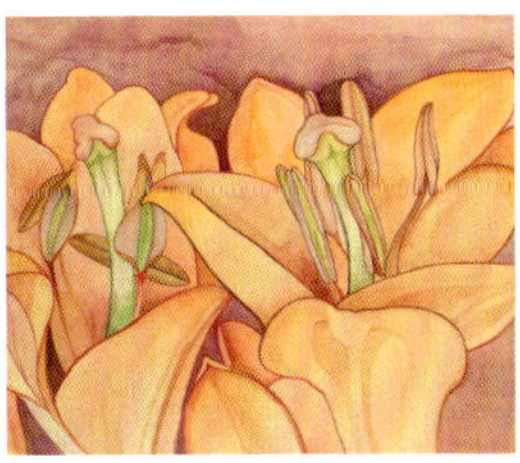
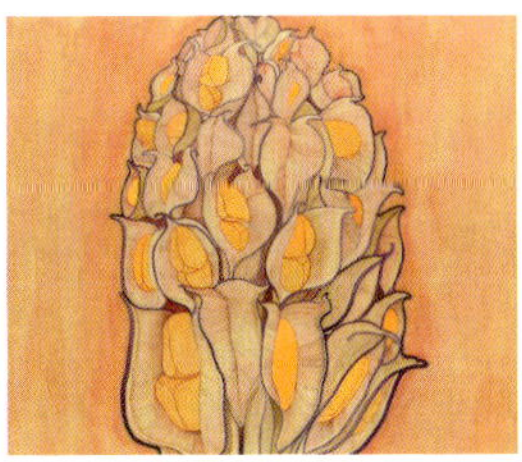
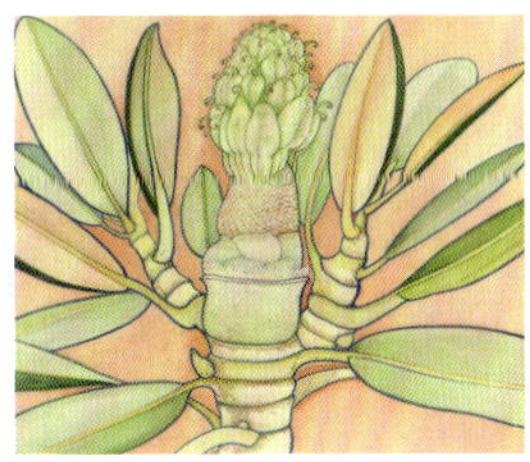
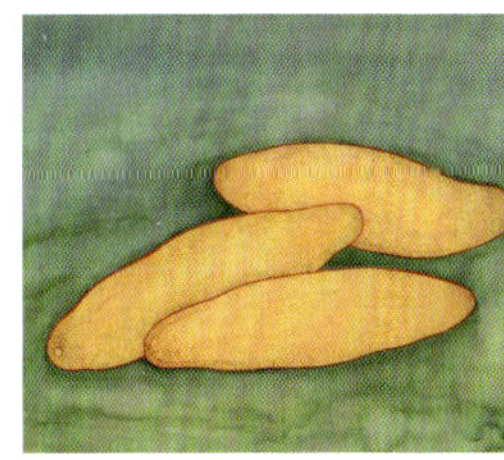

85	86	87	88
89	90	91	92
93	94	95	96

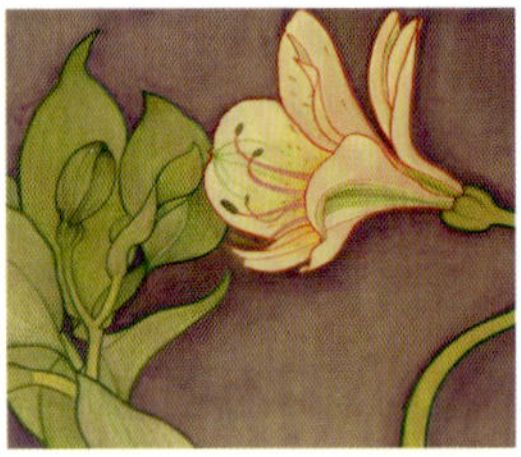
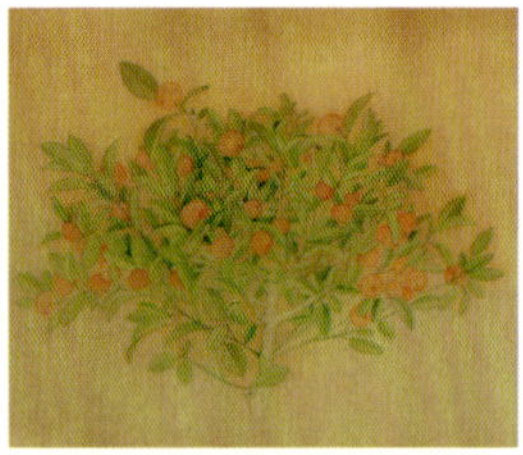
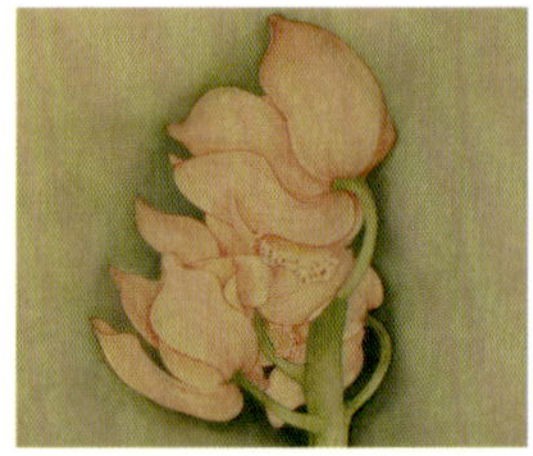
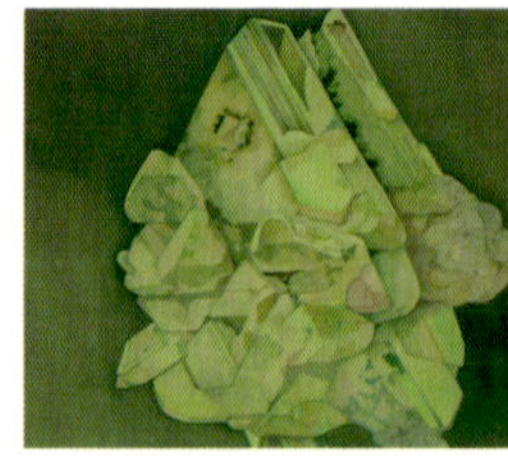
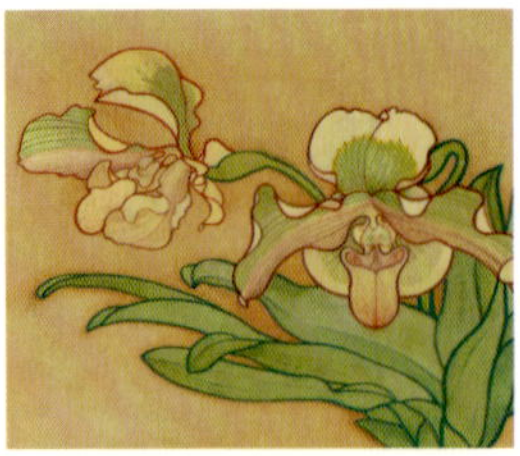
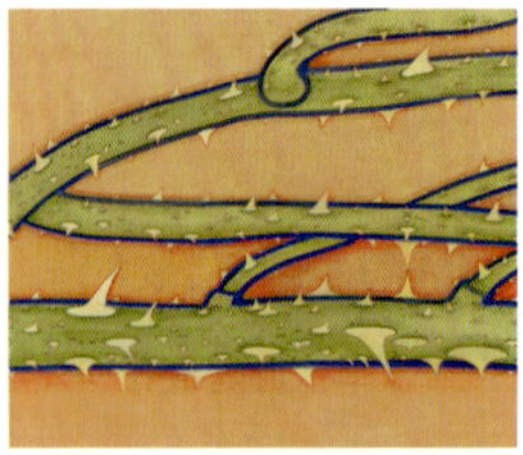
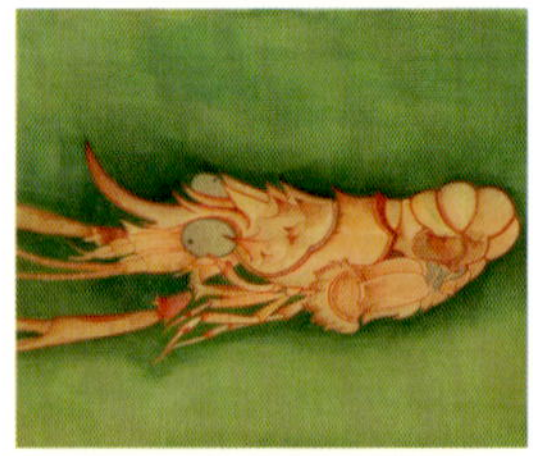
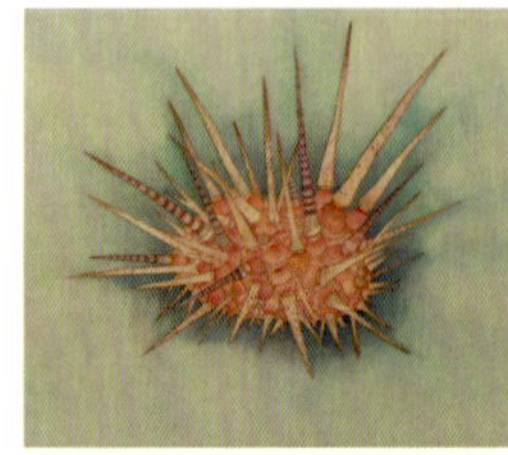
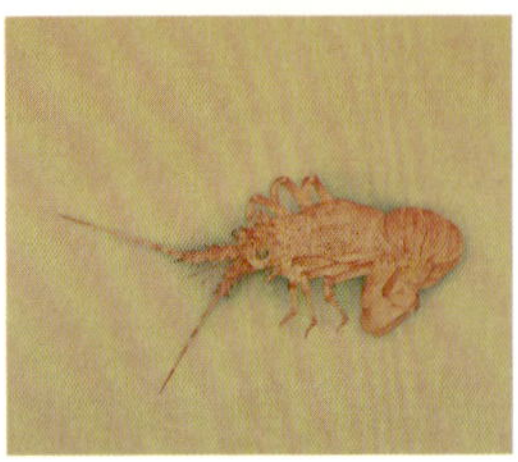
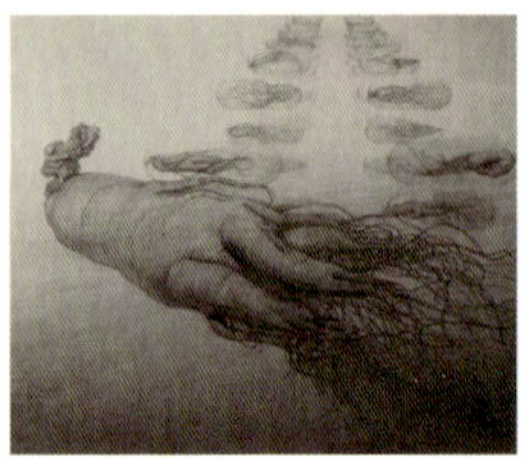
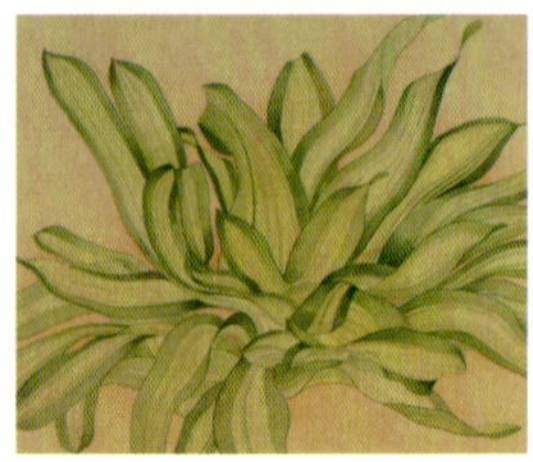
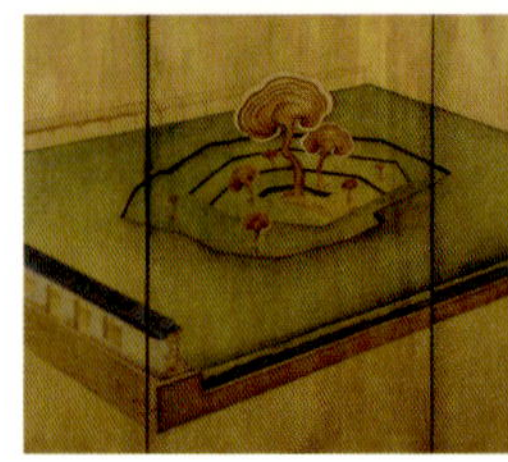

97	98	99	100
101	102	103	104
105	106	107	108

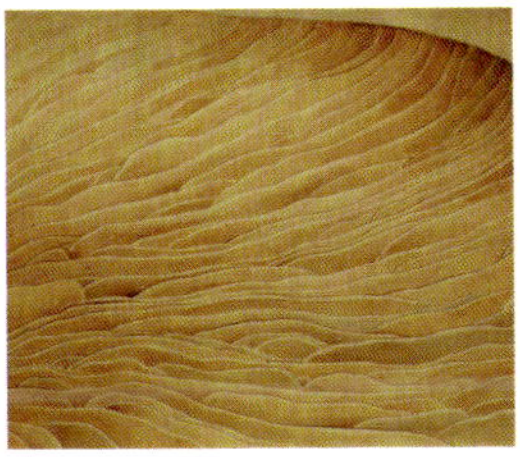
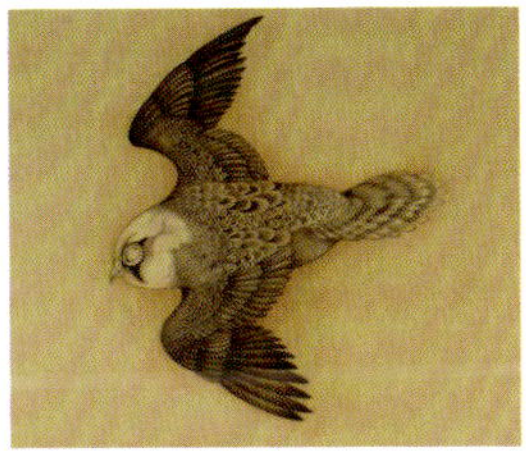
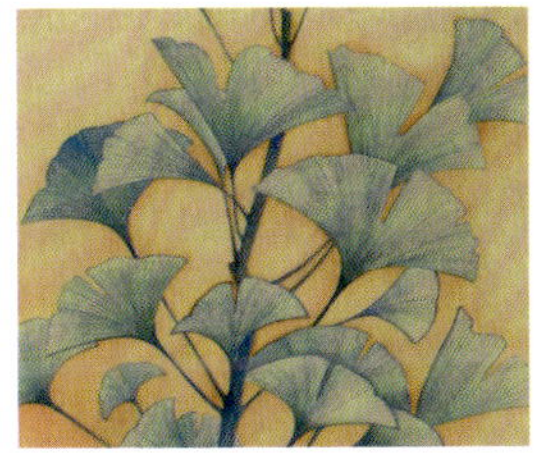
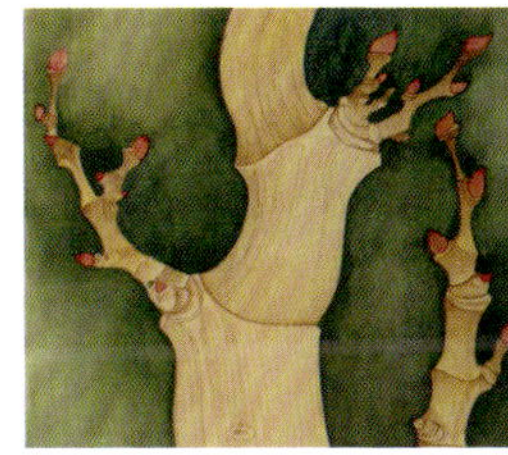
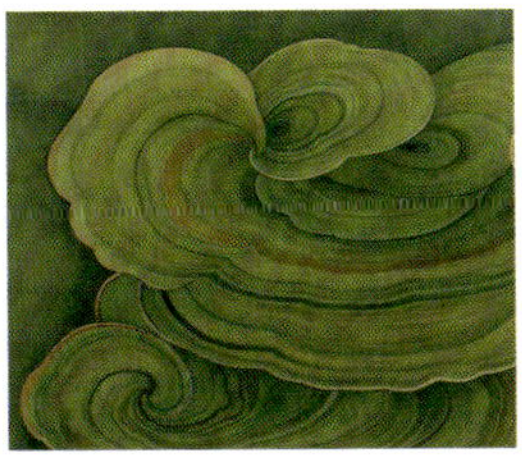
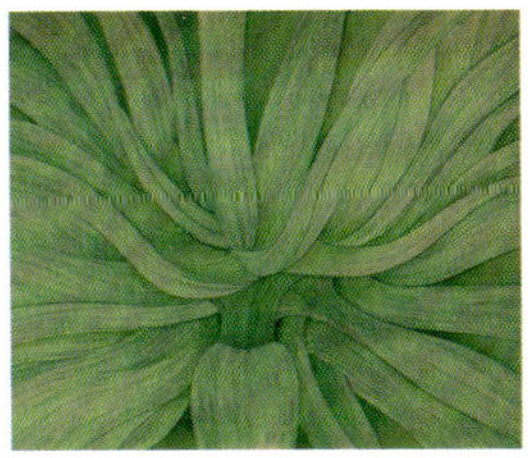
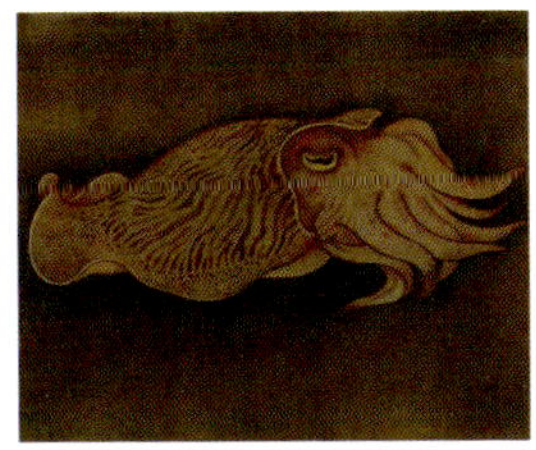
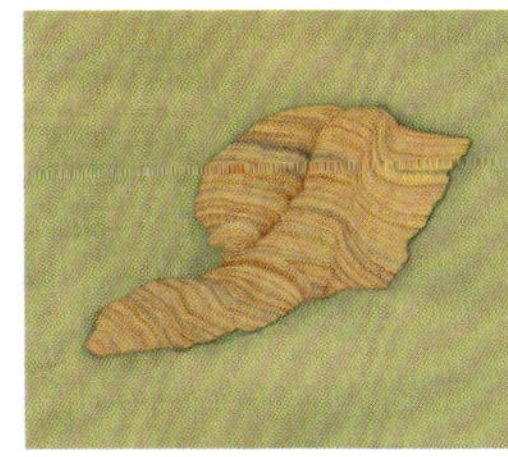
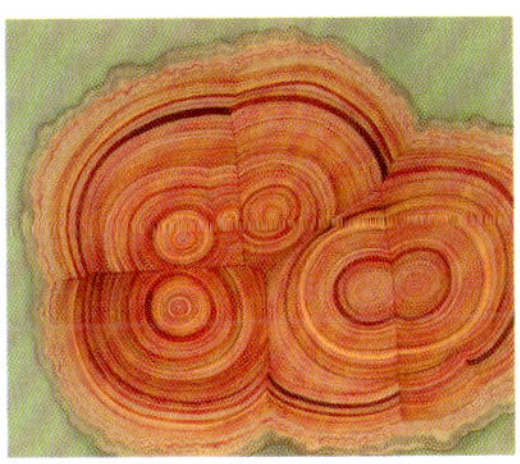
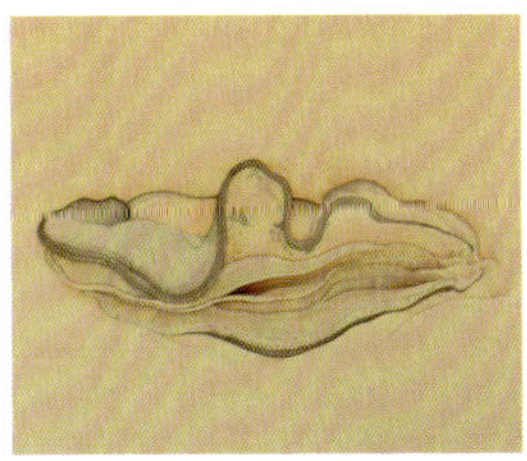
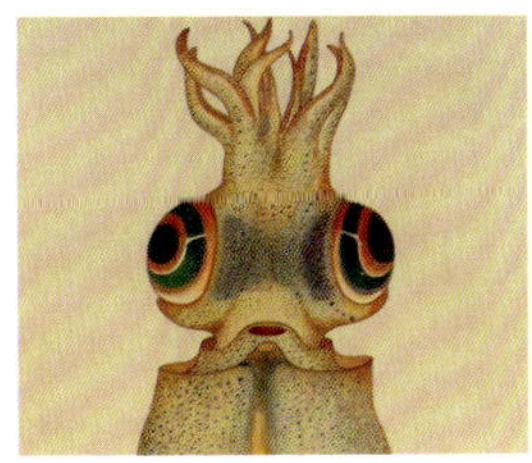
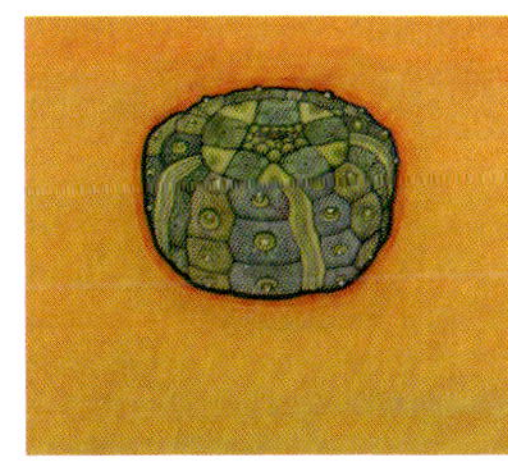

109	110	111	112
113	114	115	116
117	118	119	120

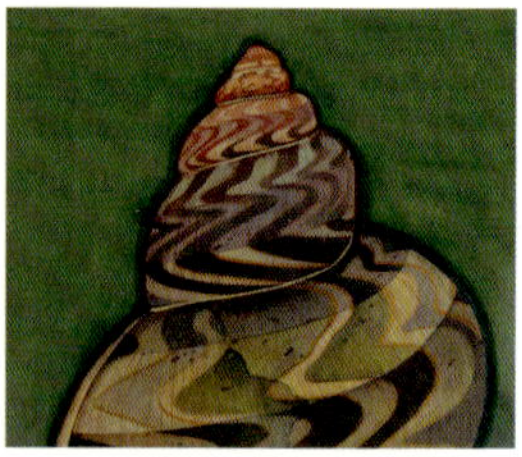
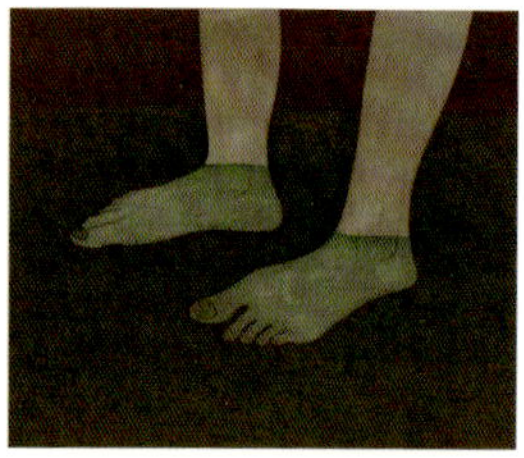
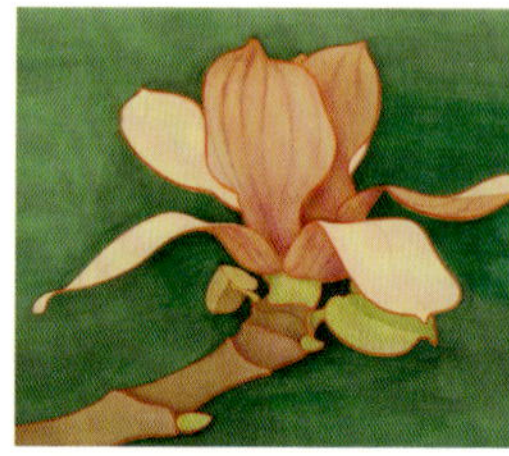
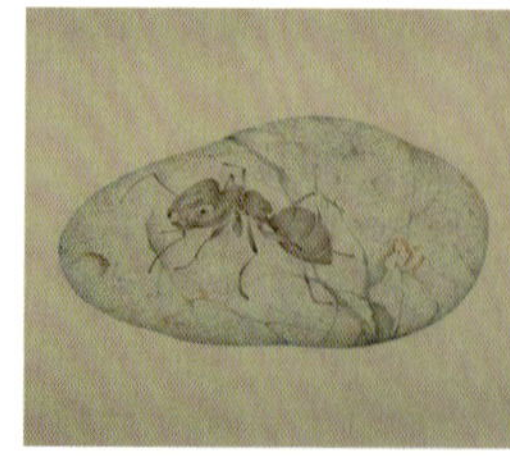
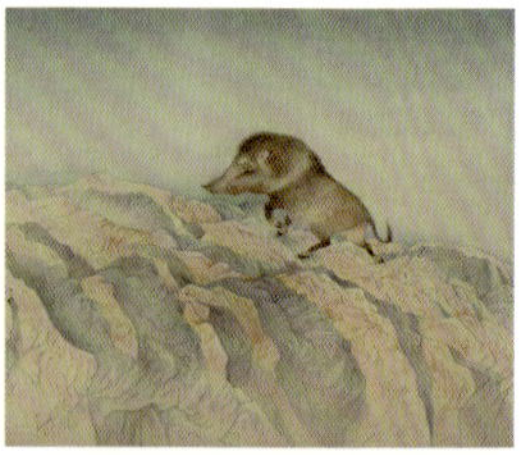
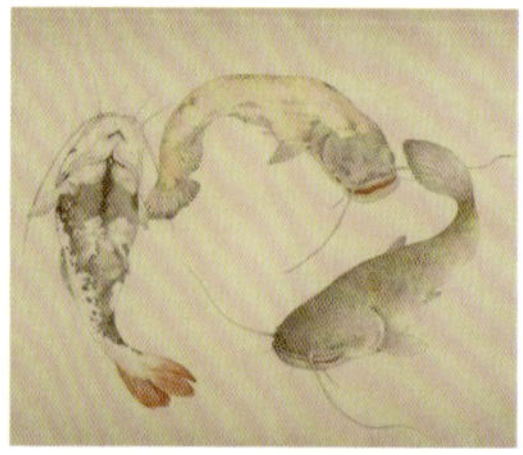
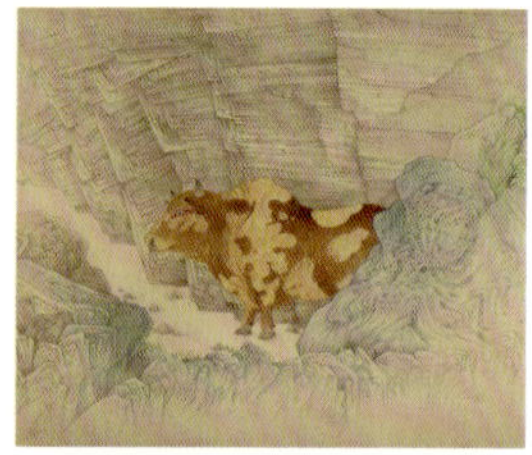
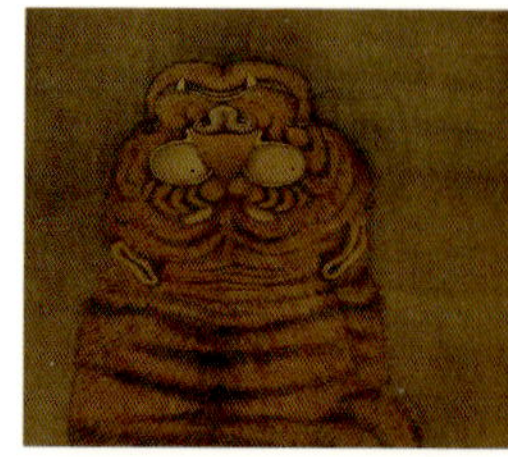
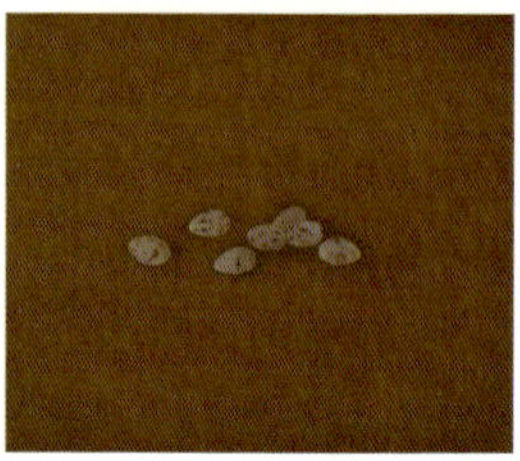
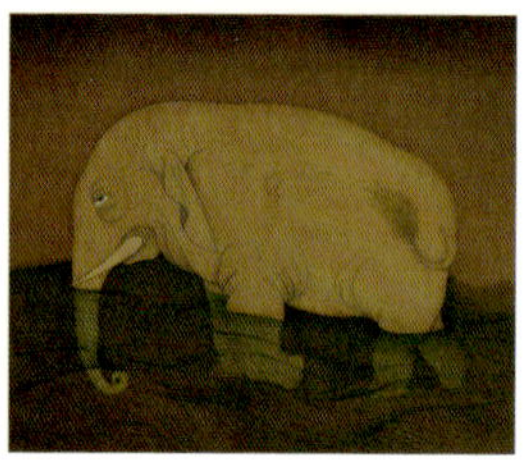
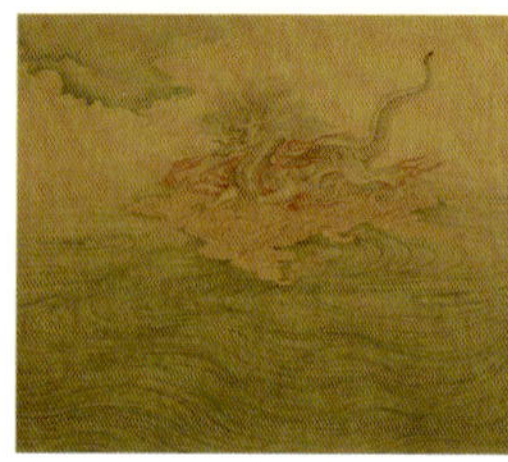
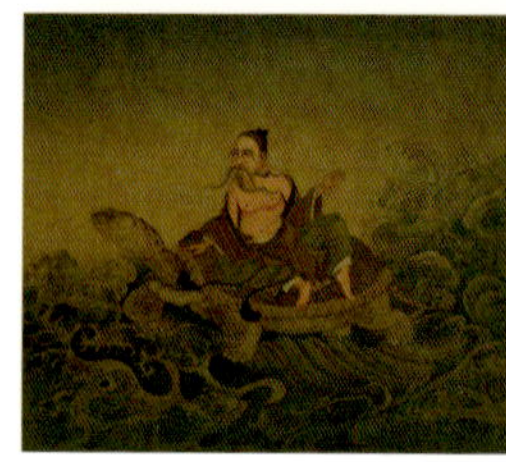

121	122	123	124
125	126	127	128
129	130	131	132

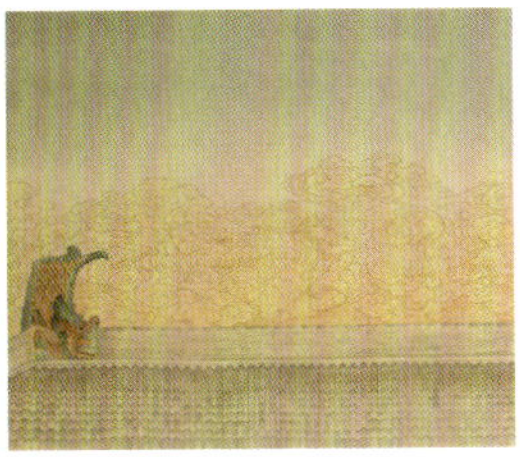
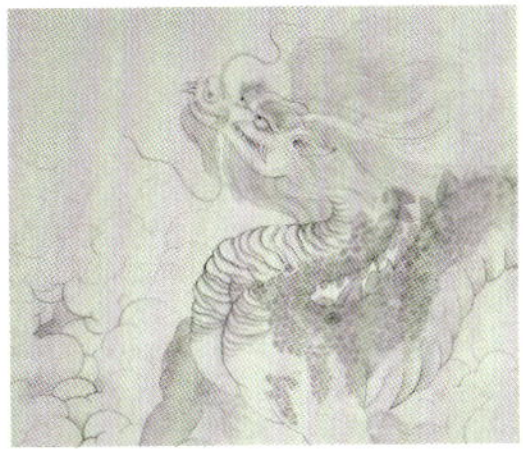
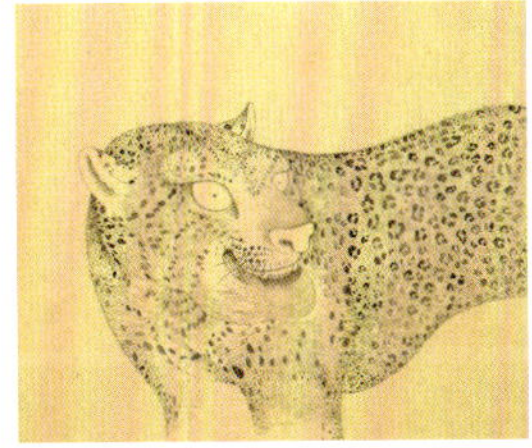
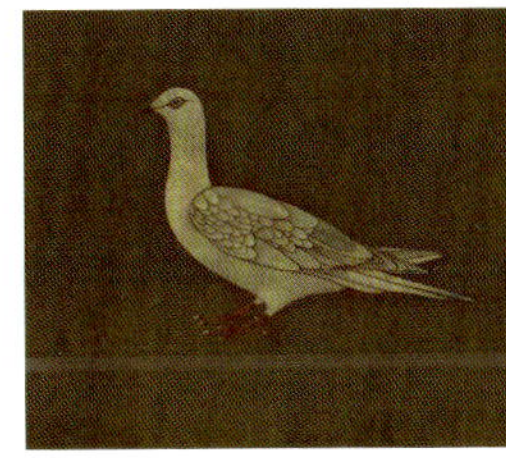
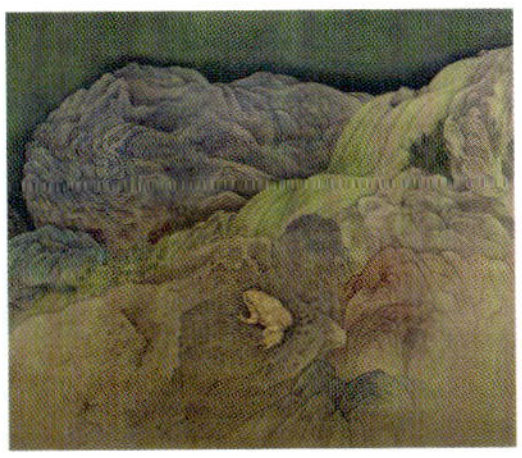
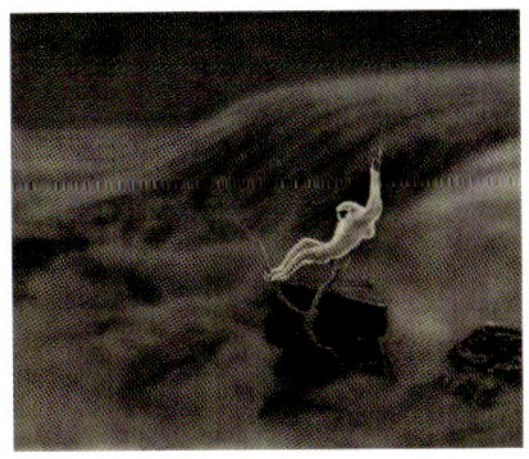
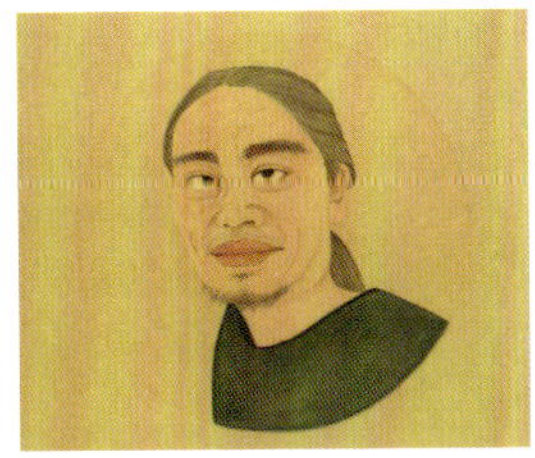
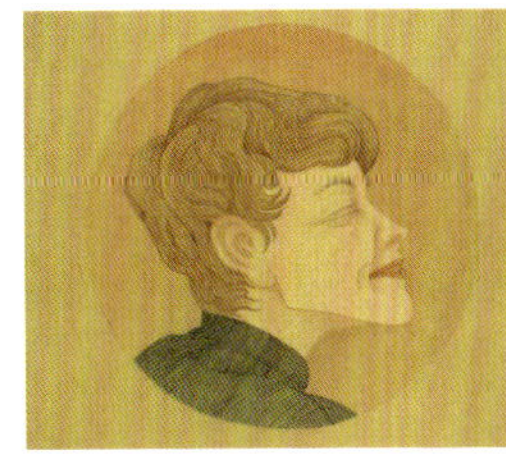
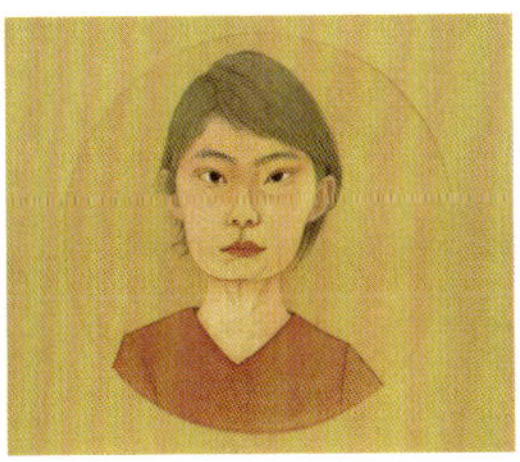
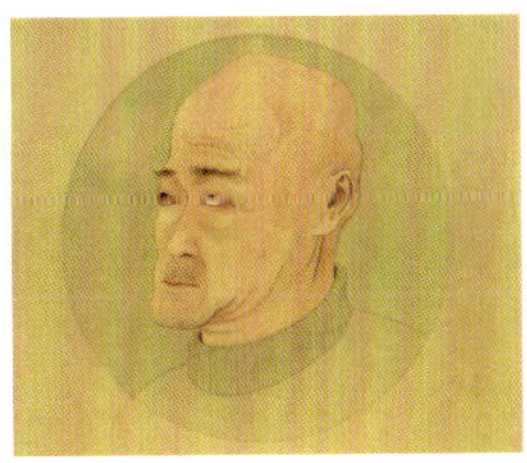
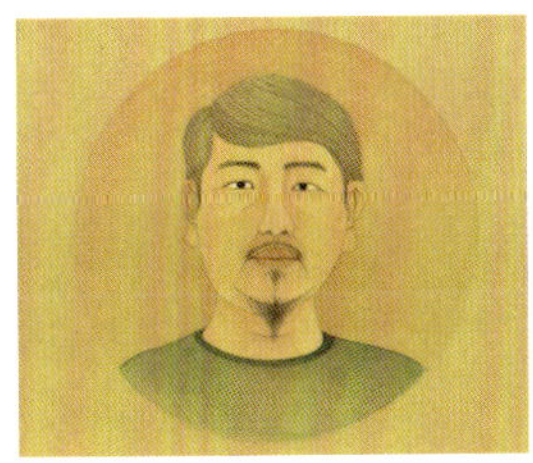
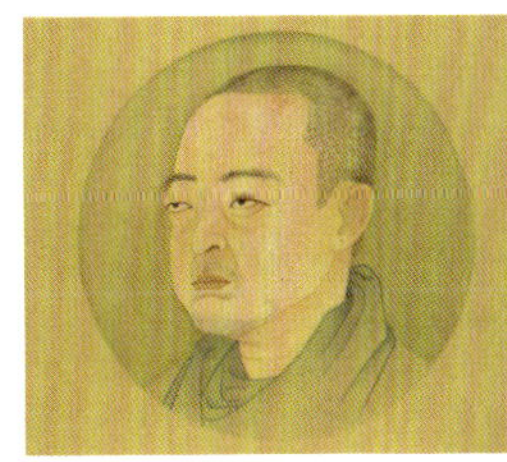

133	134	135	136
137	138	139	140
141	142	143	144

ISBN 978-1-913536-55-8

BETWEEN EARTH AND HEAVEN

Edit: Wu Yumo & Chen Duxi
Text: Bao Dong / Guo Xinran / Feng Qing / Wang Wei / Chen Duxi
Design: AnyOne / Zhang Zeyangping & Zhao Ye

Size: 170mm × 216mm
First Edition: November, 2023

6 Prospect Way, Royal Oak Industrial Estate,
Daventry Northamptonshire, NN11 8PL, UK
Tel: + 44(0) 1213 146196 -1
Fax: + 44(0) 1213 146196 -2
Web: www.lighthousebooks.net

Printed and bound in China.

Thanks: Mr GuJia